Private Capital Investing

Private Capital Investing

The Handbook of Private Debt and Private Equity

ROBERTO IPPOLITO

WILEY

Library of Congress Cataloging-in-Publication Data

Names: Ippolito, Roberto, 1969- author.
Title: Private capital investing : the handbook of private debt and private
    equity / Roberto Ippolito.
Description: Chichester, West Sussex, United Kingdom : John Wiley & Sons,
    2020. | Series: The Wiley finance | Includes bibliographical references
    and index.
Identifiers: LCCN 2019033206 (print) | LCCN 2019033207 (ebook) | ISBN
    9781119526162 (hardback) | ISBN 9781119526131 (adobe pdf) | ISBN
    9781119526193 (epub)
Subjects: LCSH: Private equity. | Investments. | Capital market.
Classification: LCC HG4751 .I67 2020 (print) | LCC HG4751 (ebook) | DDC
    332.6—dc23
LC record available at https://lccn.loc.gov/2019033206
LC ebook record available at https://lccn.loc.gov/2019033207

Cover Design: Wiley
Cover Images: © Classen Rafael/EyeEm/Getty Images, © tifonimages/Getty Images

Set in 10/12pt, TimesLTStd by SPi Global, Chennai, India.

Printed in Great Britain by TJ International Ltd, Padstow, Cornwall, UK

SKY10042084_013123

To Gaia

Contents

About the Author

Roberto Ippolito is Managing Partner of a leading hybrid capital (private equity and private debt) fund and Professor of Principal Investing at Università degli Studi Guglielmo Marconi.

Roberto has 20 years' private capital experience in sourcing, structuring, and investing in all parts of the capital structure (senior debt, junior debt, and private equity) of Italian SMEs across several industries and three years' management consulting experience (with a focus on business due diligence and performance improvement).

Former Head of Leverage Finance at General Electric Capital Italy, Roberto has held managerial roles at European Bank for Reconstruction and Development, DAM Capital (Anschutz Group), Bain & Co. He also held junior positions at Goldman Sachs (Merchant and Investment Banking) and Istituto Mobiliare Italiano (Merchant Banking).

Roberto is a Fulbright Scholar and a British Chevening Scholar. He has written academic and popular articles and books on economics and finance (with a focus on private equity and private debt) and teaches various Executive courses and Masters at the London Stock Exchange Academy and 24Ore Business School.

Roberto received an MBA from the University of Chicago, an MSc in Economics from the University of Warwick and a Summa Cum Laude BSc in Business from LUISS University. He is a CFA and CPA in Italy and FSA registered in the UK.

Acknowledgements

Writing a book on topics which have been the basis of 20 years of work is – to use Steve Jobs's words – to 'connect the dots looking backwards'. In this connection of points, there are many people who have accompanied me and to whom I owe a thanks. As always, it is easy to forget someone: in this sense, I apologise in advance to the many I have omitted or forgotten.

The first thanks goes to my parents and my grandparents who – with sacrifices and example – taught me the importance of education and work ethic.

Among the different universities where I have developed my knowledge, I will be eternally grateful to the University of Chicago Booth School of Business, the cradle of breakthrough finance ideas and Nobel prizes. Every professor of my MBA has contributed to my knowledge, but I would like to specially thank – in strict alphabetical order – Professor Eugene F. Fama, Steven Neil Kaplan, Scott F. Meadow, James E. Schrager, Pietro Veronesi, Robert W. Vishny, and Luigi Zingales.

Several university professors have taught me lifelong lessons: amongst all of them, I want to thank Luigi Zingales of the University of Chicago for opening my horizons to the knowledge of private equity in the United States and Marcus H. Miller of the University of Warwick for suggesting I protect the 20% of the time devoted to reasoning in everyday work (the remaining 80% being pure execution).

I had the honour of working for prestigious institutions and outstanding professionals: amongst all these I want to remember Robert Wardrop (DAM Capital, University of Cambridge) for sharing the sharpness and 'long' view in the difficult investment decisions in mezzanine finance, James Fenner (GE Capital) for giving an international imprinting to my knowledge of leverage finance, and Rainer Masera (IMI, Intesa Sanpaolo) whose intellectual rigour I have tried to aspire to – not only in private equity.

I have also met brilliant individuals on various deals, whose wisdom pills have enriched my professional career: of all these, I would like to mention with gratitude Luca Bassi (Bain Capital), Luigi Bartone (ICG), Luca Peyrano (London Stock Exchange and Elite), and Giuseppe Castagna (BancoBPM).

A warm thanks goes also to the investors, employers, and colleagues of the various investment initiatives (private equity and private debt funds, investment vehicles, banks) where I have developed and applied my knowledge.

I would like to thank my longtime friend Simone Strocchi, founder and managing partner of Electa, adviser in deal structuring activities for private equity and private debt funds and pioneer of innovative solutions to help the listing of successful Italian SMEs. A warm thanks to Luca Magliano, who has worked with me at GE Capital and is now Manager at Electa, who has provided invaluable modelling assistance for this book.

A warm thanks to Alessandro Bonazzi, associate at Simmons & Simmons, who has provided substantial support in the drafting and review of the chapter on legal aspects of private equity and private debt transactions. I would like to also thank my longtime friend Andrea Accornero, managing partner of Simmons & Simmons, a leading international law firm (with offices in the EU, Asia, and the Middle East) with a sector focus in asset management and investment funds and financial institutions among others.

A special thanks to all the Wiley team who supported me in this journey: Gemma Valler for her utmost professionalism and firm steering, Benjamin Elisha and Koushika Ramesh for their support and patience, Gladys Ganaden for her guidance and help, and the production editor.

Finally, the most heartfelt thanks:

To Ilaria for the support and for the patience to tolerate all the times I had to say 'sorry, I'll call you back later, I'm busy now'.

To Gaia who gave significance to my life and to whom I owe my biggest apologies for my absence in her daily life. To her, my sweetest and loving wishes of a life full of happiness, health, and success.

About the Companion Site

This book is accompanied by a companion website:

www.wiley.com/go/privatedebtprivateequity

The website includes the following materials for instructors (password: Ippolito2019) and students (open access):

Instructors:
- Test Bank
- PowerPoints

Students:
- Excel Spreadsheets.

Introduction

The alternative investment industry has grown from $1 trillion in 1999 to nearly $6 trillion in 2018 (source: PreQin) and is expected to more than double to $15 trillion by 2022 (source: PWC AWM Research Center analysis). Within the various alternative asset classes, private debt and private equity already represent a significant share and are expected to grow faster than other asset classes.

The main drivers of growth are represented, on the supply side, by regulatory changes (constraining bank lending). On the demand side, small and mid size companies find it increasingly interesting to be financed by principal investors (alternative lenders and private equity funds) which are not only mere providers of specialised capital but – from due diligence to monitoring and value creation – also support entrepreneurs in their strategic, business and financial decisions.

Alternative assets classes are also an appealing investment opportunity for institutional investors because they offer both income and capital appreciation.

These dramatic changes in the financial landscape have been only partially accompanied by adequate educational tools: no handbook on private debt is available, whilst private equity textbooks take a very partial view (the financial analysis one) of investment decisions.

The book *Private Capital Investing. Handbook of Private Debt and Private Equity* (henceforth *Private Capital Investing*) is a practical handbook on investing in the most common alternative asset classes and provides a unique insight into how principal investors analyse investment opportunities.

Unlike other textbooks available in the market, the book covers the various phases that principal investors follow when analysing a private investment opportunity. *Private Capital Investing* combines academic rigour with the practical approach used by leading investors. Every chapter is filled with practical examples, Excel workbooks (downloadable on the book companion website), and examples of legal clauses and contracts. Further reading and cases are suggested at the end of every chapter to guide further in-depth analysis and test the learning of the reader.

Purpose of the book is to build a bridge between study and real-life case studies so that the reader will be able to start working in the principal investing world without need for further training. It is intended for undergraduates and MBA students, practitioners in investment banking, consulting, private debt, and private equity business with prior academic background in corporate finance and accounting.

THE RISE OF PRIVATE MARKETS (ALTERNATIVE ASSETS) IN THE INVESTORS' ALLOCATION

The key reasons for allocating to private markets are:

- **Potential for alpha:** one of the main reasons to invest in alternative assets is to earn a premium (i.e. alpha) over the return offered by public market assets. There are at least three sources of alpha:
  - illiquidity premium: premium paid to the investor to compensate them for not having short-term access to their money, hence making private capital asset classes suited for investors with a longer time horizon (also called patient capital);
  - active premium: this derives from the active management of the private investment;
  - complexity premium: origination, structuring, and managing private assets is one of the key features and challenges of private capital investing.
- **Diversification:** alternative investments lack correlation with the major traditional asset classes of public equities and public fixed-income assets. Risk within the asset classes can be further diversified by geography, industry/sector, and capital structure (equity, senior debt, junior debt).

The private markets space is varied and hard to define in its entirety: according to McKinsey (see Figure I.1), private market assets under management (AUM) in

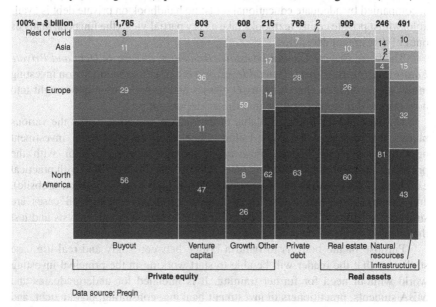

FIGURE I.1   Private market assets under management in 2018.
Source: 'Private markets come of age', February 2019, McKinsey & Company, www .mckinsey.com. (c) 2019 McKinsey & Company. All rights reserved. Reproduced with permission.

2018 totalled $5.8 trillion. Out of total AUM, private equity, growth equity, and private debt represent 54%.

Figure I.2 breaks down AUM by asset class and by region. In all regions, private equity commands the bulk of AUM, with real estate and private debt funds competing for the second place. The USA has by far the largest AUM, with China growing at the fastest pace.

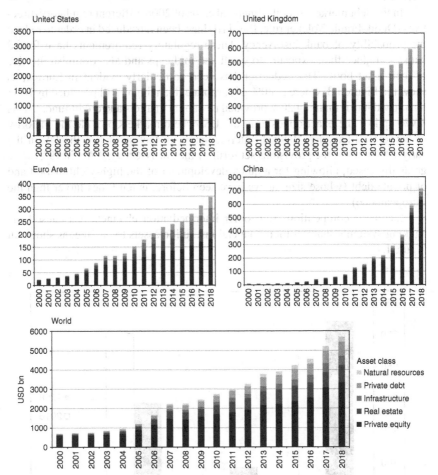

FIGURE I.2 Private market assets under management by region and by asset class in 2018 (US$ bn).

Source: © 2018, CFA Institute. Reproduced and republished from *Capital Formation: The Evolving Role of Public and Private Markets* with permission from CFA Institute. All rights reserved.

THE RISE OF PRIVATE MARKETS AS A FAVOURED ALTERNATIVE SOURCE OF COMPANY FINANCING

Private markets have also become a favoured funding alternative for corporates following the structural changes that have occurred in both debt and equity markets.

In the debt market, after the financial crisis of 2008, different regulatory directives (Dodd–Frank, Volcker rule, Basel III) have been introduced in order to reduce the probability of bank insolvency. These regulatory requirements have forced banks to reduce their exposure to small and mid caps and also diminish the size of their asset book. This reduction has been particularly evident in Europe, as shown in Figure I.3, where c. 80% of corporate financing is still provided by bank loans (with the remaining 20% provided by capital markets and credit funds). This 80/20 split is the exact opposite in the US, where markets provide the majority of corporate financing. Bank disintermediation in fact started in the US in the early 1960s, when the provisions set forth by the Glass–Steagall Act in 1933 were gradually eased, allowing for a quick development of the high-yield market and of private debt (whose size, as we have seen before, is ten times larger than the European one).

Increased competition from other intermediation channels has caused the banking system's share of total financial institution assets to decline, as shown in Figure I.4.

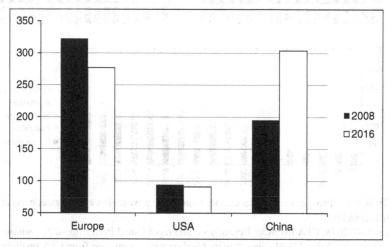

FIGURE I.3 Banking system assets as a percentage of GDP.
Source: Reproduced from Bank for International Settlements. *Structural changes in banking after the crisis.* CGFS Papers No 60, 2018.

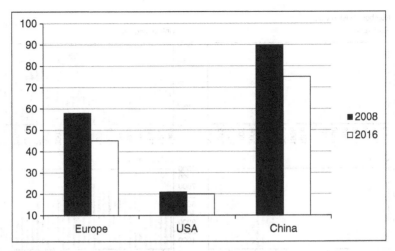

FIGURE I.4 Share of banking system assets in total financial institution assets. Source: Reproduced from Bank for International Settlements. *Structural changes in banking after the crisis.* CGFS Papers No 60, 2018.

In the equity market, according to a study of the Miken Institute,[1] in the US there are more firms owned by private equity investors than are listed on all the US stock exchanges.

Statistics on listed (see Figure I.5) companies similarly confirm that around the world (with the only exception of China) the appeal of public markets has stalled or diminished.

There are different explanations for this trend:

- **Reduced short-term pressure:** public markets are often blamed for the excessive focus on short-term financial goals.
- **Regulatory disclosure and reporting requirements:** being listed implies compliance with regulatory rules and continuous communication with the market.
- **Flexibility and speed to execute changes in strategy and operations:** operating in a private context allows owners and managers to swiftly implement changes in strategies, personnel, and operations without the need to explain and convince the market.
- **Increasing relative importance of institutional investors vs. retail investors:** the growing importance of institutional investors allows companies to raise funds without all the requirements necessary for publicly traded companies with retail investors.

---

[1] Wilhelmus, J., W. Lee. *Companies Rush to Go Private.* Milken Institute, 2018.

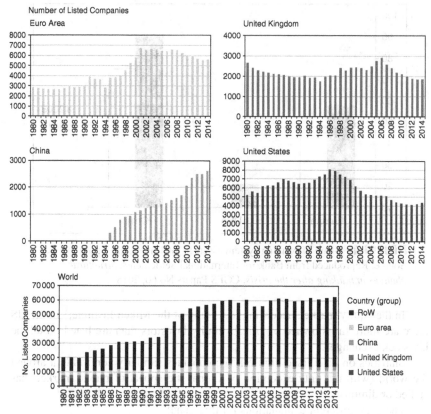

FIGURE I.5   Number of listed companies by region.

Amongst alternative investments, this book will focus on two of the most popular asset classes: private equity and private debt.

PRIVATE EQUITY

Private equity is the investment activity by institutional investors in the equity capital of non-listed companies, with the goal of increasing their equity value in order to divest it within the medium/long term. Financial scholars describe private equity as a function of the different life stages of a company, as shown in Table I.1.

Venture capital can be further divided into the following.

- **Seed financing:** investment in risk capital when there is no product at all, when the entrepreneur only has an idea or an invention.

TABLE I.1 Different types of private equity as a function of the investee company life cycle.

Life stage	Type of private equity
Start-up	Venture capital (early-stage financing)
Development	Growth equity (development or expansion capital)
Maturity	Leveraged buy out (replacement capital)
Restructuring	Distressed equity

- **Start-up financing:** the investor intervenes in the start-up phase of production, while not knowing yet the commercial validity of the product or service. Compared with the previous phase, there is a prototype (i.e., the so-called phase of experimentation has been completed). There is a company and management that has already started appropriate market research and product testing.
- **First-stage financing:** intervention in the phase following the start-up of the production activity, where the commercial validity of the product has yet to be evaluated concretely.

Growth equity is aimed at supporting development plans via organic growth (e.g. the launch of new products or penetration into new markets) or via external lines (e.g. through acquisitions) through the subscription of a capital increase or a convertible bond/loan. It generally consists of a minority stake in the company.

Leveraged buy out consists of the acquisition of a majority stake financed by a mix of equity and third-party debt.

Investors require different returns from investing in private equity as a result of the different levels of risk, as shown in Table I.2.

Figure I.6 illustrates the breakdown of private equity AUM by region and by private equity type.

TABLE I.2 The Required IRR as a function of investee company life cycle.

Type of private equity	Required internal rate of return (IRR) (%)
Start-up	>40
Distressed equity	>35
Expansion capital	>25
Leveraged buy out	>20
Quasi equity (mezzanine)	15–20
Portage and equity dressed debt	10–15

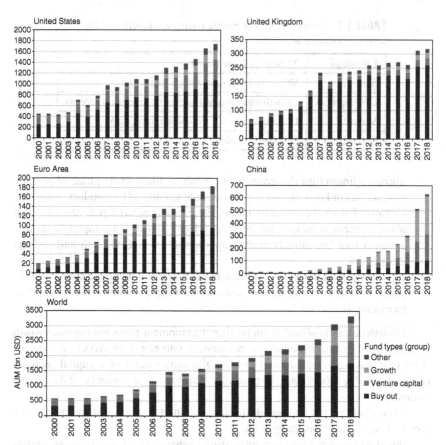

FIGURE I.6 Private equity AUM by region and type (in US$).
Source: © 2018, CFA Institute. Reproduced and republished from *Capital Formation: The Evolving Role of Public and Private Markets* with permission from CFA Institute. All rights reserved.

PRIVATE DEBT

Private debt is the financing activity by institutional investors in non-listed companies, with the goal of maximising investors' returns though a combination of fees and interest charges (and eventually capital gains). Financial scholars describe private debt as a function of the different life stages of a company, as shown in Table I.3.

A more granular definition distinguishes between:

- **Private debt:** financing by private debt funds of transactions (leveraged buy outs or LBOs) where the shareholder is a private equity fund.

TABLE I.3 Different types of private debt as a function of the investee company life cycle.

Life stage	Type of private debt
Start-up	Venture debt (early-stage financing)
Development	Growth debt (development or expansion capital)
Restructuring	Distressed debt

- **Direct lending:** financing by private debt funds of SMEs. The use of proceeds is generally aimed at supporting growth (internal or external).

Figure I.7 illustrates the breakdown of private debt AUM by region and by private debt type.

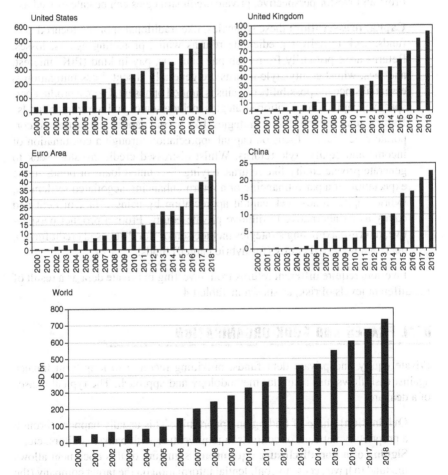

FIGURE I.7 Private debt AUM by region and type (in US$).

Source: © 2018, CFA Institute. Reproduced and republished from *Capital Formation: The Evolving Role of Public and Private Markets* with permission from CFA Institute. All rights reserved.

TABLE I.4   Required IRR as a function of debt product / fund.

Type of private debt fund	Required IRR (%)
Senior debt unlevered funds	4–6
Senior debt levered funds	6–8
Leveraged buy out funds	5–7
Mezzanine funds	8–12
Hybrid capital funds	10–15
Distressed credit funds	15–18

From an investor perspective, private credit strategies can be categorised as:

- **Capital preservation:** these strategies, like traditional sponsor-focused debt funds, seek to deliver predictable returns whilst protecting against losses. Returns arise primarily from cash pay coupons, pay in kind (PIK) interest, and fees, whilst equity style returns are generally absent. Loss mitigation is essential since the possibility of gains is limited or absent. From a product perspective, capital preservation strategies include senior and mezzanine funds.
- **Return-maximising:** these strategies, like hybrid capital and distressed corporate credit funds, focus on capital appreciation through a combination of income and equity style returns. Whilst distressed credit investors seek to generate private equity-like returns, buying discounted loans or bonds in the expectation of a par refinancing or a return-enhancing negotiated settlement, hybrid capital funds seek capital appreciation by using a mix of debt and equity as an alternative to dilutive private equity. From a product perspective, return-maximising strategies include senior (for distressed credit funds), debt, and preferred equity (for hybrid capital) funds.

Investors require different returns from investing in private debt as a result of the different levels of risk, as shown in Table I.4.

DEAL PHASES AND BOOK ORGANISATION

Private equity and private debt funds, providing medium to long-term finance against cash flows, use a similar methodology and approach. The typical phases of a deal are:

- **Origination:** phase of finding an opportunity. This usually happens through a proprietary network of contacts, a joint venture with banks, auditors, etc.
- **Signing of a non-disclosure agreement:** signature of this document allows the fund to have access to confidential information on the target company (the 'Target').

- **Preliminary analysis of the opportunity:** analysis based on available information on market opportunity, company positioning, historical financials, and the business plan of the Target.
- **Valuation** (if private equity deal): indicative valuation of the Target.
- **Deal structuring:** based on the analysis of the Target, alternative deal structures are prepared to meet the Target's needs and the fund's return objectives.
- **Letter of interest and exclusivity:** formulation of a proposal, outlining key terms and conditions of the deal.
- **Due diligence:** accounting, tax, business, environmental, and legal in-depth analysis are usually outsourced by the fund to a team of external experts.
- **Legal documentation:** set of legal documents that are needed to close the transaction.

The book is organised as follows.

CLOSED END FUNDS CH. 1   DEBT PRODUCTS CH. 2   EQUITY PRODUCTS CH. 3

The first section of the book covers the fundamentals. Chapter 1 analyses structure, economics, and the expected returns of closed end funds (the typical structure of private equity and private debt funds). Chapter 2 shows the key features of pure debt (banking and capital market) products, mezzanine, high-yield, and unitranche and provides some Excel modelling examples of debt products. Chapter 3 offers an overview of (ordinary and preferred) equity, various types of convertibles, options, and warrants and finally provides some Excel modelling examples of equity products.

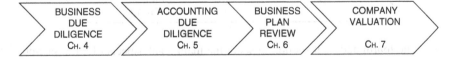

BUSINESS DUE DILIGENCE CH. 4   ACCOUNTING DUE DILIGENCE CH. 5   BUSINESS PLAN REVIEW CH. 6   COMPANY VALUATION CH. 7

The second section covers the preliminary analysis. Chapter 4 deals with business due diligence, analysing the market dynamics, competition, and positioning of the Target in order to obtain a critical view of all the 'business' aspects that affect the capacity of the Target to be profitable and to produce cash in the long term. Chapter 5 focuses on accounting due diligence and reviews quality of earnings, accounting policies, and adjustments (with particular reference to earnings before interest, tax, depreciation, and amortisation (EBITDA) and net financial position) to obtain 'normalised' (net of non-recurring items, accounting policies, etc.) figures; an analysis of cash flows and key ratios completes the accounting analysis. Chapter 6 offers a concise outline of key steps in financial projection with reference to the construction of pro-forma financials and sensitivity analysis;

a simplified Excel model of building a business plan is presented. Chapter 7 (applicable to equity deals only) presents the most used valuation methods: discounted cash flow, adjusted present value, market multiples, and transaction multiples; the chapter ends with an Excel modelling example of the valuation of a company using the abovementioned different methodologies.

GROWTH EQUITY CH. 8 → LEVERAGED BUY OUT CH. 9 → OVERVIEW OF EXITS CH. 10 → PRIVATE DEBT CH. 11

The third section focuses on deal structuring. Chapter 8 explains some fundamental concepts (pre-money and post-money, capitalisation table, equity stake calculation, dilution, anti-dilution provisions, growth capital method) and, in an Excel modelling example, analyses how to structure a growth (minority) equity transaction.

Chapter 9 illustrates in detail leveraged buy outs (LBOs): a step-by-step accounting example, capital structure analysis, value creation, valuation, and structuring are presented and a final Excel modelling example shows a LBO (majority) equity deal. Chapter 10 provides an overview of the most common exits (initial public offering (IPO), trade sale, secondary buy out) from a private equity deal.

Chapter 11 illustrates the most common methods used to structure a debt facility: among the areas covered, debt capacity, covenant, security package, and repayment structures form the core analysis. An Excel modelling example of structuring a loan facility reviews in practice all the topics.

LEGAL DOCUMENTATION CH. 12 → OVERVIEW OF DISTRESS SYMPTOMS AND REMEDIES CH. 13

The fourth and final section looks at the main legal aspects of a transaction and at the main symptoms and remedies of financial distress.

Chapter 12 covers all the legal aspects of a deal. In addition to the confidentiality agreement, the mandate, and the term sheet that characterise the pre-due diligence phase, the following contracts are used in a deal:

a) private equity: constitutional documents, investment contract, and shareholders' agreements;

b) private debt: financing contract (also typical of leveraged buy outs, or private equity majority deal through financial leverage) and security agreements.

Chapter 13 provides an overview of distress symptoms and remedies. After a review of early warning signals and the main causes of distress, legal and financial restructuring options are reviewed.

CHAPTER 1

Closed End Funds

A CLOSE UP ON PRIVATE EQUITY AND PRIVATE DEBT PARTNERSHIPS

A private equity fund is a collective investment scheme used for making minority or majority equity investments in private (i.e. non-listed) firms. A private debt fund is a collective investment scheme used for effecting loans or subscribing bonds in private firms.

At inception, investors make an unfunded commitment to the limited partnership, which is then drawn over the term of the fund. A private equity (debt) fund is raised and managed by investment professionals (who find, analyse, invest, monitor, and implement value creation actions in private firms) of a specific private equity (debt) firm. The goal of managers is to maximise investors' returns from invested capital.[1]

Institutional private equity funds are usually structured as limited partnerships (although funds that are intended for retail use often have other legal forms, such as listed vehicles) with a fixed term of up to ten years (often with annual extensions of the agreed upon investment period and fund life). A partnership has a fixed contractual term: therefore, the investment is illiquid during that time, unless the investor decides to sell the partnership on the secondary market. The main participants to a private equity (debt) partnership (see also Figure 1.1) are:

a) **General partner (GP):** the manager is called the general partner and has potentially unlimited liability for the actions of the fund. To put a cap on

---

[1] Some definitions regarding capital are worth setting out at this stage:

- **Allocated capital:** the part of the assets that has been set aside for investment.
- **Committed capital:** the capital that an investor has promised to provide to private equity (debt) funds by signing a Limited Partnerships Agreement.
- **Drawn down capital:** the amount of committed capital that has been drawn down (requested by a fund and paid to them). It has been paid on demand and includes capital to be invested in firms as well as money required for fees and costs.
- **Invested capital:** the part of drawn down capital that has been invested in portfolio firms. The other main use of drawn down capital is the payment of fees and costs.

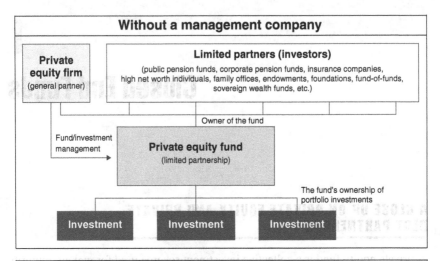

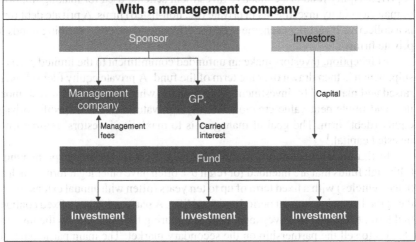

FIGURE 1.1   A typical private equity (debt) fund structure.

this potentially unlimited liability, GPs are limited companies or partnerships. The GP interest is the fund manager's participation of his capital in the fund. Technically, the fund manager invests in the general partner; however, in common usage, limited partners are investors and GPs are fund managers. GPs are compensated with an incentive allocation of capital appreciation, called carried interest. Loss carry-forwards in the partnership structure ensure that GPs do not receive their incentive allocation until all the losses of limited partners have been recovered. Similarly, claw-backs in the structure ensure that GPs do not receive an over-distribution of gains. Hurdle rates ensure that GPs do not receive an incentive allocation until investors recover their original investment and make a preferential rate of return on their investment. When the structure does not foresee a management company, the GP is entitled to also receive the management fee.

b) **Limited partner (LP):** external investors are called limited partners because their total liability is limited to the amount they invest. LPs must qualify as accredited or professional investors before they can enter an investment partnership as limited partners. In the US (but in other continents similar rules apply), the definition essentially sets a minimum net worth or minimum annual income; there are also limitations on employee benefit plan assets when admitting new LPs. A prospective LP should be aware of the percentage of the partnership assets that his or her capital represents with regard to risk as well as with regard to regulatory issues.

c) **Management company (MC):** the management company provides management services to the fund. It is usually owned by the general partners of the fund and is rewarded for its services by way of a management fee. Moreover, because GPs usually have an advisory role with the investee companies, a management company can earn advisory fees for work carried out on behalf of these companies. The partnership agreement should determine the costs that will be carried by the partnership (legal and accounting fees are usually borne by the limited partnership).

The partnerships are generally specialised by type of company, investment stage, industry, and source of transaction. Typically, a single private equity (debt) firm will manage a series of distinct private equity (debt) funds and will attempt to raise a new fund as the previous fund is fully invested. The investment management companies will usually form a new partnership every two to four years, when the prior partnership's capital is almost entirely committed to a portfolio of companies. Fundraising hence takes place at three to four year intervals: this means that in the third or fourth year of Fund I, they will be fundraising for Fund II, and so on. Some funds, such as secondary funds, have been investing more rapidly in recent years and therefore raise funds more often. New partnerships are generally formed by first contacting investors who were involved in the earlier partnership and are known to the management. Prospective investors then conduct due diligence with regard to the fund. If the outcome of that process is satisfactory, investors will commit to the fund and negotiate terms with the fund's manager. Thus, investment power is limited to the GP manager. LPs are not involved in the investment process at all. Therefore, all private equity (debt) investors are entirely passive in the legal sense. The combination of passive investment and long fund lifetimes makes this asset class unattractive for some investors, and it illustrates the need for specialist managers.

Partnership managers receive a compensation which consists of two components:

■ **Management fee:** annual payment made by the limited partners in the fund to the fund's manager to pay for the private equity (debt) firm's investment operations. Usually, the management fee is initially based on the total investor commitments to the fund (i.e. the fund size) and, after the end of the investment period (usually three to five years), the basis for calculating the fee will change to the cost basis of the fund, less any investments that have been realised or written-off (hence on the net asset value). Management fees rates will range from 1.0% (for private debt funds) to 2.0% (for private equity funds) per annum during the investment period, and will then often step down by 0.5–1.0% from the original rate through to the termination of the fund.

■ **Carried interest:** a performance fee that rewards the manager for enhancing performance. In order to receive carried interest, the manager must first return all capital contributed by the investors and then return a previously agreed-upon rate of return (the 'hurdle rate' or 'preferred return', customary at 3–4% per annum (p.a.) on private debt funds and 7–8% p.a. on private equity funds) to investors. The extra-performance over and above capital returned and the hurdle rate is then split between investors (80–85%) and the manager (15–20%). Private equity (debt) funds distribute carried interest to the manager only upon exit from all investments (loans), which may take years. Carried interest on a deal by deal basis (rather than fund) has nearly disappeared.

A slightly more complex formula for distribution is synthetised by the following clause:

1) The investors receive 100% of commitments advanced and a preferred rate of return (hurdle rate).
2) The carried interest holders receive 100% of all distributions until such time that they have received 25% of the investors' preferred return (1 above). This is referred to as 'catch up'.
3) Thereafter the remaining distributions are split as follows:
   a. 80% (or 85%) to investors.
   b. 20% (or 15%) to carried interest holders.

CASH FLOWS, J CURVE, AND RETURNS

An investment in a private equity (debt) fund is different from other asset classes because it represents an investment in a stream of cash flows. Unlike with a bond, where there is usually only one cash outflow, with a private equity fund there is a range of cash outflows as money is drawn down by the GP. When a fund needs cash, the GP will issue a draw down notice (capital call). This will request that an amount of cash be paid to a particular bank account by a certain date, and it will give details as to what the money is needed for. The LP will check that the cash is the correct amount, and that it is being used for valid purposes under the Limited Partnership Agreement. It will then make the necessary bank transfer. Importantly, funds are not usually allowed to draw down money to hold on account, though they may do so in anticipation of a particular transaction that they expect to close imminently. They will often return it and draw it down again if the transaction does not complete.

Figure 1.2 below summarises the typical timeline of a private equity (debt) fund. Before the first closing (which occurs when the minimum amount of the fund is reached), commitments are sought from investors. After the first closing, fundraising continues (usually for an additional 12–18 months) and the investment period starts. Capital calls for management fees and other costs occur from Year 1 until Year 9 or 10, while capital calls for investments occur throughout the duration of the investment period. Distributions occur when

a) dividends and divestments from a portfolio company occur in a private equity fund;

b) interest and principal repayment from a portfolio company occur in a private debt fund.

Since both the timing and number of cash flows are completely uncertain, private equity returns are not measured annually, but are measured on a compound basis. This is important to note when comparing private equity returns to returns of other asset classes. In the early years of a private equity fund, its returns will be negative because money is paid into the fund before any money is paid back by the fund upon realisation of investments. Eventually, however, the value of cash coming in will match the value of what is going out. At that point, the internal rate of return (IRR: compounded return over time) of the fund will be zero. This is referred to as the J-curve (see Figure 1.3 for a graphic representation). The J-curve is produced by consideration of the cumulative return of a fund in each year of its life: the first entry will represent the IRR of the fund for the first year of its life; whilst the second entry will represent the IRR of the fund for the first two years of its life; the third of the IRR for the first three years; and so on. An important element to bear in mind is that the IRR is likely to be more accurate toward the end of the fund than during the early stages of the fund's life (when it is still under the effect of the J-curve, both at individual transaction level and fund level). It is also important to remember that – due to the fact that the life of a fund tends to be

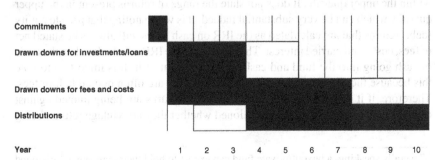

Commitments										
Drawn downs for investments/loans										
Drawn downs for fees and costs										
Distributions										
Year	1	2	3	4	5	6	7	8	9	10

FIGURE 1.2   Timeline of private equity (debt) fund.

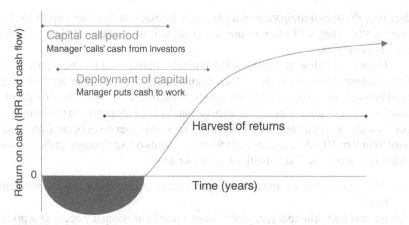

FIGURE 1.3   J-curve effect in a private equity (debt) fund.

much longer for a venture fund relative to a buyout fund[2] – IRR should therefore be used with caution during the first six years or so of the fund's life.

During the life of a fund (i.e. before it has fully divested its portfolio), investors receive an annual (or infra-annual) valuation of the fund. Valuation is one of the major issues of concern raised with regard to investment in private equity funds. One of the reasons given for this concern is that private equity returns contain a substantial element of illiquid, unrealisable capital gain that is represented only by a portfolio company having been written up by the GP.

Returns are measured on a vintage year basis. The vintage year return always states the compound return of all constituent funds formed during the vintage year, from the vintage year to a specific date. In practice the specified date is normally at the end of the last complete year for which the figures are available. The upper quartile is the data point in a sample population that is precisely one quarter down from the top in order of ranking. The upper quartile is the best way of evaluating the vintage year. The upper quartile figure describes the condition of each separate fund at the bottom of the upper quartile, not the overall condition of all the funds within the upper quartile. It does not state the range of returns present in the upper quartile, which can be very substantial indeed. It is worth noting that private equity (debt) returns that are calculated as the IRR on cash flows will always be stated net of fees, costs, and carried interest. This is because the IRR is calculated on the basis of cash going into the fund and cash being taken out of it. It is important to note this because the returns of many other asset classes are often quoted before fees. Therefore, if it is seen that private equity (debt) returns are being quoted against other asset classes, it should be questioned whether they are vintage returns being

---

[2]Generally speaking, a buyout/private fund can expect to hold their companies for around three/five years, and venture fund for around five/seven years.

compared to vintage returns, and also whether the figures for the other asset class are stated before or after fees.

Although IRR is widely accepted as the correct measure of performance, multiples are another important measure of private equity and private debt funds. The money multiple is the most important measure of performance. At company level, the money multiple is the ratio between total cash realised by disposing of that interest, by the total cash invested in a company, regardless of how many cash flows may be involved. For example, if $2.5m is paid into a portfolio company and $5m is received back, the money multiple will be 2x. It doesn't matter how many single cash flows are involved, or over what period they take place – though this is relevant to transaction IRR. Whatever money multiple is used, it can only have been generated in gross terms by the money multiple achieved on the fund's underlying portfolio companies. There is usually only one way of calculating the money multiple that is earned on a firm, and that is by considering the actual amount paid out and the actual amount received. Other typical indicators to measure a fund performance are:

a) **Distributed over paid in (DPI):** measures the ratio of money distributed by a fund against the total amount of money paid into the fund. At the start of the investment, this ratio will be zero, and will begin to increase as distributions are paid out. When the DPI is equal to one, the fund has broken even, as money paid in is equal to money distributed, and any number above this indicates that the fund has paid out more than has been paid in.

b) **Total value to paid in (TVPI):** measures the overall performance of a fund with a ratio of the fund's cumulative distributions and residual value to the paid-in capital. It calculates what multiple of the investment would be returned to investors if the unrealised assets were sold at current valuations and added to distributions that had already been received. It is very helpful in measuring the distributions received to date, as well as the residual value of the remaining investments. While DPI provides a clear measurement of the actual multiple of cash invested that has been received by an investor, TVPI provides a metric that accounts for potential returns that are the result of increased valuations of portfolio companies as they approach exit. Given this difference, many LPs rely on TVPI earlier in the life of a fund and DPI towards the end.

FINANCIAL RETURNS

Investors in private equity funds expect to receive returns of 500 to 1000 basis points (bp) more – calculated on a comparable levered basis – than they might expect to receive from public securities. Although private equity investments are viewed as being considerably more risky than public market investments, sophisticated institutional investors have been committing increasing amounts of financing in this area. Private equity has therefore become an accepted element of most diversified institutions.

Dividends and realised capital gains are the two components of the financial returns that accrue to investors.

Dividends are the portion of the company's profits paid out to shareholders. Payment takes place on a pro-rata basis depending on each shareholding percentage held in the company. Dividends are paid out if the company has realised a profit (or has sufficient accumulated reserves) and their amount depends either on the enterprise's dividend policy or on ad hoc decisions of the shareholders. There is usually no obligation for a company to pay dividends to its shareholders, except in such cases where a clause establishing a compulsory dividend pay-out ratio (always subject to the company being profitable) has been included in the shareholder agreement. Since dividend distribution affects the returns of an investor, shareholders always face the trade-off between allocating net earnings to capex (thus allowing the company to grow further) or to dividend payments.

A capital gain is a profit that results from the sale of the portfolio company at an amount higher than the purchase price. Usually, the majority of the investment's return comes from a realised capital gain on exit as opposed to dividend payments. Returns will be higher the higher the exit price and the lower the price paid at entry. The investment's degree of liquidity will also play a significant role in achieving higher, lower, or any returns at all.

As said above, IRR (investment's annualised equivalent compounded return rate or, in other words, the yield that would be produced by an investment with regular annual payments and overall same return as the one under consideration) and cash on cash multiples are the most widely used metrics to assess and compare the returns of a transaction. Time (as Tables 1.1 and 1.2 below show) plays a crucial role in determining the final outcome.

In order to make the correlation risk/reward inherently coherent, and since – in case of equity – the equilibrium between risk and return is more unstable (due to a number of factors such as company, sector, governance, exit), the expected ex ante return for equity investment tends to be significantly higher than the one for debt securities.

TABLE 1.1   IRR (%) as a function of time and cash on cash exit multiple.

Multiple/years	2x	2.5x	3x	3.5x	4x	5x	6x	8x	10x
2	41	58	73	87	100	124	145	183	216
3	26	36	44	52	59	71	82	100	115
4	19	26	32	37	41	50	57	68	78
5	15	20	25	28	32	38	43	52	58
6	12	16	20	23	26	31	35	41	47
7	10	14	17	20	22	26	29	35	39
8	9	12	15	17	19	22	25	30	33
9	8	11	13	15	17	20	22	26	29
10	7	10	12	13	15	17	20	23	26

TABLE 1.2   Cash on cash (X) exit multiple calculated as a function of time and IRRs.

IRR/years	15.0%	17.5%	20.0%	22.5%	25.0%	27.5%	30.0%	32.5%	35%
1	1.15	1.18	1.20	1.23	1.25	1.28	1.30	1.33	1.40
2	1.32	1.38	1.44	1.50	1.56	1.63	1.69	1.76	1.96
3	1.52	1.62	1.73	1.84	1.95	2.07	2.20	2.33	2.74
4	1.75	1.91	2.07	2.25	2.44	2.64	2.86	3.08	3.84
5	2.01	2.24	2.49	2.76	3.05	3.37	3.71	4.08	5.38
6	2.31	2.63	2.99	3.38	3.81	4.30	4.83	5.41	7.53
7	2.66	3.09	3.58	4.14	4.77	5.48	6.27	7.17	10.54
8	3.06	3.63	4.30	5.07	5.96	6.98	8.16	9.50	14.76
9	3.52	4.27	5.16	6.21	7.45	8.90	10.60	12.59	20.66
10	4.05	5.02	6.19	7.61	9.31	11.35	13.79	16.68	28.93

The following tables (Table 1.3 and 1.4) summarise the required return as a function of product and the company stage and product.

TABLE 1.3   Target return as a function of instrument.

Stage	Indicative target return (%)
Ordinary equity	>25
Ordinary equity (with special rights)	>20
(Redeemable, convertible) preference shares	12–25
Mezzanine (with warrants)	12–20
Loans with equity linked return interest step up, convertible	8–20
Senior unsecured debt	6–8
Senior secured debt	3–5

TABLE 1.4   Target return as a function of the company stage.

Stage	Indicative target return (%)
Start-up	>40
Early expansion capital	>30
Growth equity	>20
Quasi equity (mezzanine etc.)	15–20
Portage[3] and equity dressed debt	10–15
Senior acquisition debt	3–5
Senior capex debt	2–4

---

[3]Portage equity is an equity investment with an exit arranged that is under the private equity fund's unequivocal control, for a minimum predetermined amount, and is valid for a certain period to a creditworthy sponsor.

REFERENCES AND FURTHER READING

H. Cendrowski, L.W. Petro, J.P. Martin, and A. Wadecki. 2008. *Private Equity: History, Governance, and Operations*. Wiley Finance.

G.W. Fenn, J.N. Liang, and S.D. Prowse. 1995. 'The Economics of the Private Equity Market.' Staff Studies from Board of Governors of the Federal Reserve System (U.S.), No 168.

G. Fraser-Sampson. 2007. *Private Equity as an Asset Class*. Wiley Finance.

J. Lerner. 1984. 'A Note on Private Equity Partnership Agreements.' Harvard Business School Note 9-294-084. January.

J.S. Levin and D.E. Rocap. 2009. *Structuring Venture Capital, Private Equity, and Entrepreneurial Transactions*. Wolters Kluwer.

SUGGESTED CASES

J. Lerner. 2015. 'Yale University Investments Office: February 2015.' Harvard Business School Case 815-124.

J. Lerner. 1995. 'Acme Investment Trust.' Harvard Business School Case 296-042.

CHAPTER 2

Debt Products

INTRODUCTION

Debt is a contract where financing is provided with a defined interest rate and principal repayment schedule. It is provided by banks, credit funds, insurance companies, investment firms, and collateralised obligations vehicles. In particular:

- **Commercial banks:** provide credit, term loans, and revolving loans. Most loans are made based on historical financial performance and minimum asset collateral values. Credit is extended based on character, collateral, and capacity to pay. Banks are the lowest-risk lenders. They will not generally lend to a company with a debt-to-equity ratio greater than 2x to 3x without additional guarantee or collateral.
- **Asset-based lenders:** provide debt financing by lending against the assets of a company. Although asset-based lenders may be owned by a bank, they are typically unregulated non-bank lenders that can make highly leveraged loans based on the collateral specific to their client's business. An asset-based loan will be repaid from the liquidation of the collateral no matter what the condition of the company. An asset-based lender's primary concern is the liquidation value of its loan's underlying assets and potential management fraud. The collateral is therefore closely monitored.
- **Investment banks:** assist corporations in raising capital by underwriting or acting as the client's agent in the issuance of securities.
- **Other specialised lenders:** include credit funds (closed or open funds in which core holdings are fixed income investments like short-term or long-term bonds, securitised products, money market instruments, or floating rate debt), mezzanine funds (closed fund focused on mezzanine loans), hedge funds (investment vehicles that pool capital from a number of investors and invest in securities and other instruments), etc.

In this chapter we will illustrate a broader set of debt products of those typically used by private debt funds because the artillery of products used by companies (also when they borrow from a credit fund) entails many of them.

DEFINITION AND SOME USEFUL CLASSIFICATIONS

Debt is a liability or obligation of a company that is evidenced by a note or written obligation of the company to repay the debt with interest on a specified schedule or maturity date. A debt holder does not have voting rights and cannot participate in the company's growth or profits, except as a recipient of principal and interest repayments. However, these repayments to debt holders have priority over the rights of equity holders to receive dividends and distributions of a company, and the rights of a debt holder may be secured by a pledge of a security interest in the assets or the cash flow of the company. An important advantage to the issuance of debt is that interest payments are tax deductible (creating the so-called tax shield) and that debt holders do not dilute shareholders' ownership. Moreover, debt instruments contain specific repayment schedules, such that management can plan for the servicing of the debt. Disadvantages of debt issuance include the diversion of cash away from the operations and growth of the business through repayment of debt and interest. Management is also limited with regard to freedom to run the company since restrictive covenants in the loan documents contain terms that may limit the company's ability to engage in transactions like mergers and acquisitions, to exceed certain levels of other debt, or to effect capital expenditures to above specified levels.

There are a number of ways to classify debt instruments as a function of different variables:

- **Public vs. private:** this distinction relates to whether the fixed income instruments are sold and circulate on public capital markets or are underwritten and/or sold in private markets. In more detail:
  - Public debt:
    - *Short term*: commercial paper (unsecured promissory note with a maturity not exceeding 270 days) or money market debt instruments.
    - *Medium term*: medium-term notes or bonds (either denominated in the currency of the issuer or in a foreign currency) with a maturity usually between one and seven years.
  - Private debt:
    - *Short term*: not exceeding one year; usually consists of bank debt (see detailed section below) or money market instruments.
    - *Long term*: includes bank debt, private placement (e.g. under rule 144 of SEC), leasing (a contract under which the lessee, user of the asset object of the contract, will pay the lessor, owner of the asset, for the use of an asset).

    The advantages of public debt are: deepest investor base, better liquidity, thinner pricing, and longer maturities. The disadvantages of public debt are: a rating is required, higher issuance costs, extensive disclosure, ongoing reporting requirements, and SEC review is required.

    The advantages of private debt are: flexible structures, confidentiality and limited disclosure, lower issuance costs, and no rating required. The disadvantages of private debt are: more stringent covenants, costly pricing, limited liquidity in secondary market, thin investor base.

- **Short vs. long term:** this distinction is made as a function of the contractual duration of debt: short-term debt is up to one year, long-term is above one year.
- **Investment grade vs. non-investment grade (or junk):** distinction made on a ranking of the fixed income instrument based on its quality (i.e., capacity to repay the obligation). A rating indicates that a loan (bond) has a relatively low (investment grade) or high (junk) risk of default. Rating can be private (internal rating of banks) or public (given by rating agencies). Rating agencies use different designations (see Figure 2.1). Figure 2.1 summarises the different categories.
- **Secured vs. unsecured:** this categorisation is made to distinguish fixed income instruments which have (or have not) a security interest over the assets of the borrower. The issuance of secured debt is based mainly on the firm's ability to service the debt from cash flows of its business operations. The borrower grants a security interest in its assets or cash flow, so that in the event the company is unable to repay the debt from cash flows, the lender may take title to the assets pledged as security and then sell the assets. The proceeds of the sale may then be applied to the repayment of the secured debt. If the proceeds of the sale are insufficient to repay the principal, accrued interest, and fees associated with default, the lender will have a claim against the general assets of the borrower. In many cases, the loan is guaranteed by a shareholder of the borrower. A lender may also collect unpaid amounts from

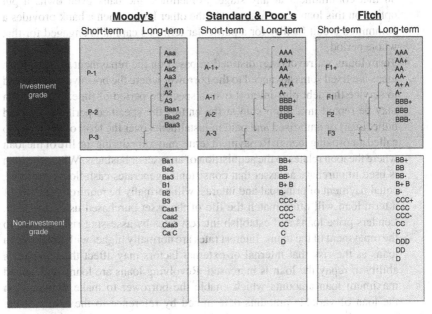

FIGURE 2.1 Comparison of rating categories per rating agency.

a guarantor or from the proceeds of the sale of any assets that a guarantor may have pledged to support the loan application. An unsecured loan is extended when the borrower has sufficient credit to insure repayment of the debt. The borrower will usually be well established, with a track record of loan repayment to secured and unsecured lenders. If a borrower takes on secured debt commitments at the same time as unsecured debt commitments, the secured debt holder has priority over the unsecured holder with regard to repayment. If a company carries both classes of debt, and there is default in the credit facilities, the unsecured lender must wait until the secured lender is paid in full before laying any claims to the borrower's assets. Unsecured loans are considered riskier due to the priority given to secured holders, and accordingly unsecured loans carry a higher interest rate than secured loans do. In Europe, inter-creditor agreements have an important role in ensuring lender security. These agreements relate to subordination and they stipulate the priority of repayment to all lenders.

- **Bilateral loan or syndicated loan:** this is a distinction based on the (number of) provider(s). A bilateral loan is a contract between two parties (the borrower and the lender), whilst a syndicated loan involves a number of banks lending to a single borrower. Usually, syndicated loans are used for substantial amounts and are common facilities in acquisition finance.
- **Committed vs. uncommitted credit facilities:** a distinction based on whether the facility drawdown is automatic or discretional. With an uncommitted credit facility, a bank may lend to a counterparty, but can go back on that commitment at any stage. Sometimes, the bank even owns a put option on this loan commitment. On the other hand, when a bank provides a committed credit facility for a particular term, its capital is engaged for that whole period.
- **Term loans vs. revolving:** distinction based on the repayment profile. Term loans are fixed sums advanced to the borrower where the borrower is expected to service the debt plus interest over a specified period of time. A term loan may be repaid in a lump sum at the end of the specified period (so called bullet loan) or amortised and paid in instalments over the term of the loan (so called amortising loans). Repayment terms may vary during the life of the loan where the loan relates to the acquisition of an asset or business. Where the loan is used to purchase an asset that consistently generates cash flow or returns, equal payment of principal and interest will normally be required. The life of a term loan will often match the life of the asset purchased using the loan. Lenders price loans and establish interest rates by assessing risks related to the repayment of the loans. Interest rates are normally higher with longer-term loans as the risk that internal or external factors may affect the company's ability to repay the loan is increased. Revolving loans are loans with stated maximum loan amounts which enable the borrower to make drawings on the loan of variable amounts determined by reference to the levels of the borrower's assets. Accounts receivable and inventory are amongst the assets

used to determine how much the company may borrow. The borrower's loan capacity increases as the level of accounts receivable and inventory increases. A borrower customarily repays a revolving loan with the collection of its accounts receivable so that availability increases as funds are applied to the loan, and decreases as amounts are redrawn. A company may draw down under a revolving loan as long as it is not in default under any term or condition of the loan agreement. Drawdowns are terminated if there is a default. Revolving loans are distinguished from term loans by the continuing increase and decrease in availability: as a term loan is paid down, availability is permanently decreased.

- **Fixed vs. floating rate:** a distinction based on how interest rate is set. Floating-rate interest payments are set based on a fixed spread to some benchmark that was predetermined at the time of issuance (e.g. London inter-bank offered rate (Libor) and Euro inter-bank offered rate (Euribor) etc.) and adjusted through the life of the debt. Fixed-rate interest (coupon) payments are set at the time of issuance and do not change over the life of the debt.
- **Asset-based vs. cash flow lending:** a distinction made on the basis of how repayment is expected. Asset-based loans are secured by specific assets and are governed by a borrowing formula or base (the most common are receivables and/or inventory lines), whilst cash flow lending (although usually secured with certain assets) relies heavily on the future expected cash flow generation of a lender to repay a loan.
- **Participations vs. syndications:** distinction based on the means by which a loan may be sold. Participations and syndications are the most common examples of underwriting activities carried out by banks. A participation loan is a single loan made to a large borrower by more than one lender. The loans are extended when the main lender is unable to lend to a large borrower because of legal or internal lending limits that restrict the amount that can be lent to one borrower. Syndications are similar to loan participations, except that the syndicate members lend directly to the borrower. The lead bank arranges a credit facility for a large borrower. The bank then sells off parts of the loan to other lenders.

Other useful terminology in fixed income instruments includes:

- **Variety of interest payments:** interest obligation can be calculated and/or paid in a variety of ways:
  - cash: paid in cash on a regular basis;
  - in kind: allows the borrower the option to pay interest/coupon either in cash but at a deferred date or in like-kind securities;
  - step-up: generally begins at a relatively low interest rate and then increases on predetermined dates/events/indicators to a predetermined higher rate;
  - zero-coupon: no interest is paid but the debt is issued at a 'deep' discount so that the principal payment at maturity will include all of the accumulated interest;

- deferred interest: payments are deferred for a specified time and at the end of the deferment period, cash interest is paid generally at a relatively high rate until maturity;
- split-coupon: they begin as a zero-coupon bond and pay no cash interest for an initial period, then cash interest is paid at a stated fixed rate until maturity;
- extendible reset: interest rate is set so that the bond trades at a predetermined price; the coupon may reset annually or only once and the reset rate is based on market conditions and reflects not only the new level of interest rates but also the new spread that investors require.

- **Variety of principal payments:**
  - amortising: the principal of the loan is paid down over the life of the loan (that is, amortised) according to an amortisation schedule;
  - bullet: the entire principal of the loan is repaid at the end of the loan term;
  - sinking-fund provision: the borrower retires a certain amount of the outstanding debt each year, beginning either the first year after issuance or after a predetermined deferment period;
  - call provision: the issuer has the right to retire the debt, fully or partially, before the scheduled maturity date;
  - put provision: the investor has the right to sell the debt back to the issuer at a designated price on designated dates;
  - dual currency: different tranches of a debt offering can be issued and repayable in different currencies, or by reference to different currencies.
- **Bonds, notes, and debentures:** debt obligations that are issued by borrowers into the public fixed-income markets and may be traded in the secondary market. They are governed by an indenture, a contract that is verified by a trustee representing the interests of the bondholders. In the US, they are registered with the Securities and Exchange Commission. There are many different types of company bonds, such as: notes (plain bonds), debentures (unsecured long-term debt), mortgage bonds, and floating-rate bonds.
- **Lender titles:** in Europe, lender titles reflect the bank's position in the arrangement and underwriting of the transaction or their administrative role. The mandated lead arranger is the most important title for the bank(s) providing the principal arrangement and initial underwriting, and receiving the majority of the fees. The main co-agent title is joint lead arranger. These make the largest underwriting commitments and receive the largest fees.
- **Private placements:** these are halfway between loans and bonds. In the US there are two types of private placements:
  - bilateral arrangements: usually between a borrower and an insurance company;
  - Regulation 144A securities: are private placements with standard documentation that can be traded by professional investors but that retail investors are prevented from trading.

- **Off balance-sheet financing:** type of financing that is kept off a company's balance sheet through various classification methods in order to lower debt figures and ratios. The most common example are operating lease, joint-venture, securitisations, and non-consolidated affiliates.
- **Securitisation:** the process of issuance of a financial instrument by a special purpose company whereby repayment of the financial instrument will take place from cash flow generated from a pool of underlying assets.

PURE DEBT INSTRUMENTS

Companies can choose amongst different debt instruments, depending on the particular need. That need should first be identified. The choices of instrument may also be specific to the market where funds are being raised. In the US, banks are not significant lenders; rather they package loans, keep a part, and sell most of it to long-term investors such as insurance companies or mutual or pension funds. In Europe or Asia, banks still play an important role in lending, but they are beginning to sell a small proportion of these loans to institutional investors. Some of the credit risks that are inherent in the debt instruments used by companies are not linked to the firm's performance, but rely on what type of instrument is used, how the different debt instruments compare with one another, and the terms and conditions determining the relationship between borrower and creditor. Other risks of debt instruments are related to the company's ability to generate cash flows when it comes to evaluating the prospects of recovery for each debt instrument in insolvency.

Bank products

The most common debt instruments offered by banks are bank loans: these are loans provided by commercial banks on a bilateral basis or with a group of banks (syndicate). Depending on their role in the syndicate, the syndicate members will claim different roles and level of fees (lead-arranger, arranger, co-arranger, lead manager, senior manager, manager). They are extremely flexible and can be provided for different maturities with differing drawdown and repayment profiles. Traditional commercial banking lending products (see Table 2.1) include:

- **Short-term loans:** with a maturity below one year, secured or unsecured, their primary use is to finance working capital. The most common are overdrafts, acceptances of credit, revolving facilities. Their repayment is usually the result of the conversion of current assets into cash:
  - Overdraft: facility that permits a company to use or withdraw more than they have in their account, without exceeding a specified maximum negative balance. Overdrafts can help with temporary cash flow issues and provide working capital, although the negative balance typically needs to be repaid within a month. They can be committed or uncommitted facilities.

TABLE 2.1 Key differences between different banking products.

		Banking products			
	Structure	Documentation	Maturity	Interest basis	Fees
Overdraft	Facility available on current account up to agreed limit. Suitable for financing short-term fluctuations in cash flows.	Uncommitted but may be advised by a simple on demand letter. Security may be required.	Repayable on demand.	Margin over bank's base rate, on a day-to-day basis and debited to account monthly or quarterly.	None.
Money market facility	Funds advanced for fixed period in amounts of $1m or multiple at a fixed interest rate. Can be available in currency.	Facility is uncommitted but can be unadvised or advised by a simple facility letter. Lender may require some covenants or negative pledge.	Usually 6 months or shorter.	Rate fixed by reference to interbank market rates. Based on 360/365 day year payable at maturity.	None.
Acceptance credit	Funds available by borrower drawing bills on a bank which accepts (guarantees) the bill and discounts it in the market. Borrower receives discount proceeds less commission. To be eligible for discount, the bill must refer to a trade transaction.	Uncommitted or committed. Facility letter covering total amount, commissions, maturities, etc. Covenants similar to any short-term facility. May include financial covenants depending on length of facility, which may be 12 months or longer.	Bill drawn for 1, 2, 3, or 6 months.	Based on eligible bill rates, similar to money market rates but can be lower. Charged up front as a discount. Acceptance commission of 0.125% for top credits charged on face amount of the bill's net proceeds.	Commitment fees.

Revolving credit	Funds available as short-term loan or by acceptance credit up to total facility amount. Amounts drawn and repaid become available for drawing again. Often syndicated. Can be multi-currency.	Committed facility evidenced by fairly lengthy agreement containing, inter alia, financial covenants.	Commitment of up to 5 years but can be 7 years for top credits.	Interest charged at margin over bank's base rate or as for acceptance credit.	Management fee. Commitment commission. Agency fee if syndicated.
Term loan	Funds usually drawn down in one amount and fixed until maturity. Often used to finance asset purchases and therefore secured by the asset financed, e.g. property.	Similar to above with security clauses if appropriate.	Can be long term. Repayment can be in one amount (bullet) or amortising over a period.	Interest can be fixed for the period or floating i.e. reset each 6 months at margin over bank's base rate.	Arrangement fee.
Leasing and hire purchase	Asset-based finance where the lender (lessor) retains title to the asset. Enables lesser credits to secure finance since the lessor can reclaim the assets at short notice.	Ranges from short standard form documentation for small leases to long and very complex agreements for big-ticket leases.	Typically 1 to 3 year term, but up to 25 years for large fixed asset lease.	Usually fixed rate for short leases; bank's base rate for long. Net cost depends on tax position of lessee.	May be commitment fee and/or arrangement fee.

Source: Based on data from Ganguin and Bilardello (2004).

- Money market facility: these are funds advanced for a fixed period in amounts of $1m or multiples at a fixed rate of interest.
- Banker's acceptances: these represent the bank's commitment to pay a certain amount on a certain date. The commitment arises when the bank agrees to pay the obligations of a purchaser to improve its creditworthiness. The commitment is established when a seller prepares a time draft stipulating that the buyer must pay for goods purchased on their receipt. The draft becomes a banker's acceptance once when the purchaser signs it and the purchaser's bank 'accepts' it. The liability accepted by the bank is called banker's liability. The banker's acceptance is a short-term instrument which typically lasts for six months or less. The purchaser repays the bank from the proceeds of the re-sale of the purchased goods. The banker's acceptance is a negotiable instrument and therefore its holder may sell it to a third party, or the bank, to receive immediate payment. The banker's acceptance can therefore be used as a form of accounts receivable financing.
- Revolving credit: with a duration between one and four years, secured or unsecured, its primary use is to finance permanent working needs (when equity and trade credit cannot support growth). Revolving facilities are committed facilities that allow a company to borrow from a bank up to a maximum amount at any time during the life of the facility. As long as the borrower stays below the committed amount, it can borrow and repay as many times as it likes (as far as it is in compliance with covenants and loans provisions). If the revolving line is structured to renew automatically at maturity, then it is called evergreen.
- **Long-term loans:** with a maturity beyond one year, usually secured, their primary use is to finance the purchase of fixed assets, acquisitions, or refinancing of short-term debt. They typically require the signing of a loan agreement. Their repayment derives from future cash flow. The most common long-term loans are term (senior) loans, high-yield, and bonds:
  - Term loan: term loans are taken in order to acquire fixed assets or businesses. They are committed facilities that involve the advance of a particular sum over a determined period of time, with a set schedule for repayment. The loans vary in length of time from several years for computers, to 40 years for real estate. Rates are charged based on the creditworthiness of the borrower and the marketability of the assets.
  - Leasing: leasing is the use of an asset (e.g. machinery or equipment) by another party (lessee) whilst the legal ownership of the asset remains with the lessor. The lessee will compensate the lessor for the use of the asset by making periodic payments. Depending on accounting principles governing the accounts, the lease will be treated as finance (capitalised) lease or an operating lease. Under a finance lease, the lessee will show the asset and the net present value of the corresponding liability on its balance sheet. The lease payment will be divided into an interest and repayment element

(i.e. similar to a loan) and the asset will have to be depreciated. If treated as an operating lease, the asset and the related liabilities will remain off balance sheet and the lease payment will show up in the profit and loss account as an operating lease expense or rental expense. The total of the future amounts due under the operating lease will only appear in the company's footnotes to the annual report.

Capital market products

Typical capital market products (see Table 2.2) include:

- **Short term:** with a maturity below one year, secured or unsecured, their primary use is to finance working capital. Examples are:
  - Commercial paper: essentially an 'IOU' issued by a company in return for short-term debt (typically one, three, six, and twelve months), it is only available to creditworthy firms. Banks act as intermediaries between issuers and investors, and may also provide a back-up facility in case an insufficient number of investors can be found. Obligations are typically unsecured and proceeds are normally used to finance working capital needs and used by finance companies of large equipment manufacturers (e.g. General Electric, Siemens, etc.). The issue of commercial paper is subject to different rules regarding maturity, size, type of issuer, etc. in different countries. Commercial paper issues can be rated by the major rating agencies. The principal risk to investors is that market conditions and the credit strength of the borrower could change drastically during the borrowing term, precluding a renewal or rollover of the borrowings for a new term. Therefore, companies often arrange other refinancing sources, called commercial paper 'back up lines'.
- **Long term:** with a maturity beyond one year, usually secured, their primary use is to finance the purchase of fixed assets, acquisitions, or refinancing of short-term obligations. Examples are:
  - Corporate bonds: debt securities raised on the capital markets to finance long-term needs such as mergers and acquisitions (M&A), capital expenditures, etc. Particular examples of bonds are:
    - ○ *Eurobonds*: corporate bonds issued by an issuer outside their home country (e.g. US company issues US bonds in Luxembourg). Eurodollar bonds make up the largest segment of the Eurobond market and are dollar denominated bonds issued and traded outside the jurisdiction of any single country.
    - ○ *Yankee bonds*: bonds issued by non-US issuers who register with the SEC, borrow dollars, and sell primarily to the US market.
  - High-yield: debt securities issued by corporations with lower-than-investment grade ratings. High-yield is used to support growth, M&A, and working capital. Given the non-investment grade nature, this instrument offers a higher interest rate, and in certain cases additional investor-friendly features to compensate for bondholder risk and to attract investors' interest.

TABLE 2.2 Key differences between different banking products.

Capital market products					
	Structure	**Documentation**	**Maturity**	**Interest basis**	**Fees**
Commercial paper (CP)	CPs are short-term unsecured promissory notes issued by borrower and sold by a dealer to an investor. In most markets requires a credit rating since investors have less ability to analyse credit than bank lenders. In theory the paper is liquid, but is invariably held by one investor to maturity.	Documentation sets out the terms by which the dealer(s) will market paper issued under the programme. Back-up bank facility is also required since the dealer is not committed to purchase and distribute paper.	CP has a maximum maturity of 12 months but most issuance is for 30–45 days.	CP is sold at a discount to face value. Depending on credit strength, close to or below bank's base rate.	Rating agency fees and dealer up-front and annual fees.
Corporate bonds	Medium- or long-term paper issued to institutional investors. Can be secured. If not secured, market is restricted to AAA/AA credits. Bonds are transferable and are in registered form. Issue minimum $75m.	Documentation is fairly standard and includes financial covenants and negative pledge. Bond is launched on the basis of an Offering Circular containing outline documentation and information on the issuer.	Maturity is typically 5 to 15 years.	Interest is paid semi-annually and is fixed at time of issuance for the entire period. Priced by reference to a margin over a government bond of similar maturity.	Managing and underwriting fees.

Medium-term notes	Medium-term debt securities issued intermittently under a programme similar to CP. Offers the issuer flexibility of issuing large or small amounts in different maturities. Rating is required.	Documentation provides a legal framework under which securities may be issued. Can be complex and expensive to document but is becoming more standardised.	Usually 1 to 7 years securities but can be longer.	Usually fixed rate bond basis but can be floating, zero-coupon, or index-linked if investor requires.	Dealer commission payable up front on value of notes issued.
Private placements	Debt securities in amounts of $15m to $50m issued in the international market to a single investor or a small group. Usually restricted to 'household names' and other top credits. Ratings may be Required	Similar to Eurobond or bank loan depending on investor's requirements, e.g. domestic tax issues. Financial covenants may be required but usually minimal if maturity up to 10 years.	Typically 5 to 10 years but can be much longer.	As agreed with investor but usually similar to and slightly higher than equivalent public bond.	Arrangement fees.

Source: Based on data from Ganguin and Bilardello (2004).

- Medium term notes (MTN): medium term notes are regularly issued under an MTN programme (similar to a commercial paper programme, but longer dated paper).

Other specialised debt products

Other specialised loans and credit products include the following.

- **Accounts receivable financing:** the lender advances funds to the client's bank account against a line of credit based on a percentage of the eligible outstanding receivables. Before receiving the funds, the client company normally prepares a report detailing the calculated availability and the amount of credit required. The lender can then closely monitor the collateral supporting the loan. Loans are extended against presentation of accounts receivable satisfactory to the financial institution. The advance formula used states that the amount that can be lent should be roughly equal to 80% of eligible accounts receivable (A/R).
- **Inventory financing:** inventory financing is usually combined with A/R financing. Adding inventory to an A/R line of credit normally increases the total credit available. The inventory loan does not usually exceed the accounts receivable line of credit or factoring.
- **Factoring:** factoring is an agreement between the lender (factor) and the client company whereby the factor purchases the accounts receivable generated by the company's product or services. In this way, a weak company may be able to fund new sales more easily, albeit at a higher cost than through traditional bank financing. The advantages of factoring include exploiting supplier discounts for early payments and cash discounts, fewer lending covenants than a traditional bank line of credit, and not losing business to better financed competitors. There may be no limit to the credit made available; limits are based on the creditworthiness of the client company's customers. For factoring to be an option, the company must have a significant gross margin, low overhead cost, and/or enough flexibility to be able to pass the cost of factoring to the buyer to absorb the cost. Factoring can be either non-recourse (factor assumes the risk of customer payment) or recourse (factor does not assume the risk of customer payment), and can involve notification to the customer that a receivable has been sold. The advance formula roughly equals to 80% of eligible A/R.
- **Letters of credit (LC):** these contain a conditional promise to pay and are not usually negotiable. They substitute the bank's credit for that of its customers by providing a guarantee of payment of the third party upon satisfaction of specified conditions. In trade finance, the LC is usually issued by the purchaser's bank, which agrees to pay the purchaser's obligation to a seller on receiving proof that a specified delivery has been made. The purchaser agrees to pay the bank the sales amount plus a fee. The duration of an LC is usually related to the expected amount of time needed to complete the transaction. It may be revocable or irrevocable. A revocable LC can be withdrawn without

notice at any time prior to actual performance of the transaction. An irrevocable LC may not be withdrawn before it expires. With standby letters of credit, the issuing bank agrees to pay the LC beneficiary only if its client defaults on payment to the beneficiary. The seller would collect from the issuing bank only on default of the purchaser.

- **Purchase order financing:** purchase order financing can be used to finance the purchase or manufacture of particular goods that have already been sold. It can be used to pay for supplies, for issuing letters of credit, and for paying for raw materials and labour. It works well for importers.
- **Royalty financing:** this is an advance against future product or service sales. The investor who issued the advance receives a percentage of the product or service revenues by way of repayment. The approach is suitable for mature companies that have a product or service, or emerging companies that are ready to launch a product with high gross and net margins. Royalty financing is traditionally used in mining, energy, and life science markets.

HIGH-YIELD BONDS

A high-yield bond (non-investment-grade bond, speculative-grade bond, or junk bond) is a bond that is rated below investment grade at the time of issue. These bonds have a higher risk of default or other adverse credit events, but typically pay higher yields and in certain cases have additional investor-friendly features to compensate for bondholder risk and to attract investors' interest. From a process perspective, a bond issuance involves investment bankers preparing a prospectus (or offering a memo or red herring), negotiating the terms with potential investors, then syndicating and allocating the security to bondholders, and finally starting trading on the market.

Some key terms are relevant when analysing high-yield bonds:

- **Repayment profile:** typically bullet.
- **Maturity:** between seven to ten years.
- **Coupon:** typically fixed-rate and pay twice annually, it is not infrequent to see deals with a floating-rate coupon (so called 'floaters or 'FRNs'), which usually pay interest quarterly. Further, there are bonds which pay no coupon at all ('zero-coupon bonds', 'zeros', or 'zips') and are sold at a steep discount to face value by companies that might not have the cash flow to pay interest for a number of years. Finally, there are bonds with pay in kind coupons (called 'PIK' notes), which clearly provide the issuer breathing room, just as with zero-coupon bonds.
- **Call protection:** this term limits the ability of the issuer to call the bond for redemption and is typically half the life of the bond itself.
- **Call premium:** starting at the end of the period of call protection, the premium on the first call date is typically par plus 50% of the coupon, declining thereafter each year (e.g. for a 10% note due in eight years with a non-call four, the bond is callable at 105% of par upon the fourth year protection).

- **Make-whole call:** provision on a bond allowing the borrower to pay off remaining debt early. The borrower has to make a lump sum payment derived from a formula based on the net present value (NPV) of future coupon payments that will not be paid because of the call. The payment plan is composed of the earliest call price and the net present value of all coupons that would have been paid through the first call date, which is determined by a pricing formula utilising a yield equal to a reference security (e.g. US Treasury due near the call date) plus the make-whole premium (typically 50 bp).
- **Put provision:** provision allowing bondholders to accelerate repayment at a defined price due to certain events (e.g. change of control, merger, etc.).
- **Equity warrants:** often attached to highly speculative bond issues, each bond carries a defined number of warrants to purchase equity in the issuer at a later date (usually for a 2–5% stake, but they can go up to 10–20% for start-ups).
- **Equity clawbacks:** provision that allows the issuer to refinance a certain amount of the outstanding bonds with proceeds from an equity offering, whether initial or follow-on offerings.
- **Covenants:** looser than those on bank loans, they provide the issuer with more operating flexibility and enable the company to avoid the need for compliance certification on a quarterly basis. The indenture includes the description of covenants.
- **Registration (for USA):** to access the market quickly (the SEC registration process adds several weeks), to avoid extensive reporting requirements in the US, and to possibly avoid road shows and costly bridge financing, some issuers issue under the SEC Rule 144a. These securities are sold to the initial purchasers (acting like an underwriter), then resold to qualified institutional investors (usually within moments of the initial purchase). Quite often these securities are sold with registration rights, whereby the securities are to be registered with the SEC within a specified period of time, usually 90 to 180 days. Since the SEC registration increases the securities' liquidity, if the securities are not registered the issuer must pay liquidated damages (usually 50 basis points per annum) until the securities have been registered. Upon registration, holders of 144a securities are asked to actually exchange their securities for a registered security.

Other useful terms of a high-yield bond are:

- **Yield to maturity:** interest rate that equates the present value of a bond's cash flow to its current price (thus assumes that the bond will be held to maturity, and that all interim cash flows will be reinvested at a rate equal to the yield to maturity).
- **Yield to call:** yield on a bond assuming the bond is redeemed by the issuer at the first call date.
- **Yield to worst:** lowest yield generated, given the stated calls prior to maturity.
- **Current yield:** yield on a bond based on the coupon rate and the current market price of the bond (not on its face or par value). Current yield is calculated

by dividing the annual interest earned on a bond by its current market price. For example, a $1000 bond selling for $850 and paying an 8% coupon rate (or $80 per year) has a current yield of 9.41% (the ratio of $80 to $850). The coupon rate in this example is 8% (80/1000).

- **Duration:** measure of a bond or bond fund's price sensitivity to changes in interest rates. It is calculated as the weighted average term to maturity of a security's cash flows, where the weights are the present value of each cash flow as a percentage to the security's price. The greater a bond or fund's duration, the greater its price volatility in response to changes in interest rates. Duration provides an estimate of a bond's percentage price change for a 1% change in interest rates.

MEZZANINE

Mezzanine financing is a capital resource that sits between (lower risk) senior debt and (higher risk) equity that has debt features and can have (when warranted) equity features as well. Mezzanine capital is a subordinated debt, long-term instrument with a claim on a company's assets which is senior only to that of the common shares. It is used typically in connection with LBO (leveraged buy out), corporate acquisitions, growth, and re-capitalisation and is often combined with warrants. Usually unrated or rated below-investment grade, mezzanine capital is typically more expensive than senior debt due to the major risk that it carries: in fact it is usually repaid entirely at maturity (bullet repayment instead of amortising) and has no (in the US version) or junior (European version) obligation in a company's capital structure (i.e. in the event of default, the mezzanine financing is less likely to be repaid in full after all senior obligations have been satisfied). From a structuring perspective, mezzanine is usually provided at operating company level in order to enjoy a contractual subordination, but it is not uncommon to see it at the level of a holding company (in this case being this structurally subordinated). Due to the hybrid nature of mezzanine as a debt product, the specific structural characteristics vary with each transaction. However, there are a number of key structural aspects that apply to mezzanine loans:

- **Contractual subordination:** mezzanine is usually provided at the same company level as the senior secured debt and is subordinated to it by virtue of a contract ('inter-creditor agreement'). This avoids concerns about the structural subordination typical of high-yield bonds.
- **Second ranking and junior secured:** mezzanine loans are typically secured over the same or similar collateral as the senior secured lenders but they consent through the inter-creditor agreement to the senior lenders having priority over the cash flow and assets for repayment of interest and principal at all times until the senior debt is repaid. However, this shared security means that the mezzanine lenders cannot be set aside in any restructuring negotiations. They will be entitled to a 'seat at the negotiating table', as they cannot

be unilaterally dispossessed of their security. The inter-creditor agreement between the senior debt and mezzanine funders will also incorporate a standstill arrangement whereby the mezzanine providers will not be able to take action for a certain period of time in the event of a default (payment, financial covenant, or any other default).

■ **Interest is both cash and PIK:**
  ● Cash interest: periodic payment of cash based on a percentage of the outstanding balance of the mezzanine financing. The interest rate can be either fixed or floating throughout the life of the loan.
  ● PIK interest: pay in kind interest is a periodic form of payment in which the interest payment is not paid in cash but rather accrues by increasing the principal amount by the amount of the interest. It is then paid at maturity.
■ **Equity kicker:** in the majority of cases, a mezzanine loan is combined with a warrant, providing the mezzanine debt provider a share in the upside value of the company.
■ **Other fees:** these may include arrangement fee, up-front fee, etc.

For a company considering introducing mezzanine financing to their balance sheet, the following pros and cons should be weighed up:

■ Pros:
  ● it is less costly and less dilutive than a direct equity issuance (institutional equity typically has a return expectation of 20%+);
  ● mezzanine financing provides more flexibility (looser financial covenants, reduced amortisation, fewer restrictions) than traditional bank loans and allows companies to achieve goals that require capital beyond senior debt availability;
  ● there are fewer control-type provisions than typical minority private equity;
  ● a mezzanine-led recapitalisation often results in the existing owner retaining majority control of the company, controlling the board, management, etc.
■ Cons:
  ● mezzanine financing is more costly than senior debt;
  ● terms for a mezzanine financing include financial covenants and creditor rights;
  ● there is often a prepayment penalty for a period following issuance;
  ● mezzanine financing may involve some equity dilution, which is typically small, and may be in the form of attached warrants or another structure.

It is worth noting some differences between high-yield bonds and mezzanine (apart from high-yield bonds being a capital markets instrument, historically underwritten by different investors). The all-in cost of mezzanine (taking account of the equity warrants and their dilutive impact on equity) will tend to make it more expensive than high-yield bonds after the first three years on average, despite the greater up-front costs in arranging a high-yield bond issue.

However, mezzanine – by virtue of its deferred interest payments, back-ended structure, and equity warrants – puts less stress on the initial cash flows of the company. In the majority of cases, high-yield bonds are structurally subordinated to the senior secured creditors and therefore not only rank after the senior debt but also all the trade creditors of the group operating companies; whilst mezzanine is usually placed on the operating company. From a time perspective, arranging a high-yield bond issue takes considerably more time than that of mezzanine: therefore, in circumstances where the arranging bank or the company are keen to issue high-yield bonds but are faced with tight time constraints, it is not unusual to see a bridge loan facility arranged. This may well take the form of a mezzanine facility (with the interest margin ratcheting up over time together with equity options), thereby giving added protection to the provider against re-financing risk should a situation prevail where the high-yield bond does not eventually proceed. From a size perspective, mezzanine tranches fall in the range $5–200m, whilst high-yield have a minimum size of $150m. Finally, from a flexibility point of view, mezzanine can handle confidential restructuring and early repayment is simplified by the fact that it is a private security; whilst high-yield has a public profile and its nature of add-on financing simplifies corporate growth and equity listing. In summary:

- information: in mezzanine transactions, all reporting is on a private, confidential basis whereas high-yield reporting and trading are public;
- structuring: mezzanine is of great use for bespoke structures, since its various flexibility features accommodate the requirements of issuer and investor; whereas high-yield has flexibility within acceptable parameters of public market;
- relative value: mezzanine provides superior returns, higher interest income, similar credit risk, and stronger covenant protection (and control);
- size: mezzanine focuses on smaller transactions with no minimum size; whereas high-yield focuses on larger levels of financing, although with minimum limits on size;
- certainty of terms: upon signing the mezzanine, the borrower has certainty about key features (amount, price, tenor, etc.); whereas the final terms of high-yield are determined by the market through a 'discovery' process;
- flexibility: in mezzanine, the speed of execution is high as well as potential restructurings; unlike high-yield.

As shown in Table 2.3, it is important to highlight that mezzanine in Europe exhibits more 'loan-type' characteristics compared to a US mezzanine, which is more akin to a high-yield bond or PIK instrument. A US mezzanine will be provided by way of fixed-rate funding and comes with heavy pre-payment premiums attached. It is considered more deeply subordinated within the capital structure than a European mezzanine and will usually have no collateral; although similar to a European mezzanine, it will often have equity warrants to boost upside returns and will often allow for interest to be paid in kind.

TABLE 2.3 Key differences between European and US mezzanines.

	Europe	USA
Ranking	Second secured bank debt with same guarantees and security as senior debt (but on a subordinated basis).	Unsecured.
Amount	Usually 10–25% of total debt facilities arranged, typically in the €25–150m range, but much larger mezzanine facilities can be arranged.	Seldom exceeds $50m in size, and often significantly smaller.
Interest	Floating rate (Libor/Euribor), often a mixture of cash pay and PIK (rolled up interest).	Generally fixed rate, often a mixture of cash pay and PIK.
Call rights	Moderate prepayment penalties, e.g. 3% in Year one, 2% in Year two, and 1% in Year three.	Higher pre-payment penalties designed to compensate lenders for expected fixed-rate return.
Financial covenants	Often set at same level as those for senior debt, but sometimes set at approximately 10% lower.	Generally include a 'cushion' vis-à-vis those for senior debt (typically ranging from 10–25%).
Standstill	Typical standstills on enforcement are 90 days for non-payment, 120 days for breach of a financial covenant, and 150 days for other breaches.	Typically one standstill period. Length ranges from 60 to 180 days but usually between 90 and 150 days.
Payment block	Senior lenders can generally block mezzanine debt payments for up to 150 days, by giving notice following a senior debt default.	A senior debt payment default typically blocks mezzanine debt payments indefinitely. A senior debt covenant default will block mezzanine debt payments only for a semi-annual period, and this is often subject to other limitations on the number or length of blockage periods.
Amendments	Tight restrictions on amendments of senior documents without mezzanine lender consent. Tight restrictions on amendment of mezzanine documents without senior lender consent. Some headroom allowed for future senior debt – typically 10%.	Senior lenders limit the right to amend subordinated debt to make it more restrictive. Subordinated lenders' right to limit negotiated on a deal by deal basis, but is typically narrower than the senior lenders' corresponding right (often limited to pricing-type amendments).

(continued)

TABLE 2.3 *(Continued)*

	Europe	USA
Inter-creditor	Standardised inter-creditor arrangements and documentation.	Less standardised inter-creditor arrangements. Negotiated on a deal by deal basis.
Monitoring	Often accompanied by board observer rights.	Same for private equity and venture capital.
Buy-out of senior	Mezzanine lenders typically given the option to purchase all senior debt if senior lenders accelerate or take enforcement action.	No equivalent rights generally granted to US mezzanine lenders.
Warrants	Smaller deals normally have warrants. The majority of larger buy-out deals are warrantless or there is a mixture of cash interest, PIK, and/or warrants.	Whilst the proportion of deals with warrants has been declining due to market conditions, the majority of deals have warrants or at least an equity component (e.g. through a co-investment), as investors typically still desire an equity return to achieve overall targeted returns.

UNITRANCHE

Unitranche debt is a hybrid loan structure that combines senior and subordinated debt into one facility. The borrower of this type of loan pays a blended interest rate that falls between the rate of the senior debt and subordinated debt. In Europe, until now, the primary demand for unitranche has come from private equity firms, whilst in the US it has also been used by corporates. In its original form, unitranche combined senior and mezzanine into one facility, but it has now evolved to replicate the senior/second lien structures and stretched senior loans.

Some of the private debt funds providing unitranche are unwilling or unable to provide undrawn commitments, revolving or capex facilities, or other services, particularly hedging or clearing; on the other hand some banks are keen to participate in the unitranche facility too, but are unwilling to assume the riskier, first-loss piece of the unitranche. This has created the space for unitranche facilities as the role of private debt funds has emerged.

Unitranche facilities are private and by definition bespoke in nature. Although several variations exist, some common features can be cited:

1. **Borrowers benefit from a single loan agreement:** one of the main advantages of unitranche is that all facilities are documented in a single loan agreement, which typically includes at least two facilities (revolving credit facility (RCF) and unitranche facility), each with their own margin. Where the facilities have been clubbed, different relationships can exist:
   a. Where each lender provides the unitranche facility on a *pari passu* basis, each provider is a lender of record.
   b. Where the unitranche is provided by two or more parties with one provider, typically a private debt fund taking the junior part and the other party (bank) taking the senior portion, this can be handled in three ways:
      o each provider is a lender of record and the margin split and subordination of the junior piece can be covered in an agreement among lenders;
      o each provider is a lender of record and the loan would have two unitranche facilities (Unitranche A and Unitranche B), each with their own margin, with the subordination being covered either in an inter-creditor agreement
      o there is only one lender of record who sells down part of the unitranche as a sub-participation with margin and ranking being covered in the sub-participation agreement.
2. **Security:** since all secured facilities share the same first lien security package, the ranking is achieved through an inter-creditor agreement between those parties.
3. **Bullet structures and tenor:** the unitranche facility is often structured as a bullet repayment with a tenor of five to seven years.
4. **Call protection:** typically a soft-call protection structure with a 'make-whole' in the first year and 101 in the second year (i.e. a penalty of 1% on the outstanding amount).
5. **Margins:** priced on a floating rate basis with a margin over an underlying reference rate. The blended margin on unitranche tends to be slightly more expensive than would be obtained from a traditional senior/junior structure.
6. **Covenants:** maintenance covenants.
7. **Facility size:** in Europe, unitranche facilities have fallen in the €40–150m range, whilst in the US it is not uncommon to see unitranche facilities around $15m.
8. **Use of proceeds:** acquisitions.
9. **Leverage:** up to 5.5x leverage ratio.

Table 2.4 summarises some key features of the senior, mezzanine, high-yield, and unitranche.

Debt products: some modelling examples

Figure 2.2 shows modelling examples of some debt products illustrated in this chapter (the related Excel file can be found on the companion website).

TABLE 2.4 Key differences among senior, mezzanine, high-yield, and unitranche.

	Senior secured	European mezzanine	US mezzanine	Traditional high-yield	Unitranche
Security	Yes, first lien	Yes, second	No	No	Yes, first and second (via inter-creditor)
Ranking	Senior	Contractually subordinated	Contractually/ structurally subordinated	Structurally subordinated	Senior (and contractually subordinated via inter-creditor)
Covenants	Maintenance.[1] Generally comprehensive	Maintenance. Track senior covenants	Maintenance. Track but behind senior covenants	Incurrence.[2]	Maintenance. Generally comprehensive
Term	5–7 years	6–8 years	6–8 years	6–10 years	5–8 years
Income	Cash pay – floating	Cash pay – floating + PIK	Cash pay – fixed	Cash pay – fixed	Cash pay – floating + PIK
Warrants	No	Yes	Yes	No	No
Pre-payment	Yes, usually at no penalty	Yes (3% in Year 1, 2 % in Y2, 1% in Y3)	3-year non-call rules apply. Declining penalty thereafter	3–5 year non-call rules apply. Heavy penalty thereafter	Make-whole in Year 1 and 1% in Y2
Funding	Usually fully underwritten	Usually fully underwritten	Usually fully underwritten	Subject to market conditions/ liquidity	Usually fully underwritten
Providers	Banks, credit funds, asset based lenders	Credit/mezzanine funds	Credit/mezzanine funds, insurance companies	Institutional investors	Bank and credit /mezzanine funds
Up-front fees (%)	1–2	2–3	2–3	None	2%
Required IRR (all in) (%)	3–5	10–15	15–22	8–12	8–12

(continued)

TABLE 2.4 (Continued)

	Senior secured	European mezzanine	US mezzanine	Traditional high-yield	Unitranche
Other costs					
- legal	- only in case of LBO	- extra cost	- extra cost	- paid out of underwriters' spread	- extra cost
- accounting	- only in case of LBO	- piggy-back senior dd in case of LBO	- piggy-back senior dd in case of LBO	- 3-year US GAAP reconciliation	- only in case of LBO
- rating	- usually none	- none	- none	- paid by issuer	- usually none
- marketing	- none	- none	- none	- roadshow and prospectus	- none
- listing	- none	- none	- none	- paid by issuer	- none
- ongoing	- agency	- agency	- agency	- reporting and trustee	- agency
Leverage limit (indicative)	Up to 4x	Up to 5.5x (incl. senior)	Up to 5.5x (incl. senior)	Up to 6x	Up to 6x
Advantages	- Lowest cost of the capital structure - High certainty of execution - No prepayment penalties	- Bullet repayment - Longer maturity - More flexible than senior - Less costly than equity	- Bullet repayment - Longer maturity - More flexible than senior - Less costly than equity	- Bullet repayment - Fixed rate - Less restrictive incurrence-based covenants - Longer maturity - Unsecured	- Bullet repayment - One loan document - Limited pre-payment penalties
Disadvantages	- Amortisation schedule - Shorter maturity - Security - Restrictive maintenance covenants - Floating rate	- More costly than senior - Covenanted - Prepayment penalty - May be dilutive	- More costly than senior - Covenanted - Prepayment penalty - May be dilutive	- Reporting requirements - Listing - Call protection - Rating required	- More expensive - Treatment by tribunal uncertain (since no case history) - Coordination complexities when many parties

[1] Maintenance covenants require a borrower/issuer to meet certain financial tests on a regular basis.

[2] Incurrence covenants require that if an issuer takes an action (e.g. taking more debt), it would still need to be in compliance.

Debt structure	Term (Years)	Amort.	x EBITDA	Amount (€M)	Base rate	Margin	Interest rate
Senior Debt							
Term Loan A	5	Amortising	0.5x	10.00	-0.1%	2.50%	2.40%
Term Loan B	5	Bullet	0.5x	10.00	-0.1%	3.00%	2.90%
Revolving Cash Facility	7	RCF	0.5x	10.00	-0.1%	2.00%	1.90%
Mezzanine							
Mezzanine PIK	6	Bullet	0.5x	10.00	-0.1%	4.00%	3.90%
Mezzanine CASH					-0.1%	4.00%	3.90%
Bonds					Issue value	Coupon	
Step-Up Bonds	5	Bullet	0.5x	10.00	100%	3.00%	4.50%
Zero-Coupon Bonds	5	Bullet	0.5x	10.00	90.00%		
Split-Coupon Bonds	5	Bullet	0.5x	10.00	95.0%	3.00%	
Extendible Bonds	4	Bullet	0.5x	10.00	100.0%	2.50%	
High-Yield Bonds	5	Bullet	0.5x	10.00	100.0%	5.00%	
PIK Bonds	6	Bullet	0.5x	10.00	100.0%	2.50%	

Debt repayment schedule

Term Loan A

	2018	2019	2020	2021	2022	2023	2024
Interest rate		2.40%	2.40%	2.40%	2.40%	2.40%	2.40%
Amortisation schedule		20.00%	20.00%	20.00%	20.00%	20.00%	0.00%
Opening balance		10.00	8.00	6.00	4.00	2.00	0.00
Principal repayments		-2.00	-2.00	-2.00	-2.00	-2.00	0.00
Interest expense		-0.22	-0.17	-0.12	-0.07	-0.02	0.00
Closing balance	10.00	8.00	6.00	4.00	2.00	0.00	0.00

Term Loan B

	2018	2019	2020	2021	2022	2023	2024
Interest rate		2.90%	2.90%	2.90%	2.90%	2.90%	2.90%
Amortisation schedule		0.00%	0.00%	0.00%	0.00%	100.00%	0.00%
Opening balance		10.00	10.00	10.00	10.00	10.00	0.00
Principal repayments		0.00	0.00	0.00	0.00	-10.00	0.00
Interest expense		-0.29	-0.29	-0.29	-0.29	-0.29	-0.15
Closing balance	10.00	10.00	10.00	10.00	10.00	0.00	0.00

FIGURE 2.2 Some modelling examples of debt products.

Debt repayment schedule	2018	2019	2020	2021	2022	2023	2024
RCF							
Interest rate		1.90%	1.90%	1.90%	1.90%	1.90%	1.90%
Commitment fee		1.00%	1.00%	1.00%	1.00%	1.00%	1.00%
Commitment	10.00	10.00	10.00	10.00	10.00	10.00	0.00
Undrawn	10.00	10.00	10.00	10.00	10.00	10.00	0.00
Opening cash balance		15.60	23.53	33.55	47.92	52.43	16.97
Cash increase/decrease		7.93	10.02	14.37	4.50	-45.45	8.28
Closing cash balance before RCF		23.53	33.55	47.92	52.43	6.97	25.25
Minimum cash balance	20.0						
Draw down/repayment		0.00	0.00	0.00	0.00	10.00	-5.25
Interest expenses		0.00	0.00	0.00	0.00	-0.10	-0.14
Commitment fee		-0.10	-0.10	-0.10	-0.10	-0.10	-0.05
Opening balance		0.00	0.00	0.00	0.00	0.00	10.00
Closing balance	10.00	0.00	0.00	0.00	0.00	10.00	4.75
Mezzanine							
Interest rate - PIK		3.90%	3.90%	3.90%	3.90%	3.90%	3.90%
Interest rate - cash		3.90%	3.90%	3.90%	3.90%	3.90%	3.90%
Amortisation schedule		0.00%	0.00%	0.00%	0.00%	0.00%	100.00%
Opening balance		10.00	10.00	10.00	10.00	10.00	10.00
Principal repayments		0.00	0.00	0.00	0.00	0.00	-10.00
Interest expense - PIK		-0.39	-0.39	-0.39	-0.39	-0.39	-0.20
Interest expense - cash		-0.39	-0.39	-0.39	-0.39	-0.39	-0.20
Closing balance	10.00	10.00	10.00	10.00	10.00	10.00	0.00
Step-Up Bonds							
Interest rate		3.00%	3.00%	3.00%	4.50%	4.50%	
Amortisation schedule		0.00%	0.00%	0.00%	0.00%	100.00%	
Opening balance		10.00	10.00	10.00	10.00	10.00	0.00
Principal repayments		0.00	0.00	0.00	0.00	-10.00	0.00
Interest expense		-0.30	-0.30	-0.30	-0.45	-0.23	0.00
Closing balance	10.00	10.00	10.00	10.00	10.00	0.00	0.00

FIGURE 2.2 (Continued)

Zero-Coupon Bonds

Interest rate	ZC	ZC	ZC	ZC	ZC	ZC
	0.00%	0.00%	0.00%	0.00%	0.00%	0.00%
Amortisation schedule	0.00%	0.00%	0.00%	0.00%	100.00%	0.00%
Opening balance	10.00	10.00	10.00	10.00	10.00	0.00
Principal repayments	0.00	0.00	0.00	0.00	−10.00	0.00
Interest expense (under par by competence)	−0.20	−0.20	−0.20	−0.20	−0.20	0.00
Closing balance	10.00	10.00	10.00	10.00	0.00	0.00

Split-Coupon Bonds

Interest rate	ZC	ZC	ZC	3.00%	3.00%	3.00%
	0.00%	0.00%	0.00%	3.00%	3.00%	3.00%
Amortisation schedule	0.00%	0.00%	0.00%	0.00%	100.00%	0.00%
Opening balance	10.00	10.00	10.00	10.00	10.00	0.00
Principal repayments	0.00	0.00	0.00	0.00	−10.00	0.00
Interest expense (under par by competence)	−0.10	−0.10	−0.10	−0.10	−0.10	0.00
Interest expense (coupon)	0.00	0.00	0.00	−0.30	−0.30	−0.30
Closing balance	10.00	10.00	10.00	10.00	0.00	0.00

Extendible Bonds

Interest rate	2.50%	2.50%	2.50%	2.50%	2.50%	2.50%
	0.00%	0.00%	0.00%	0.00%	0.00%	0.00%
Amortisation schedule	0.00%	0.00%	0.00%	100.00%	0.00%	0.00%
Opening balance	10.00	10.00	10.00	10.00	0.00	0.00
Principal repayments	0.00	0.00	0.00	−10.00	0.00	0.00
Interest expense	−0.25	−0.25	−0.25	−0.13	0.00	0.00
Closing balance	10.00	10.00	10.00	0.00	0.00	0.00

High-Yield Bonds

Interest rate	5.00%	5.00%	5.00%	5.00%	5.00%	5.00%
	0.00%	0.00%	0.00%	0.00%	0.00%	0.00%
Amortisation schedule	0.00%	0.00%	0.00%	0.00%	100.00%	0.00%
Opening balance	10.00	10.00	10.00	10.00	10.00	0.00
Principal repayments	0.00	0.00	0.00	0.00	−10.00	0.00
Interest expense	−0.50	−0.50	−0.50	−0.50	−0.25	0.00
Closing balance	10.00	10.00	10.00	10.00	0.00	0.00

PIK Bonds

Interest rate	2.50%	2.50%	2.50%	2.50%	2.50%	2.50%
	0.00%	0.00%	0.00%	0.00%	0.00%	0.00%
Amortisation schedule	0.00%	0.00%	0.00%	0.00%	100.00%	0.00%
Opening balance	10.00	10.00	10.00	10.00	10.00	0.00
Principal repayments	0.00	0.00	0.00	0.00	−10.00	0.00
Interest expense	−0.25	−0.25	−0.25	−0.25	−0.13	0.00
Closing balance	10.00	10.00	10.00	10.00	0.00	0.00

FIGURE 2.2 (*Continued*)

A CLOSE UP ON SYNDICATED LENDING

A syndicated loan is a loan provided by a group of lenders. It is structured and administered by commercial or investment banks called arrangers. Syndicated loans are more efficient to run, and less expensive, than traditional bilateral or individual lines of credit. With this type of loan, two or more banks (the syndicate of lenders) contract with the borrower to extend credit (typically medium-term) on conditions governed by a common document. Credit provisions extended by a small group of banks are also referred to as *club deals*. In syndicated credits, borrowers choose one or more banks to act as arrangers, with one member of the bank group normally being appointed as the agent bank. The agent facilitates all the negotiations, payments, and administrations between the parties to the transaction.

The advantages of the syndicated credit market are:

1. flexibility and swift execution;
2. risk is shared with other banks;
3. banks can dispose of their exposure through the secondary market if necessary.

An important limitation of the syndicated credit market is that credit is not available for longer than ten years. By comparison, the bond market can extend easily to 30 years for counterparties with good quality credit. The main types of syndicated credits are term loans and revolving credit facilities.

There are three types of syndicate:

- **Best efforts:** the manager markets the loan under agreed terms and conditions, but the loan will not be made if the syndication is not fully subscribed. With this syndication, the arranger group commits to underwrite less than the entire amount of the loan, leaving the credit to the vicissitudes of the market. If the loan is under-subscribed, the credit may not close or may need major changes to clear the market. Traditionally, best-efforts syndications were used for risky borrowers or for complex transactions. Since the late 1990s, however, the rapid acceptance of market-flex language has made best-efforts loans the rule even for investment-grade transactions.
- **Underwritten deal:** the lead bank agrees to extend the loan, irrespective of its ability to fully syndicate it. Here, the arrangers guarantee the whole commitment and syndicate the loan to other banks and institutional investors. If the arrangers cannot fully subscribe the loan, they are forced to absorb the difference, which they may later try to sell to investors. This is easy, of course, if market conditions, or the credit's fundamentals, improve. If not, the arranger may be forced to sell at a discount and, potentially, even take a loss on the paper. Or the arranger may just be left above its desired hold level of credit. There are two main reasons why arrangers underwrite loans: first, offering

an underwritten loan can be a competitive tool to win mandates; and second, underwritten loans usually require more lucrative fees because the agent is on the hook if potential lenders balk.

■ **Club deal:** This is a smaller loan (€150m or less) that is pre-marketed to a group of relationship lenders. Each lender gets a full, or nearly full, cut of the fees.

In a syndicate, the borrower pays interest plus fees, which typically are:

■ Up-front fee: paid to cover the work of the bank.
■ Commitment fee: based on the amount of the credit and the undrawn portion.
■ Management fee: paid to the syndicate managers for putting together the syndicate and servicing the loan.
■ Participation fee: paid to syndicate participants based on the amount of their commitments. Participation fees range from 0.25–1.50%.
■ Agency fee: paid to the bank servicing the loan, can range from $55 000 a year to $500 000 a year.
■ Pre-payment fee: paid in case the loan is repaid before its contractual end.

From a process perspective, after the mandate has been awarded, the arranger prepares an information memo (IM) or 'bank book' describing the terms of the transactions. The typical content of an IM is: executive summary (description of the issuer, an overview of the transaction and rationale, sources and uses, and key statistics on the financials); investment considerations (management's sales pitch for the deal); a list of terms and conditions (pricing, structure, collateral, covenants, and other terms of the credit); an industry overview (company's industry and competitive position); and a financial model (historical, pro forma, and projected financials including management's best, worst, and base case). The confidential offering contained in the IM will be shown only to qualified banks and accredited investors; if the issuer is speculative grade and seeking capital from non-bank investors, the arranger will often prepare a public version of the IM (that will not contain confidential material such as management financial projections). Whilst the bank book is being prepared, the syndicate desk will solicit informal feedback from potential investors on what their appetite for the deal will be and at what price they are willing to invest. Once this intelligence has been gathered, the agent will formally market the deal to potential investors. Most new acquisition-related loans are kicked off at a bank meeting at which potential lenders hear management and the sponsor group describe what the terms of the loan are and what transaction it backs. Once the loan is closed, the final terms are then documented in detailed credit and security agreements. Subsequently, liens are perfected and collateral is attached.

The main investor constituencies are banks (a commercial bank, a savings and loan institution, or a securities company in the USA; a commercial bank in Europe) and institutional investors.

REFERENCES AND FURTHER READING

R. Bagaria. 2013. *High Yield Debt*. Wiley Finance.

B. Ganguin and J. Bilardello. 2009. *Standard & Poor's Fundamentals of Corporate Credit Analysis*. McGraw Hill.

K.H. Marks, L.E. Robbins, G. Fernandez, et al. 2009. *The Handbook of Financing Growth*. Wiley Finance.

S.P. Mason and S.L. Roth. 1991. 'A Note on Bank Loans.' Harvard Business School Note 9-291-026. January 1991.

L. Nijs. 2013. *Mezzanine Financing: Tools, Applications and Total Performance*. Wiley Finance.

Standard & Poor. 2007. *LCD High-Yield Bond Marker Primer*. Standard & Poor.

SUGGESTED CASES

G.C. Chacko, P. Tufano, and J. Musher. 2001. 'Diageo plc.' Harvard Business School Case 201-033.

K. Froot. 1992. 'Intel Corp.-1992.' Harvard Business School Case 292-106.

M. Jensen and B. Barry. 1998. 'Wisconsin Central Ltd. Railroad and Berkshire Partners Series TN.' Harvard Business School Teaching Case 899-050.

D. Narayandas and V.K. Rangan. 1995. 'Dell Computer Corporation.' Harvard Business School Case 596-058.

CHAPTER 3

Equity Products

INTRODUCTION

Equity capital is capital raised by a company in exchange for an ownership interest in the firm. Equity as a financial instrument has the following defining features:

- it refers to an investment in a company's share capital, via the purchase of shares of the company, entitling the holder to a pro-rata ownership of the business;
- the rights of the shareholder are defined by the company laws and by the commercial laws of the countries where the company is located;
- in case of default, there is no protection in terms of security;
- it involves an indefinite, open-ended commitment with no automatic right to return of capital;
- unlike debt securities, there is no contractual obligation entitling regular payments to holders;
- if the company performs well, shareholders will benefit from dividend payments and capital appreciation (the so-called upside of the business).

Therefore, the advantages of equity financing are: 1) no repayment is necessary; 2) longer-term funding can provide long-term support where the returns are not certain; 3) availability of assets for other funding is not restricted; and 4) there are fewer limitations on the use of funds and business operations.

The disadvantages of equity financing are: 1) ownership and control are diluted; 2) the original owners must share the upside; 3) sources of equity financing are limited; 4) it is more expensive to raise; and 5) investors require very high returns.

As a byproduct of the features described above, equity investments require a significant degree of engagement since they generally involve the fulfilment of a governance role (as shareholder and as a board director of the investee company), the use of persuasion and the need to engage in negotiations (as opposed to the simpler process of covenant monitoring in debt transactions), and involvement in elaborating the business strategy.

ORDINARY SHARES

The owners of the common shares are the ultimate owners of the company. They will receive the excess over liabilities, however much that is, and without limit. Ordinary shareholders are entitled to: 1) receive dividends if any are available after dividends on preferred shares are paid; and 2) their share of the residual economic value of the company should the business be liquidated. These shares are the riskiest form of investment in a company.

Ordinary shares represent a unit of ownership, typically carrying voting rights that can be exercised at a shareholders' meeting of the company. Shareholders vote on a variety of topics including issues relating to corporate policy, the appointment of directors and auditors, whether to accept a dividend proposal by management, and changes to the company's constitution documents. It is worth noting some recurring terms used in conjunction with ordinary shares:

- **Nominal or par value:** issue value of the share; it is the value written on the share certificate or in the shareholders' register.
- **Share premium:** excess paid by the investor, at issue, over the nominal value of the share. It will be accounted for in the share premium reserve or capital surplus account.
- **Authorised share capital:** maximum number of shares that can be issued by the company.
- **Treasury shares:** shares (issued but not outstanding) that the company has repurchased but not cancelled or re-issued. They are held in the company's 'treasury' until they are cancelled or resold. Repurchasing shares can be a tax efficient and flexible means of returning 'surplus' capital to shareholders. Repurchase of shares is often used by management in an effort to support share price or for staff remuneration packages. Treasury shares do not carry voting or dividend rights.
- **Class A/Class B shares:** such shares are differentiated by the level of voting rights and/or dividends that shareholders receive (e.g. a Class A shareholder might have ten votes per share and a Class B shareholder might have five votes per share).
- **Dividend:** a distribution of a portion of a company's earnings to its shareholders.
- **Market value:** the amount at which a share can be bought/sold to another investor. It may be radically different from the nominal value.
- **Market capitalisation:** total number of shares outstanding multiplied by the market value of a share.
- **Tracker shares:** shares issued by a company whereby returns are linked to the performance of a part of its business. They normally do not give the holder any ownership or voting rights.

PREFERENCE SHARES

Preference shares are included in shareholders' funds, but they do not constitute equity share capital. Preference shares are a form of equity that is very close to debt since they have a definite participation in the assets and return. Holders of preference shares are entitled to dividends at a pre-determined, usually fixed,[1] rate. However, that amount will be reduced, sometimes to nothing, if the company does not make enough profit. There is often a provision in the structuring that unpaid dividends will be paid at a time when there are enough profits. They come before common stock both in the payment of those dividends and in the claim on the remaining company assets in an event of default. Holders of preference shares do not typically benefit from especially good performance by the company, since any profits over what was expected are given to ordinary shareholders. Preference shares do not usually carry the right to vote, unless the dividend is in arrears, or unless there is liquidation. Preference shares have a liquidation preference over common stock. In other words, in the case of liquidation or sale of the company, the face value (or its multiple) of the preferred stock is paid ahead of the common stock. It is also possible to specify that preference shares will attract a multiple of face value in the event of specified occurrences, such as the sale of the company.

Amongst the advantages of preference shares for the issuing company are the following.

- **Dividend optionality:** there is no legal obligation to pay preference dividends every year, which gives the company more flexibility.
- **Leverage:** if a firm cannot raise finance by borrowing, but wants to grow, preference shares are an interesting option because they can also be issued without conferring voting rights.
- **Floor on return:** used to create a downside protection.
- **Cap on return:** the limits placed on the return to preference shareholders mean that the ordinary shareholders receive all the extraordinary profits when the firm is doing extremely well.

Amongst the disadvantages of preference shares for the issuing company are the following.

- **High cost:** the higher risk attached causes preference shareholders to demand a higher level of return than debt holders.

---

[1]The preference dividend is fixed at the time of issue (e.g. 5% preference dividend $0.25). This is a preference share with a nominal value of $0.25 per share that carries a dividend of 5%, that is 5% of $0.25 every year for every share issued. If a company has issued 100 000 of these shares at par, then it will have received: 100 000 × $0.25 = $25 000 from shareholders at the time of issue. It will pay an annual dividend of $25 000 × 5% = $1250 each year.

- **Dividends are not tax deductible:** because preference shares are regarded as part of shareholders' funds, preferred dividend is not tax deductible.

There are three main categories of preferred shares (see Table 3.1).

a) **Redeemable:** also called straight preferred since it has no convertibility into normal equity. In the case of redeemable preferred shares, the company[2] has agreed to buy back the shares at a pre-determined price and time in the future. The price can be at par value or it may include a premium. Its intrinsic value is its face value. It always contains the timing when the company shall redeem it (usually IPO or five to eight years). It is usually combined with warrant and common stock.

b) **Convertible:** a preferred stock that can be converted into ordinary shares at a shareholder's option at a future date and depending on certain conditions or trigger events (e.g. when preferred dividends are not paid for a number of years or when there is a change of ownership). Terms always contain a mandatory conversion term. Many convertible preferred stocks contain anti-dilution provisions that adjust the price down if the round of financing takes place at a price lower than the one the investor paid.

TABLE 3.1   Key differences among preferred shares.

Amount of proceeds	Redeemable preferred	Convertible preferred	Participating convertible preferred
Up to face value (FV) of preferred	All to investor	All to investor	All to investor
From FV to implied enterprise value (IEV) at time of investment	FV plus common equity proportion of increment over FV to investor	FV only to investor	FV plus common equity proportion of increment over FV to investor
From IEV to public offering (PO)	FV plus common equity proportion of increment over FV to investor	Common equity proportion to investor	FV plus common equity proportion of increment over FV to investor
Above PO	FV plus common equity proportion of increment over FV to investor	Common equity proportion to investor	Common equity proportion to investor

Source: Based on data from Lerner and Hardymon (2001).

---

[2]Under IFRS, redeemable preference shares are treated as a financial liability and preference dividend payments as interest expenses.

c) **Participating convertible:** a convertible preferred stock with the additional characteristic that in the case of sale or liquidation (and often also merger) of the company, the holder has the right to receive the face value and the equity participation as if the stock was converted. Always carries mandatory conversion in the case of IPO.

The following features can be attached to preference shares.

- **Increasing fixed coupon:** the fixed preference dividend will increase automatically over time. For example, 5% and increasing by 0.5% per year.
- **Floating-rate coupon:** the preference dividend is reset every dividend period based on a pre-determined interest base rate and margin (e.g. Euribor + 5%).
- **Cumulative:** if the preferred coupon is not paid in a particular year (e.g. due to lack of sufficient cash generation), it will accumulate to the following year and so on until it is paid. In the case of non-cumulative preferred shares, there exists no obligation to pay the preferred dividend in the year following the one in which the company was unable to pay the preferred dividend.
- **Zero-dividend (also called 'capital shares'):** are not required to pay a dividend to their holder. The owner of a zero-dividend preference share will earn income from capital appreciation and may receive a one-time payment at the end of the investment term.
- **Prior:** preference shares with a higher claim on assets and dividends than other issues of preferred shares.
- **Perpetual:** the investment will remain in the company for the entire existence of the company (similar to ordinary equity).
- **Puttable:** the company[3] is committed to buy back the shares at a future point in time, at the request of the holder of the preference shares. The price may be pre-agreed at par value or at a pre-agreed premium above par, at fair market value, or according to a pre-agreed valuation method or formula.
- **Callable:** The company has the right to buy back the shares at a point in the future.
- **Exchangeable:** preference shareholders have the option at a future date of converting the preference shares into ordinary shares issued by another company depending on certain conditions.

The features of preference shares vary widely. No preference shares have all the abovementioned features; the precise details are specific to each issue.

CONVERTIBLES

Convertible securities (also referred to as 'convertibles' or 'converts') include convertible loans, convertible bonds, and convertible preferred shares, plus variations

---

[3]A preference share with a put option to the company or ordinary shareholder is sometimes referred to as portage equity.

on these themes. These securities enable investors (i.e. subscribers of convertible securities) to convert their fixed income investments into pre-specified amounts of an issuing firm's common stock through the establishment of a 'conversion price'. The securities combine features from both debt and equity and have therefore been described as 'hybrid' instruments. The standard convertible security is a fixed income security with an option to convert the fixed income investment into common stock. The fixed income instrument – usually a loan, a bond, or a preferred share – offers a set schedule of 'fixed' cash flows in the form of interest, coupon, or dividend payments. The option to convert the security gives the right to exchange the bond or preferred share for a certain number of shares of the issuer's common stock. The security can be issued such that it can be traded for common stock at a set share price ('conversion price'). If a conversion price is given, the conversion ratio is easily calculated, and vice versa. Convertible bonds are, in other words, corporate bonds with a call option (right to purchase) on the company's shares: the convertible bondholder is in fact in a similar position to that of a holder of a bond plus a warrant (equal to a call option), but the position is different in that, at conversion, the convertible bondholder will give up the bond in order to exercise the call option. The bond-warrant holder can exercise the warrant for cash and keep the bond. Warrants are often 'detachable' from the underlying loan and continue to be valid even after the loan's maturity and full repayment.

In essence, a convertible transaction entails (see Figure 3.1 for a pictorial representation):

▪ **At issue:** the company receives initial cash proceeds at issue from investors in exchange for the convertible loan.

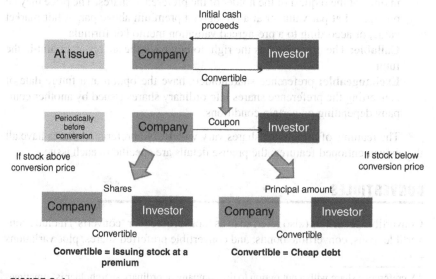

FIGURE 3.1 Convertible fundamentals.

- **Periodically before conversion:** the company pays a coupon to investors.
- **At conversion time:**
  - If the stock price is above the conversion price: the company issues shares (or uses treasury shares) in exchange for conversion of debt. Obviously, no cash payment takes place at the time of conversion.
  - If the stock price is below the conversion price: the company will redeem at par on maturity and extinguish its debt.

From a cost perspective, a convertible is cheap debt (see Figure 3.2): it is easy to show that a seven-year high-yield paying a 7% coupon with a par value of $1000 is equivalent to a seven-year (non-call 3) convertible paying a 4% coupon and with a 25% premium or 125% strike price (option value equal to $165 + bond value equal to $835).

There is a wide range of securities in the convertible family. Ranking the products in order in an ideal debt-equity spectrum, the closest to debt are zero-coupon convertible, then premium-redemption convertible, conventional convertible, resettable convertible bond, and finally mandatory convertible bond (the closest to equity). Below is a short description of the most common.

- **Zero-coupon:** this security is a convertible bond with no coupon issued at a discount to the face amount of the security. There is a rising conversion price over time since the investor must forego accretion if the security is converted; they usually feature tax deductibility of amortisation of the original issue discount. It is considered debt from an accounting treatment perspective, the earnings per share (EPS) impact is computed under the if-converted method, and issuers show the more dilutive of the interest expense or the underlying shares. The main advantages of zero-coupon include: a) cheap debt with limited equity content; b) preservation of senior debt capacity; c) tax and cash flow advantages; and d) highest 'effective' issuance price upon conversion. Amongst the disadvantages worth mentioning: it is the least likely convertible debt security to be converted; it is highly unlikely to receive equity treatment; and finally there is a put risk/growing debt obligation.

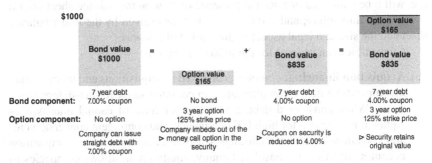

FIGURE 3.2 Example of a convertible security.

- **Convertible debt:** convertible debt is a traditional security that offers the issuer the ability to finance at a low after-tax cost by incorporating into a debt instrument the sale of an option to purchase equity at a fixed premium to the current share price. It is considered debt from an accounting treatment perspective and the EPS impact is computed under the if-converted method; issuers show the more dilutive of the interest expense or the underlying shares. It features a lower current cash coupon relative to straight debt and gives the company the ability to send a 'bullish' signal to the market. The main advantages of convertible debt include: a) cheaper after-tax financing cost versus convertible preferred stock or common stock; b) most likely convertible debt security to be converted; c) the market will accept a long maturity date; d) less dilutive than common stock and other securities with stronger equity features; and e) can be executed on an expedited basis using Rule 144A. Amongst the main disadvantages, we cite a high current cash interest cost relative to discount and zero-coupon alternatives and a required principal repayment at maturity if stock does not appreciate (and debt is not converted).
- **Convertible preferred:** a security that incorporates into a preferred stock the sale of an option to purchase equity at a fixed premium to the current share price. Considered preferred stock from an accounting perspective, the EPS impact is computed under the if-converted method and issuers show the more dilutive of the interest expense or the underlying shares. In the US, it is typically structured through a Delaware Trust to allow for tax deductibility of coupons.
- **Mandatory:** this is the security that most closely resembles common stock. There is a three-year maturity in which the investor bears full downside exposure in stock. The investor gives up a portion of the upside (e.g. first 20%) in exchange for an incremental yield over the common stock.

The advantages of issuing a convertible are: a lower cost debt (than ordinary loans); the possibility of selling equity/shares at a premium if converted; the flexibility of the instrument (call feature, cash settlement, structuring); a relatively quick execution; the possibility of tapping into a new investor base; and its tax efficiency. The disadvantages of this instrument are the uncertainty of outcome (i.e. will it be converted or not); the presence of debt on the balance sheet until it is converted into equity; and certain size constraints (given by the issuer balance sheet and the size and legal aspect of the market of issuance).

Convertibles can be used for the following reasons:

a) **Acquisition financing:** companies involved in acquisitions and mergers may use convertible debt as an alternative to common stock for tax-deferral purposes. When considered debt, it is a cheaper form of capital than issuing equity, it is accretive for high P/E companies, and contingent conversion creates 'breathing space' for earnings-sensitive companies before acquisition becomes accretive. If considered equity, equity credit allows companies to maintain a desired credit rating.

b) **Debt repayment:** in this case, the convertible is issued to repay higher yielding debt. Thus, the company realises significant cash savings from coupon differential and may increase senior debt capacity.

c) **Share repurchase:** typically used by healthy companies that believe their stock is undervalued, the company realises an immediate EPS benefit from share reduction.

d) **Opportunistic:** as an attractive source of primary financing with no specific use of proceeds, it can be used for general purposes, such as to raise accretive financing or for use as an acquisition war chest.

Convertibles are also issued to sell a shareholding, to privatise at a premium, and to exploit market conditions.

Conversion can normally be exercised at an agreed time or during a range of times in the future. Convertible loans will generally charge a lower interest rate than 'ordinary' loans, as they offer the option to participate in and profit from an upside of the business via conversion into shares. However, if the company performs poorly, the share price (if listed) or valuation (if unlisted) will remain below the conversion price or not sufficiently above it to make conversion attractive and, in such a case, the debt is held to maturity and the lender simply receives the usual payments of principal and interest. Since existing shareholders face the risk of dilution if conversion happens, the company will need existing shareholders' approval before issuing convertible debt. Convertible debt will typically be either unsecured or subordinated to senior bank debt and usually implies covenants, but these will generally be less restrictive than for senior loans.

Some key terms are relevant when analysing convertible (bonds):

- **Investment value:** the value of the bond without its conversion option. A ten-year convertible bond with an annual coupon of 7% has an investment value equal to the present value of the bond's cash flows. Since a convertible bond's coupon is typically lower than the issuance of straight debt, it normally has a lower investment value.
- **Conversion value:** a convertible bond's conversion value is calculated by multiplying its conversion ratio by the issuer's common stock price. For example, if a bond was convertible into 25 shares and the issuer's common stock were trading at $10, the conversion value of the bond would be $250.
- **Investment premium:** the investment premium is the difference between the convertible bond's market price and its investment value. The investment premium (usually expressed as a percentage of the investment value) is a useful way of measuring the downside risk of the convertible due to changes in its underlying stock price. If a convertible bond had a market value of $1000 and an investment value of $800, the investment premium would be 25% [($1000 − $800/$800)];
- **Conversion premium:** the conversion premium is the difference between the market value of the convertible and its conversion value, divided by its conversion value. This ratio, quoted as a percentage, expresses the higher value

or premium that the investor pays for the issuer's common stock by investing in the convertible rather than in the stock directly. The market price of a convertible is higher than its conversion value to take into account the value of the call option embedded in the bond.

■ **Break-even calculation:** also known as payback period analysis; this is used to compare the cost premium of stock inherent in convertibles with their higher coupon yields. The break-even or payback period calculation gives investors an idea of the time it takes to earn back the convertibles' conversion premium through the bond's relative income yield. The calculation is the bond's conversion premium divided by the difference between the coupon rate and common stock's dividend rate.

■ **Key issuance terms:**

● Principal and par value (face value): the principal amount of a bond is the amount borrowed by the issuing firm left outstanding. The par or face value of a bond is the amount to be repaid to the investor at the bond's maturity. The values are typically quoted on a per-bond basis. Bonds that make fixed interest payments are usually priced at par, where principal and par value match. 'Zero-coupon' bonds (which do not make interim payments) are priced below par or priced at a discount. The difference between the principal and par value of a 'discount bond' constitutes the investor's return over the life of the bond.

● Maturity: a convertible bond's maturity is the date set for the debt to be repaid and the date when the investor receives par amount for the bond.

● Coupon: the coupon payments of convertible bonds are similar to coupon payments of ordinary bonds. They fix interest payments made from the borrowers to the lenders and are expressed as a percentage of the bonds' par value. Coupon payments are a means by which investors can be compensated for the risk of their investments. If a bond is priced at par, the coupon payments are the main sources of the bond's return.

● Conversion price and conversion ratio: a bond's conversion price is related to its conversion ratio through the following equation: Conversion Price = Par Value / Conversion Ratio.

● Call provision: if a bond is 'callable', the issuer may redeem the security before the final maturity date. A bond's 'call schedule' establishes the dates and prices at which the bonds may be called. Most convertible bonds are callable by their issuers. If a bond's call price at a certain date is lower than the value of the bond converted into common shares, the issuing company can call the bond and 'force conversion'. In these ways, companies are able to convert their debt into equity and manage the leverage on their balance sheets. Whilst investors retain the right not to convert, companies expect rational investors to choose the higher value and in doing so use their conversion options.

- Put: an option granted to investors to sell the bonds back to the issuer at discrete points in time, usually at par.
- Subordination: convertible bonds rank above common shares, preferred stock, and other equity securities, but are usually subordinate to senior debt. It is important for investors in convertible bonds to fully understand their securities' subordination terms and the risks they are accepting: a debt portion's subordination determines when its investors are repaid in the event of bankruptcy.
- Contingent conversion: all convertible bonds have a conversion price; that is, the price one pays in order to exchange the bonds for stocks. Contingent convertible bonds have a second, higher price that the underlying stock must meet before a bondholder is allowed to convert. For example, the conversion price for a convertible bond may be $20 per share, but if the stock price is below $40 per share, the investor may not convert the bond.
- Contingent accretion: contingency whereby the yield on the convertible bond will increase after Year 3 if the stock price is below a trigger level that reduces the likelihood of investors exercising a put, and also achieves significant tax savings for issuer.
- The following table shows a very simple example:

Face value	$1000
Coupon	4%
Stock price	$100
Conversion premium	25%
Conversion price	$125
Conversion ratio	8 (=$1000/$125)
Parity (at issue)	$800 (=$1000 * 8)
Issuer call features	Non call (3 years)
Provisional (or soft call)	Callable if stock price exceeds 130% of the conversion price
Put	100% after 3 years
Contingent conversion	Convertible only if stock price > 110% of conversion price
Contingent accretion	Yield increase from stated yield to 6% if stock price is lower than 60% of conversion price

Thus, the company gets $1000 and pays $40 per annum. Then, if the stock price rises above $125, the company issues eight shares; if instead the stock price is below $125, the company will repay $1000.

OTHER EQUITY INSTRUMENTS

Shareholder loans

These instruments are loans to a company that are provided by the ultimate share-holders or a holding company and are usually subordinated and structured to be ranked only just prior to ordinary shares. They are usually (upon debtholders' request) 'deeply subordinated' to all other debt obligations and preferred share-holders through a longer tenor of the loan, bullet repayment, fixed zero-coupon interest, structural subordination, and inter-creditor agreement.

Options and warrants

Options enable the owner to buy common shares at a given time and at a given price. They are often used as an incentive for managers and may also give the investor the right to increase its interest in a company in certain situations, such as the failure to achieve a particular milestone. Options allow an owner to become more involved in a transaction by deferring an equity entry decision via a right to purchase equity at a pre-agreed value or by a pre-agreed formula as part of a convertible loan/equity instrument or a loan. This may either be to take a material stake in the business or to enhance the yield on a loan by taking a small stake.

Warrants and options are similar in that the two contractual financial instruments allow the holder the right to acquire common shares in the future. Both are discretionary and have expiration dates. Warrants are usually attached to bonds or preferred stock as a sweetener, allowing the issuer to pay lower interest rates or dividends. They can be used to enhance the yield of the bond and make them more attractive to potential buyers. Warrants can also be used in private equity deals. Frequently, these warrants are detachable and can be sold independently of the bond or stock. In the case of warrants issued with preferred stocks, stockholders may need to detach and sell the warrant before they can receive dividend payments. Thus, it is sometimes beneficial to detach and sell a warrant as soon as possible so the investor can earn dividends. The main characteristics of a warrant are:

- **Premium:** a warrant's 'premium' represents how much an investor has to pay for the shares when buying them through the warrant as compared to buying them directly.
- **Expiration date:** the date the warrant expires. An investor must exercise the warrant before the expiration date. The more time remaining until expiry, the more time for the underlying security to appreciate, which, in turn, will increase the price of the warrant (unless it depreciates). Therefore, the expiry date is the date on which the right to exercise ceases to exist.
- **Restrictions on exercise:** like options, there are different exercise types associated with warrants, such as American style (holder can exercise any time before expiration) or European style (holder can only exercise on expiration date).

Company - Base Case

Share Capital (USD M)	10.00	Nominal/Par Value per share (USD)	1.00
Outstanding ordinary shares (M)	10		
Company Valuation/Market Capitalisation (USD M)	250	Market Value per share (USD)	25.00

Ordinary Shares with different voting rights

Voting rights:

		Issued shares:		
Voting rights per A share	4	Outstanding A shares	4
Voting rights per B share	1	Outstanding B shares	6
		Total shares	10

Shareholders	# of A Shares	# of B Shares	Total Shares	% of Equity	% of Voting Rights
X	4	1	5	50%	77%
Y		5	5	50%	23%
total	4	6	10	100%	100%

Preference Shares (Redeemable)

Shares issued:

Ordinary - A shares	40
Preferred - B shares	20
Preferred yield B shares	8%
Issue date	01/01/19
Redemption/Trigger Event date	20/12/24
Exit Equity Value	70

FIGURE 3.3 Some modelling examples of equity products.

Value allocation (waterfall) at Exit (no preferred dividend payments before exit):

1. Preferred Return to B Shares   11.67

2. Redemption of the Face Value of B Shares   20

3. Face Value of A shares   38.33   *DOWNSIDE DUE TO PREFERRED RETURN TO B SHARES*

4. Upside to A shares   0

Total value to A shares	38.33	54.76%
Total value to B shares	31.67	45.24%

Preference Shares (Convertible)

Shares issued:

Ordinary - A shares	40
Preferred - B shares	20
Preferred yield B shares	8%
Issue date	01/01/19
Redemption/Trigger Event date	20/12/24
Exit Equity Value	70

Value allocation (waterfall) at Exit in the hypothesis of (i) no preferred dividend payment over years and (ii) Conversion at Exit:

Initial Ordinary - A shares	40	
Accrued value of Preferred - B shares	31.67	
A shares resulting from B shares conversion	31.00	*>>round-down to unit*

1. Exit Value to ordinary equity

Initial A shares	39.44	
A shares resulting from B shares conversion	30.56	

Total value to A shares	39.44	56.34%
Total value to ex B shares	30.56	43.66%

FIGURE 3.3 (*Continued*)

Preference Shares (Participating Convertible)

Shares issued:

Ordinary - A shares	40
Preferred - B shares	20

Preferred yield B shares	8%
Issue date	01/01/19
Redemption/Trigger Event date	20/12/24
Exit Equity Value	70

Value allocation (waterfall) at Exit (no preferred dividend payments before exit):

1. **Preferred Return to B Shares** — 11.67

2. **Redemption of the Face Value of B Shares** — 20

3. **Face Value of A shares** — 38.33 *DOWNSIDE DUE TO PREFERRED RETURN TO B SHARES*

4. **Upside to A and B shares**

    0.00 A shares
    0.00 B shares

Total value to A shares	38.33	54.76%
Total value to ex B shares	31.67	45.24%

FIGURE 3.3   *(Continued)*

Convertible Bond

Shares issued:

Ordinary shares   100

Bonds issued (zero coupon):

Aggregate nominal value	50
Number of bonds	50
Under par	89%
Issue date	01/01/19
Maturity date	20/12/24
Implied interest rate	1.97%
Conversion ratio	1 bonds to get 1 share
Conversion value	1.33 per bond
Conversion price	1.00 per bond
Investment value	0.89 per bond

Equity value	200
Equity value per share	1.33

flows (no conversion):

	01/01/19	20/12/24
	44.5	−50

Value allocation (waterfall) at exit:

1. Bonds   Conversion control   YES   0.00

2. Shares

	Shares	%
Original shareholders	100	66.67%
Converted bondholders	50	33.33%
	150	100.00%

		133.33
		66.67

		%
Total value to original shareholders	133.33	66.67%
Total value to ex bondsholders	66.67	33.33%

FIGURE 3.3 (*Continued*)

Warrant

Shares issued:

Ordinary shares	100
Equity value per share	10.00
Total equity value	1.000

Warrant issued:

# of warrants	10
Strike	12
Premium	2.00

Equity value at warrant exercise (pre-money)	1.500
Equity value per share (pre-money)	15.00 *WARRANT IN THE MONEY*
Compendium shares (from exercise of warrant)	10.00
Money injection (from exercise of warrant)	120
Equity value post-money	1.620
New amount of shares outstanding	110
Value per share post-money	14.73

FIGURE 3.3 (Continued)

Warrants are very similar to call options. However, there is one key difference between warrants and equity options: warrants issued by the company itself are dilutive. When the warrant issued by the company is exercised, the company issues new shares of stock, so the number of outstanding shares increases. When a call option is exercised, the owner of the call option receives an existing share from an assigned call writer (except in the case of employee stock options, where new shares are created and issued by the company upon exercise). Unlike common stock shares outstanding, warrants do not have voting rights.

Equity products: some modelling examples

Figure 3.3 shows modelling examples of some debt products illustrated in this chapter (the related Excel file can be found on the companion website).

REFERENCES AND FURTHER READING

G. Chacko and E.P. Strick. 2002. 'Convertible Securities.' Harvard Business School Note 9-202-129.
J. Lerner and F. Hardymon. 2001. 'A Note on Private Equity Securities.' Harvard Business School Note 9-200-027.

SUGGESTED CASES

B.C. Greenwald. 1984. 'MCI Communications Corp.– 1983.' Harvard Business School Case 284-057.
W.C. Kester and K. Backstrand. 1996. 'Netscape's Initial Public Offering.' Harvard Business School Case 296-088.

CHAPTER 4

Business Due Diligence

INTRODUCTION

A number of important factors affect and determine the proper functioning and financial success of a corporation. Amongst these are: management risk; financial capitalisation and liquidity risk; project completion risk; technical and operational risk; market risk; financial risk (foreign exchange, interest rate, and commodity price); industry risk; production risk; legal, tax, regulatory, and environmental risk; and many others. Although analysis incorporates a certain degree of subjective judgement, several private equity and private debt fund methodologies converge towards a framework of segmentation of risks: some risks are a result of country conditions, others may be common to all participants in the industry, while yet others are company specific. This chapter is structured into sections that represent phases in the business due diligence process of both private equity and private debt funds.

MACRO FACTORS

A company's business can be strongly impacted by the conduct of the sovereign government of the country where it is located. This impact can be far-reaching. Macro factors are those that influence a company's business environment within the country it is located: government regulations, political and legal elements, infrastructure, financial markets, and macroeconomic environment are among the most relevant. We can classify the main sovereign and country risks as follows:

- **Macroeconomic factors:** in a broader sense, these include economic risks, social issues, political risks, government regulations, licensing, barriers, and incentives. Economic indicators are used to capture several trends. They can be summarised as follows:
  - leading indicators: new constructions, building permits, new orders of consumer goods, consumer expectation index, stock prices, etc.;
  - coincident indicators: industrial production, manufacturing sales, etc.;

- lagging indicators: consumer price index of services, inventory to sales ratio of manufacturing sector, etc.

  Inflation and interest rates are other key economic variables to watch for. Where the rates of inflation are high, a company's stability may hang on business regulations with pricing flexibility that allows the pass-through of increasing expenses. When interest rates are high, local borrowing can be costly. On the other hand, when interest rates are consistently high, it may not be possible to access international capital markets. In that case, local borrowing will be the principal borrowing option. Foreign exchange risk must also be considered in every country. The greatest risks occur when revenues and costs are denominated in different currencies.

- **Government regulations:** government regulations may cover export and import limitations, competition, antitrust laws, standards of service, subsidies, and percentage of local or foreign ownership. These rules may well affect a company's business strategy. A foreign company wanting to sell its product in a particular country may be subject to taxes or tariffs imposed by a host country's government that is seeking to reduce the demand for the company's product to the benefit of local suppliers. Moreover, income taxes are the main means by which a sovereign government can collect the revenue it needs to finance its programmes. Finally, when a government is pressed financially, it will also seek to control the flow of revenue by imposing foreign control exchange controls.

- **Political and legal risks:** the success or failure of a company can be heavily influenced by the political and legal environment of a country. The country's economic condition can determine its government's decisions with regard to taxation and currency control. Economic stress can influence how the population at large responds, and that response may impact certain businesses or the business community as a whole. When considering whether to invest or lend in a certain country, it is important to analyse the country's legal system and be confident in the rule of law and independent judiciary system found there.

- **Infrastructure:** natural resources such as gold, forests, and farmland usually determine which businesses can do well in a particular country. The physical infrastructure of a country is vital to the success of business, because it enables the movement of goods and people. Moreover, the quality of education and training available to workers will also affect the sophistication and growth of a business community. It is also important to understand the influence and bargaining power of labour unions present.

- **Financial markets:** a strong economic system has financial agents that connect suppliers with buyers, and price the transactions. These agents include insurance companies, investment banks, mutual funds, hedge funds, commercial banks, and private capital funds. It is important that there be a well-developed banking system to lend the capital required to finance the start and development of a business. Analysts must also consider the different accounting and disclosure systems found amongst companies and within geographic areas.

From a historical perspective, the main country risk factors that have affected financial performance of companies have been:

- GDP contraction and reduced domestic demand for a prolonged period, leading to economic depression;
- unfriendly or unexpected changes in regulations or changes in tariffs and taxes;
- sudden contraction of liquidity, combined with a general weakening of the financial system and a possible freezing of bank deposits;
- currency mismatch on operations and financial obligations combined with sharp local currency depreciation;
- delayed payments from sovereigns themselves or sovereign-owned entities;
- forced conversion of foreign currency-denominated obligations into local currency.

INDUSTRY RISK ANALYSIS

Industry risk is defined as the risks associated with any entity operating in the industry. Industry risk can be described as the risk of loss of market share or revenue; or suffering financial decline because of industry changes, business cycles, changes in consumer preferences, advances in technology, augmented competition, or reduction in barriers to entry. The main industry risks are related to industry structure, competition, growth dynamics, and industry profitability (opportunities and threats). The risks of doing business in some industries can be so significant as to put a limit on the credit quality of some, and possibly all, players in that industry. Analysis of an industry involves consideration and assessment of long-term industry basics and changes to those basics, industry trends and firms' adaptability, competitive dynamics of the industry, and peer-comparisons within the industry and across industry groups.

To properly evaluate an industry, it is important to evaluate the industry's long- and short-term actual and potential size and growth (as well as factors that may impact them) and evaluate the strength of the company within the industry (especially as it relates to competitors).

The key areas to look at when evaluating an industry are as follows.

Business definition

Although it may appear trivial, it is very important to find the appropriate business definition. Market definition establishes the relevant market segment that relates to the target company. It helps identify what drives superior profitability in an industry, indicates whether two business segments can be compared, and serves as the foundation for strategic analysis and sound decision making. According to Chris Zook, we can say that if two business segments have the same customers, the same cost structure, and the same competitors, they are one business. If they are different on all of these dimensions, they are separate businesses. Elements often used to define a market are products and geography.

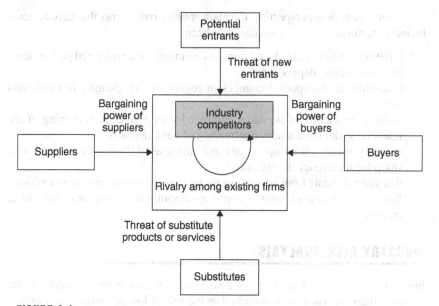

FIGURE 4.1   Porter Five Forces model.
Source: Grant (2016). © John Wiley & Sons, Inc. Reproduced with permission.

Attractiveness

The degree of competitiveness and maturity of an industry affects the performance of the companies of that sector. The industry structure also has an impact on the possibility for a company to grow market share or raise margins (to the levels needed to repay the debt on time). The response from competitors or substitute products is also an important factor affecting the profitability of an industry. The most known and used framework used to evaluate the attractiveness of an industry in terms of its ability to earn high returns is Porter's Five Forces model (depicted in Figure 4.1).

According to this model, competitive advantage in an industry is dependent on five primary forces:

- threat of new entrants
- bargaining power of buyers/customers
- bargaining power of suppliers
- threat of substitute products
- rivalry with competitors.

The degree of these threats determines the attractiveness of the market: intense competition allows minimal profit margins; while mild competition allows wider profit margins. In greater detail:

1. **Threat of new entrants:** profitable markets attract new firms. This results in many new entrants, which eventually will decrease profitability for all firms

in the industry. Unless the entry of new firms can be blocked by incumbents, excess profits will be wiped away (perfect competition). The following factors can have an effect on how much of a threat new entrants may pose:

- Barriers to entry: the height of the barriers against this threat and the determination to get over them defines the industry's profitability. Sectors with material barriers to entry tend to have lower competition and better profit margins and pricing flexibility than those that do not (and, generally, a stronger credit risk profile). There are many different forms of barrier to entry in a given industry, and they can be financial or non-financial. Every industry has particular requirements that are necessary to achieve for a company to be able to carry on doing business in that industry. For some companies those requirements can be met, although there has to be investment in resources, assets, skills, and time to develop reputation, relationships, and experience. Other barriers may be insurmountable because the requirements are so costly and geographically prohibitive. The main barriers to entry are listed below:
  - *Hurdle cost:* certain elements need to be evaluated to determine if there are hurdles. The expense of building facilities or the capital intensity of an industry can present a major barrier to entry. An industry's entry capital requirements can directly impact a company's ability to improve its profitability, or to be profitable at all. Capital-intensive industries that are also challenged by heavy competition and limited growth potential usually have low profit margins to deal with as well. Such industries include integrated steel, rubber, homebuilding, and mining. Conversely, industries that can generate more revenue with their capital and that can also vary spending according to cycles (e.g. branded consumer products, pharmaceutical manufacturers, publishing, and broadcasting) have more positive revenue and expense characteristics. Limits to credit strength also arise when industries are compelled to spend their available cash to maintain or grow their business (e.g. oil and gas production, whose producers have to constantly develop and explore for more oil and natural gas using their own cash).
  - *Technology:* keeping up with technology is a substantial barrier for many companies.
  - *Access to customers:* the location and efficiency of distribution to customers is vital to the success of companies. Reputation amongst customers is also important.
  - *Suppliers:* companies must be able to access suppliers and raw materials. A country's infrastructure is very important here. It is obviously vital to have access to harbours, airports, roads, and electricity in order to function as a business.
2. **Bargaining power of buyers/customers:** this primarily depends upon their price sensitivity and their bargaining leverage. A buyer group is powerful if there is:
  - Price sensitivity: this depends upon the purchaser's relative cost importance to the buyer. A number of things can reduce price sensitivity: brand loyalty

and differentiation; customer's own profitability; and decision-makers' incentives (e.g. quality, etc.).
- Bargaining leverage: several factors determine the amount of leverage buyers have. These include: buyer concentration and volume (relative to seller's sales); buyer switching costs; buyer information; threat of backward vertical integration by buyers; existence of substitutes; differentiation; and quality.

3. **Bargaining power of suppliers:** this is the differentiation of the inputs, and it matters when the organisation's process needs a rare commodity. Contributory factors to this force are:
- Switching costs of changing to an alternative supplier: when these costs are high, then suppliers are relatively powerful since the organisation would face significant costs if it were to leave them. Where a supplier is in a monopoly position – for example, electricity supplies – their power is extremely high since changing to gas causes high switching costs.
- Availability of substitute supplies: when substitutes are available, the power of the supplier is reduced; for example, if the fuel used can be changed from electricity to gas.
- Supplier concentration: the more unique the supplier is, the higher their power. The extreme of this is the monopoly supplier situation. When suppliers are not concentrated, their power is lowered.
- The importance of volume to suppliers: if the volume of sales represented by that customer is less significant, then the supplier bargaining position is strengthened.
- Cost relative to the purchasing industry's total costs: supplier power is low when goods provided form a cost-significant input. Bargaining power increases when their ratio to the users' total costs falls.
- Impact of product to cost or differentiation: supplier power is higher when their product is significant to the buyer organisation's overall costs or chances of product differentiation. Their power is weaker if the quality or cost of the supplies is not significant to the quality or cost of the purchaser's product.
- Threat of forward integration by suppliers: when suppliers find it easy to forward integrate into the purchaser's industry, then they have high bargaining power. If pushed to lower prices, they will themselves produce the 'finished product'. Where the barriers to such integration are high (see threat of new entrants), then the power of suppliers is weakened.

4. **Threat of substitute products:** when this threat is high, the 'safe' profit margin is low as customers more readily change when prices are high. Substitute products that deserve the most attention are those that compete in price with the industry's products and are produced by industries earning high profits. In particular:
- Relative price and performance of substitutes: if a similar product or service is available at the same, or lower, price then the threat is high. If potential substitutes are more expensive, or inferior, then the threat is low.

- Switching costs for customers: this factor determines the threat of substitutes as well as determining the height of the entry barrier. If no extra costs are incurred, then change is likely.
- Buyers' propensity to substitutes: apathetic or satisfied buyers are not likely to change; militant or dissatisfied ones are. Generally, the more significant the purchase is to the customer, the higher their propensity to switch.

5. **Rivalry with competitors:** this rivalry can range from intense in a cut-throat industry, to mild in an affluent and affable one. When rivalry is high, profits will tend to be low. The most important contributory factors are:

- Industry growth: industries that are static or in decline will have more intense rivalry than those which are rapidly growing.
- High fixed costs or high storage costs: when these are high the volume of sales must be maintained and so rivalry heightens.
- Intermittent over-capacity: rivalry is more intense when, either because of demand fluctuations or production constraints, the industry experiences periods of over-capacity.
- Product differences, brand identity and switching costs for customers: where there is no brand loyalty, i.e. no differentiation, then the customer depends upon price, and when switching costs are small this is very elastic, so rivalry will be heated. Conversely, when differentiation or switching costs are high, then demand is less elastic and rivalry is cooled.
- Number of organisations and their size: if there are lots of organisations of a similar size in the same pool, then rivalry will be intense. Fewer firms or one of a dominant size reduce rivalry and enforce 'orderly' competition.
- Diversity of competitors: the greater the degree of similarity between the different organisations, the lower the level of rivalry is. An industry with structurally, culturally, and geographically diverse players will have intense rivalry.
- Corporate stakes: the rivalry of the industry will vary with the importance of it to the players. Side-line industries have low rivalry, whilst single product industries have very intense rivalry.
- High exit barriers: if leaving the industry will cost a lot either physically or emotionally, then the rivalry will tend to be intense.

With respect to the five forces used by Porter to rate an industry, we can say that an industry is attractive when:

1. **Threat of new entrants:** there is one or more of the factors listed hereafter: economies of scale, proprietary product differences, high brand identity, high switching costs, high capital requirements, difficult access to distribution, high absolute cost advantages, restricting government policy, expected retaliation.
2. **Bargaining power of buyers/customers:** there is low bargaining leverage (low buyer concentration vs. firm concentration, low buyer volume, high buyer switching costs relative to firm switching costs, limited buyer information, low ability to backward integrate, few substitute products)

or low price sensitivity (low price/total purchases, high product differences, high brand identity, high impact on quality/performance, high buyer profits).

3. **Bargaining power of suppliers:** there is one of more of the factors listed hereafter: low differentiation of inputs, low switching costs of suppliers and firms in the industry, large presence of substitute inputs, low supplier concentration, high importance of volume to supplier, low cost relative to total cost/purchases, low impact of inputs on cost or differentiation, low threat of forward integration relative to threat of backward integration by firms in the industry.

4. **Threat of substitute products:** there is low relative price performance of substitutes, or high switching costs, or low buyer propensity to substitute.

5. **Rivalry with competitors:** there is one of more of the factors listed hereafter: industry growth above GDP, lower fixed (or storage) costs/value added, low intermittent over-capacity, high product differences, high brand identity, high switching costs, high concentration, high diversity of competitors, low corporate stakes, low exit barriers, low cyclicality.

Structure: Porter's value chain analysis (summarised in Figure 4.2) is a tool that can be used to understand how an industry is structured (though its use can be adapted to firms and activity value chains). An industry value chain analysis is a systematic method for disaggregating an industry into its major discrete components to understand sources of competitive advantage. The simplest value chain is made of supplier, company, buyer or supplier, manufacturer, retailer, and end user.

An example from the personal computer industry will help here. The good that the end customer receives is a combination of hardware, software, and support services. Intel supplies components, Dell builds the case and provides the services, and Microsoft supplies the operating software. Since the component supplier Intel and the software supplier Microsoft both operate in more or less of a monopoly position, they are able to extract most of the value added which goes into the final product. Dell has to compete in a marketplace with many competitors and low barriers to entry, and will thus receive a much smaller portion of the cumulative value added. Thus: margin = total value to buyers - cost of producing value.

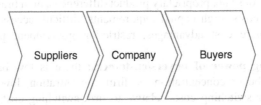

FIGURE 4.2   Porter's industry value chain.

Size

Looking at the revenues and profits generated by an industry as a whole (also called revenue or profit pool), it is a good way of measuring that industry's condition. Market sizing establishes the:

- market potential for target company (total size);
- growth potential of company (relative to market growth);
- frame of reference for size of target company (relative to total market).

Profit (revenue) pools are the total profits (revenues) earned in an industry at all points along the industry's value chain. Companies that recognise the variability of profitability and that can control choke points can influence the distribution of profits amongst competitors and can earn superior returns. A proper analysis should examine different sectors within the industry separately to make the best comparisons. It is also important to analyse the patterns of both unit sales and price per unit, as revenue is made up of both these elements. Industries with good appeal to private equity and private debt funds are obviously those that are growing consistently as well as growing in size. Furthermore, an industry's value is appealing when demand is greater than supply, enabling the seller to set the price (this is the concept of pricing power).

Growth

A growth industry is one that has a strong potential for sales growth (>5%) in new markets, but which has not yet achieved sales in every available market. A mature industry has already achieved sales in most possible markets and its growth prospects are usually around −5 to 5% compared to that of other industries. Niche industries are narrow, small businesses within larger industries. Within niche industries there are more growth opportunities for smaller firms and usually negligible potential for larger companies. A global business is usually an established company making sales internationally. Sales growth potential for global participants can be substantial, although political and logistical issues can be very challenging. New products coming onto the market also impact sales demands in mature industries. Although new products are not always successful, they can still influence the dynamics of supply and demand. For example, a new product can render an existing product obsolete because it is a better product at a similar price. Moreover, a new product may provide an alternative to a current product. New products can also create a new demand for all related products. Industry growth can slow, and ultimately reverse, because of the following drivers:

- technological change, leading to industry substitution (e.g. typewriters for word processors and PCs);
- competing business models, leading to disintermediation (e.g. local retailers by mega retailers);
- maturing economic and demographic environment, leading to market saturation (e.g. very low growth rates in the European car sector).

Capacity utilisation

Not all mature or established industries have stable growth patterns, and funds' analysts need to be aware of this. Use of plant capacity can indicate the condition of the manufacturing industry, and in particular its pricing power. Industries with low capacity utilisation (<80%) normally experience flat or reduced prices until demand increases (usually because of seasonal or economic changes). High use of capacity promotes higher prices and an increase in workers' hours or the building of new plants.

Capital intensity

Companies in this sector display higher risk, as return and/or break-even horizons are often longer term because of the need to invest heavily in fixed assets and/or production capacity. Operating leverage and capacity utilisation are major business risk factors. In sectors that are capital intensive and highly competitive (e.g. autos, shipping, metals, and mining), profitability is highly sensitive to high-capacity utilisation or a fixed high-cost basis. Capital-intensive sectors often have a tendency to over-expand capacity in growth periods (leading to surplus capacity that can create intense price competition and thus erode margins) and frequently produce products that are commodity-like (with poor pricing power). From a financial risk profile perspective, they also tend to have above-average risk, as financing needs are long term and require substantial debt. Cash flow volatility and high debt service make these sectors higher risk.

Cyclicality and seasonality

Not all industries are affected in the same way by shifts in their businesses or the economy. Business cycles need to be factored in when assessing risk. Analysts should assess the size and timing of the highs and lows of the cycles of different industries in order to anticipate these swings. Cyclical industries are challenged by the need to achieve consistent sales, as they are strongly impacted by shifts in the economy and vulnerable to changes in supply and demand patterns that cause financial stress. Industry cycles are produced by demand volatility, but also by swings in supply capacity. Addition of new capacity often occurs in response to cyclical upswings in demand, and over-building of production capacity exacerbates competitive and earnings pressure – especially in a downturn (the dynamics seen in bulk chemicals, shipping, housing, paper, metals, and mining). In cyclical downturns, companies with weak competitive positions can see profitability and cash flow disappear and credit risk is additionally worsened by the presence of gearing of a company. Many companies in the cyclical sector opt for diversification to offset swings in performance. It should be noted that there is no normal cycle for any industry. In the twenty-first century, cycles of business have been faster than in the twentieth century. However, one should expect that weak companies become weaker and more unstable during lows in the business cycles. Most defaults occur during the lows. For some companies, the speed and degree of shifts in market conditions can signify the difference between survival and failure. Business cycles come in different forms. The general business cycle covers economic activity as a whole as well as national or global business demand. Demand-driven cycles are normally found within individual sectors, such as the product-replacement cycles that occur in the PC industry. Supply-driven cycles are reflected in the capacity growth and plant closure usually present in manufacturing sectors (paper, metals, chemicals). Seasonality is another form of cycle which only impacts certain industries, such as toys, agriculture, utilities, and energy. Analysts need to fully evaluate the individual seasons of companies in this category. Shifts in the consistency of business strategies and financial policies during the different stages of business cycles and seasons are actually vital to the performance of every company. As a way of illustration, a synthetic categorisation of sectors as a function of cyclicality is reported below:

- Early in the economic cycle: leisure, gaming, lodging, building materials, homebuilders, real estate, retailers, restaurants, textiles and clothing, automotive and auto suppliers.
- Consistent throughout the cycle: health care, consumer products, food and beverages, tobacco, food and drug retail, utilities.
- Late in the cycle: cable television, capital goods, airlines and aerospace, paper, containers, chemicals, oil and natural gas, telecommunications, metals, mining, technology, broadcasting and media, publishing and printing.

Regulation

Industry regulations and legal issues impact profitability and credit strength. For example, significant restrictions can be imposed on earnings growth by the regulated return on equity prescribed for utilities. One may think that if cyclicality and instability are negatives, then the stability afforded by governmental or regulatory rules would be positive – but that is not always the case. So the analyst must determine the impact of regulations on the revenue and income of the business, and on its ability to compete. Analysts should consider whether the regulations set a minimum on financial performance, or whether they a set a maximum. Moreover, do the regulations provide a safety net, or do they tie the company's hands?

Global vs. niche sectors

It is important for analysts to follow supply and demand trends in order to understand sales growth and pricing power in mature industries. Niche companies focus on a limited line of products in order to try and take advantage of the inefficiencies of larger companies. They are often small suppliers supporting products made by larger companies, and they depend on the success of those larger companies. They face huge competition and are normally considered high risk. Global companies carry all the risks and opportunities of mature businesses, but on a greater and more complex scale. Only large companies can operate on a global level, as a global business is one in which competitors, manufacturers, suppliers, and distributors produce and deliver from all over the world.

In a nutshell, key risks to assess in this phase are:

- declining or limited growth;
- distressed/negatively-trending industry profitability (e.g. commoditisation, maturing, globalisation, delayering);
- intensely competitive market;
- low barriers to entry;
- strong/difficult to manage cyclicality;
- poor or declining regulatory relations;
- product substitution.

Sectors that historically have displayed higher degrees of credit default and/or credit downgrades have a significant degree of correlation with industries featuring greater concentrations of key high-risk industry characteristics. Factors that have amongst the highest levels of impact on credit risk are: cyclicality, degree of competition, capital intensity, technological risk, regulation and/or deregulation, and energy cost sensitivity.

Finally, it should be noted that industry risk profiles can change materially over time due to: trends in key industry drivers and characteristics, industry maturation, deregulation, and emergence of new technologies.

Examples of industries in transition are deregulated utilities and telecoms. Industries undergoing rapid transition in their competitive landscapes usually also have a higher incidence of governance problems because management is tempted to overly optimistically present their business prospects and financial performance.

Equally, it should be noted that some industries that have become old fashioned in certain countries or continents can become rejuvenated in emerging markets. For example, in China and India, sectors such as auto manufacturing, capital goods, and steel, which are mature industries in developed countries, are growth sectors. In industries that developing countries seek to attract, foreign companies often initially benefit from government assistance and inducement such as tariff protection, the barring of other foreign entrants, and tax breaks.

With all the caveats related to generalisations, we summarise below various sectors of an economy as a function of levels of 'inherent' industry risk:

1. **Highest risk:**
   - metals and mining, especially integrated steel;
   - large-scale manufacturers, especially auto;
   - airlines and aerospace;
   - homebuilding;

- merchant electricity generators;
- paper and wood products.

2. Medium risk:
- oil and natural gas;
- technology and telecommunications equipment;
- restaurants and retail;
- health care;
- hotels and gaming;
- basic transport.

3. Lowest risk:
- branded consumer products;
- pharmaceutical and medical instruments;
- regulated utilities;
- publishing and broadcasting;
- military defense manufacturers;
- agriculture, meat, and poultry.

(Ganguin and Bilardello, 2004)

COMPANY ANALYSIS

Company positioning and strategy

Company analysis involves assessment of the company's competitive position in each line of activity, its ability to maintain or improve its competitive position, the level of balance and diversity of the company's portfolio, and the diversity of the company's end markets and customers, and is fundamental to evaluating a company's competitive position and sustainability vis à vis its competitors based on key success factors and sources of competitive advantage. Differences in competitive positioning can justify substantial differences in profitability amongst various industry players. A strong business profile score can be achieved via a very strong and distinct competitive positioning and it generally goes hand in hand with sustained profitability and stable revenue and cash flow; conversely a relative or absolute weak competitive position – even in a favourable industry environment – is unlikely to result in a solid profitability and credit standing.

Michael Porter defined the two types of competitive advantage a company can achieve relative to its rivals: lower cost or differentiation. This advantage derives from attribute(s) that allow an organisation to outperform its competition, such as superior market position, skills, or resources. In order to measure quantitatively the competitive advantage of a company vs. its competitors, the analyst must look at:

- cost advantage: compare a company unit costs (with special reference to those most significant and relevant to a particular business) with those of its competitors;
- differentiation: compare price positioning of a company vs. its competitors.

The most used tool to assess a company's positioning is the company Five Forces model by Porter (see above for the analytical framework). Based on these strategies, analysts can map the borrower against the industry they operate in inorder to understand the competitive advantage (key success factors or economic profit drivers for the industry that allow it to earn excess returns). Depending on the different industry types (although it is worth noting that many industries display a combination of these characteristics), a company can analyse its competitive advantages (if any) and benchmark them vis à vis the competitors as follows:

- **Commodity:** cost is the main differentiating factor (e.g. steel). Very limited room for differentiation through premium, innovation, or customer relations. The key purchasing criteria is price; the key success factor is low relative cost position. The competitive advantage is cost and the sources of cost advantage are:
  - Scale: driven by volume (production) or focus (concentration on value chain, customer segment, etc.). An example is the Multijet diesel engine.
  - Process effectiveness: mainly due to management and workforce skills (e.g. supply chain, distribution, etc.). An example is Amazon's process management.
  - Factor costs: typically labour, raw material, capital, information, etc. An example would be the Chinese producers of labour-intensive sectors.
  - Privileged assets: natural resources, regulation, patents, etc. An example would be De Beers mines.
- **Premium category:** brand identity is the main differentiating factor (e.g. athletic footwear). An industry is premium when 50% of the products are sold 30% above private label prices. The key purchasing criteria is perceived quality; the key success factor is high premium price realisation. The competitive advantage is differentiation and the sources of differentiation advantage are:
  - Quality: design, performance, and features are all factors of differentiation.
  - Range: breadth of offering is the main differentiation feature.
  - Price: value for money and perceived luxury are key differentiators.
  - Privileged assets: physical assets, location space, access, distribution or sales network, and patents are some examples of variables of differentiation.
  - Distinctive capabilities: innovation skills represent some of the sources of differentiation.
  - Brand: image, prestige, and premium are key differentiators.
- **Relationship driven:** customer relationships are the main differentiating factor (e.g. banks). Customer retention is instrumental. The key purchasing criteria is trust; the key success factor is high customer retention. The competitive advantage is differentiation and the sources of differentiation advantage are:
  - Quality: reliability is a key differentiation factor.
  - Customer service: delivery time is one example of differentiation.

- Special relation: trade and customer relationship are often variables at the root of differentiation.
- Distinctive capabilities: management skills represent a source of differentiation.
- **Innovation driven:** technological innovation is the main differentiating factor (e.g. mobile phones). Successive new product launches and product innovations are crucial. The key purchasing criteria is technological sophistication; the key success factor is short time to market. The competitive advantage is differentiation and the sources of differentiation advantage are:
  - Quality: reliability and ease of use represent key differentiators.
  - Range: interoperability is a factor of differentiation.
  - Privileged assets: patent is a differentiation variable.
  - Distinctive capabilities: innovation skills are a source of differentiation.

Another useful framework used to analyse synthetically a company vs. its competitors is the SWOT (Strengths – Weaknesses – Opportunities – Threats) analysis. SWOT analysis helps with identifying the internal and external factors that are favourable or not to achieve the objective of a given strategy. More particularly:

- Strengths: characteristics of a company that give it an advantage over others.
- Weaknesses: characteristics that place the business at a disadvantage relative to others.
- Opportunities: elements that the company could exploit to its advantage.
- Threats: elements in the environment that could cause trouble for the business.

SWOT analysis thus groups key characteristics of a company into two main categories:

- internal factors – the *strengths* and *weaknesses* internal to the organisation;
- external factors – the *opportunities* and *threats* presented by the environment external to the organisation.

Another widely used framework (though increasingly criticised) is the so-called Boston Consulting Group Matrix (see Figure 4.3). The Growth/Share Matrix divides a corporation's portfolio of businesses according to the market potential and relative competitive position of each business. Future market growth is used as a proxy for market potential (10% or above real growth is considered high growth) and Relative Market Share[1] (greater than 1.0 means business is #1 in market share, around 1.0–1.5 is a tenuous position since the second largest player is a close second) as a proxy for relative competitive advantage. Using this

---

[1]The relative market share (RMS) for the market leader is calculated in relation to the #2 player; the RMS for all other players is calculated in relation to the market leader. The metric most often used for the calculation is sales revenues.

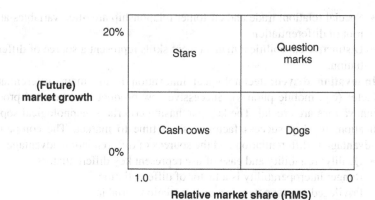

FIGURE 4.3   Boston Consulting Group Matrix.

2 × 2 matrix, it is possible to rank the business units (or products) on the basis of their relative market shares and growth rates.

- **Cash cows:** a company with high market share in a slow-growing industry. These typically generate cash in excess of the amount of cash needed to maintain the business. They produce stable cash flows in a 'mature' market and are to be 'milked' continuously with as little investment as possible, since such investment would be wasted in an industry with low growth.
- **Dogs:** companies/business units with low market share in a mature, slow-growing industry. These units typically 'break-even', generating barely enough cash to maintain the business's market share. These units are worthless since they depress group profitability, although careful attention should be given to potential synergies with other business units of the company.
- **Question marks (also known as problem children):** businesses operating in a high market growth, but having a low market share (the usual starting point for most businesses). Question marks have a potential to gain market share and become stars, and eventually cash cows when market growth slows. If question marks do not succeed in becoming a market leader (after years of cash consumption), they will degenerate into dogs when market growth declines. Question marks must be analysed carefully in order to determine whether they are worth the investment required to grow market share.
- **Stars:** companies/units with a high market share in a fast-growing industry.

It should be noted that it is the sustainability over the future of a competitive position, rather than the position itself on an absolute scale, which is critical for a superior equity and credit quality. The lack of a clear competitive advantage in cost leadership or diversification leads to below-industry-average profitability: in fact, even if a company in such a situation can still generate attractive profits when the industry grows, the sustainability of its business performance can be severely challenged during downturns. Analysts consequently should focus their analysis on the underlying sustainability of existing business positions and on the tangible prospects for improvement, rather than on absolute market shares.

In summary, key risks to assess in this phase are:

- insufficient/declining advantage of products and services (e.g. maturing, under-invested);
- insufficient sustainability of advantage (absence of self-re-enforcing scale, intellectual property);
- declining market share;
- excessive profit dependence of few products, regions, etc.;
- volatility of profitability – e.g. cyclicality, blockbuster product dependence, etc.;
- poorly integrated acquisitions;
- inability to accommodate growth – space, controls, systems, access to labour pool, etc.;
- workforce inadequacy – poor training, high attrition rate, poor trade relations, etc.;
- lacking discipline – overstaffed, overcompensated, etc.;
- approaching minimum efficient scale.

Competitor's analysis

Analysis of a company's profitability derives from hard numbers and historical evidence and therefore appears less subject to differences in interpretation. Profitability ratios, for instance, provide strong evidence of a company's relative positioning and are one of the easier factors to compare among companies. Since there are margins of subjectivity in reporting or valuing certain items of the P&L and balance sheet, it is opportune to analyse profits over a number of years and compare with competitors in the same sector or segment. Profit serves three main factors: a premium for risk, a source of capital for growth, and a measure of business effectiveness. Different stakeholders measure business success using different criteria:

- investors: focus on ROE and EPS to compare the return of capital invested vs. alternative investment opportunities;
- lenders: view profits as a component of cash flow;
- management: use gross and net profit margins to measure efficiency of processes and labour force;
- labour and government: try to capture excess returns of capital to investors.

From a comparative point of view, it is important to understand the allocation of profits:

- gross margin: profits that remain after operating costs associated with the primary business activity;
- profit before interest and taxes: profits that remain after the primary business activity and administrative expenses, but before interest and taxes;

- profit before taxes: profits that remain after the primary business activity, administrative, and financial expenses, but before taxes;
- net profits: profits that remain available for reinvestment in the company or for distribution to shareholders.

The following table summarises the advantages and disadvantages of the different profit measures.

Profit variable	Pro	Con
Gross margin	Captures operating efficiency	Cost of goods sold (COGS) calculation may differ across competitors
PBIT	Highlights efficiency of administration and management	Ignores effects of gearing to generate profit
PBT	Incorporates (positive or negative) effects of financial policies on profits	Ignores effects of tax planning to reduce taxes through transfer pricing, international operations, etc.
Net profit	Captures tax and financial policies as well as production and administration efficiency	Assumes management is accountable for changes in interest rates and taxes

Pricing advantages, efficiency differences, and asset utilisation are each attributable to a situation in which the firm or management conducts its operations more effectively and efficiently than its competitors (it possesses a unique advantage). Performance or profitability ratios (classified hereafter as a function of what 'type' of profitability they are trying to measure) should be thus jointly analysed. It is suggested that when comparing companies, only simple ratio calculations should be used, and these ratios should be calculated consistently. Simple ratio measures to analyse are:

- **Profit margins:**
  - Gross profit margin: gross profit measures the raw profit net of cost of goods sold. Usually, companies with high turnover display low margin and vice versa. Typical ratios used are:
    - *Gross profit margin:* (Gross Profit / Sales) * 100. The gross margin reflects the relationship of prices, volume, and costs and therefore any change of the margin may result from a change in one or more of those variables. In this sense, a comparative analysis of prices, volumes, and COGS vs. competitors may shed light on different advantages or policies.
    - *Cost of goods sold ratio:* (COGS / Sales) * 100.

- Net profit margin:
  - *EBITDA margin:* (EBITDA / Sales) * 100. EBITDA allows a comparison of profitability between different companies, by discounting the effects of interest payments from different forms of financing (by ignoring interest payments), political jurisdictions (by ignoring tax payments), tax and accounting policies (by ignoring depreciation of assets), and different M&A histories (by ignoring amortisation often stemming from goodwill). It is quite common to make adjustments to EBITDA to normalise the measurement, which then allows comparison of the performance of one business to another. Since EBITDA is often used as a quick proxy for cash, it must be noted that, while a negative EBITDA indicates that a business has fundamental problems with profitability and cash flow, on the other hand a positive EBITDA does not necessarily mean that the business generates cash (since it ignores changes in working capital, capital expenditures, taxes, and interest).
  - *Earnings before tax (EBT margin):* (EBT / Sales) * 100. This ratio takes into account the financial policy of a firm, but comparison across an industry may be distorted by different gearing and interest costs (not always under management control).
  - *Net profit margin:* (Net profit / Sales) * 100. Very popular since it shows how good a company is at converting revenue into profits available for shareholders, it is relevant especially for listed companies (although has several weaknesses since it is prone to creative accounting and sensitive to different tax regimes and financial policies).
- **Asset utilisation ratios:**
  - Total asset turnover: TATO (Sales / Average Total Assets)[2] is a measure of sales generated per unit of assets available. This indicator suffers from the fact that it does not take into account the different assets (fixed, current), can be distorted by accounting values significantly different from market values, and does not account for multiple product lines with different levels of capital intensity.
  - Fixed asset turnover: FATO (Sales / Average Net Property, Plant and Equipment (PP&E)) measures a company's ability to generate net sales from fixed-asset investments.
  - Account receivable turnover: ARTO (= Sales / Average Accounts Receivable) and average collection cycle (= 365 / ARTO) are the indicators used to measure how many times a business can collect its average accounts receivable during the year.
  - Inventory turnover: INVTO (= COGS / average inventory) and average holding period (= 365 / INVTO) show how many times a company's inventory is sold and replaced over a period.

---

[2]It is sometimes useful to look at its reciprocal to have a capital intensity ratio.

- Account payable turnover: APTO (= Purchases[3] / Average Accounts Payable) and days payable (= 365 / APTO) show how many times a company can pay off its average accounts payable balance during the course of a year.
- Net trade cycle (or cash conversion cycle): NTC (Avg. Collection Cycle + Avg. Holding Period – Days Payable) measure the length of time, in days, that it takes for a company to convert resource inputs into cash flows by looking at the amount of time needed to sell inventory, collect receivables, and pay its payables.

Return:

- Return on assets: indicator of how profitable a company is relative to its total assets. ROA gives an idea as to how efficient management is at using its assets to generate earnings and is calculated as follows: (Net income / Average Total Assets). Using the Dupont method and defining profit margin (PM) as (Net Income / Sales), one can further decompose ROA as PM * TATO (the latter can be further decomposed) to better understand the drivers of ROA.
- Return on capital employed: calculated as (EBIT / Average Total Assets)[4] measures how efficiently a company makes use of its available capital to generate profits. ROCE also can be decomposed (EBIT margin * TATO) to better understand its components. Warning signals are a downward trend and when ROCE is below the cost of borrowing.
- Return on equity: preferred by equity investors, it is calculated as (Net Income / Shareholders' Equity) and measures the efficiency of a firm at generating profits from each unit of shareholder equity. As with the other indicators, it can be broken down into: (Net Income / Sales) * TATO * (Average Total Assets / Average Shareholder's Equity), in other words Profit Margin * Total Asset Turnover * Asset Leverage.

As a very general rule, profit margins and returns on investment over 20% are considered strong; between 10 and 20% are average, lower than 10% are weak.

SUMMARY STEPS FOR A STRATEGIC ANALYSIS OF A BUSINESS PLAN

At the end of this section, it is useful to summarise the different steps to perform in a strategic analysis of a business plan:

1. define the sector boundaries;
2. analyse the sector attractiveness, profitability drivers, and sources of competitive advantage;

---

[3]Purchases = COGS + Δ inventory.
[4]An alternative formulation uses NOPAT [= EBIT * (1-marginal tax rate)] instead of EBIT.

3. analyse the competitive positioning of the target company;

4. quantify the profit and revenue pool of the sector (together called sector full potential);

5. measure the full potential of the target company and its distance from it;

6. define the strategies and list the investments needed to reach the profit potential;

7. analyse the consistency between the target company business plan and the previously analysed market scenario;

8. review the business plan's sustainability;

9. develop sensitivity.

REFERENCES AND FURTHER READING

B. Ganguin and J. Bilardello. 2004. *Standard & Poor's Fundamentals of Corporate Credit Analysis*. McGraw Hill.

R. Grant. 2016. *Contemporary Strategy Analysis: Text and Cases Edition*. Wiley.

C. Zook and J. Allen. 2010. *Profit from the Core*. Harvard Business Review Press.

SUGGESTED CASES

G. Stuart. 1994. Humana, Inc.: 'Managing in a Changing Industry.' Harvard Business School Case 294-062.

D.B. Yoffie and R. Kim. 2011. 'Wal-Mart Update, 2011.' Harvard Business School Case 711-546.

D.B. Yoffie and M. Slind. 2005. 'Intel Corporation 2005.' Harvard Business School Case 706-437.

CHAPTER 5

Accounting Due Diligence

INTRODUCTION

After developing a contextual understanding of the firm, its industry, and management's plans, we evaluate its financial performance. Financial risk measures the stability, flexibility, variety, and cost of a company's funding structure. The level of a firm's business and financial risks should be inversely correlated. Companies with low levels of business risk (steady and stable cash flow) can afford higher levels of financial risk than those with high business risk.

Different industries and companies may have varying factors that are important to assess. However, the main thing is to ensure that obligations are repaid in cash and that equity value creation is not a mere accounting exercise conducted with accounting adjustments. To this end, it is important to analyse the following elements:

a) a review of the quality of earnings (or quality of the accounting) that forms the basis of the financial analysis;
b) ratio and cash flow analysis;
c) creative accounting.

QUALITY OF EARNINGS

Whereas financial risk analysis should be conducted on the basis of financial statements audited by a reputable auditor, it is important to start the financial analysis with a review of the quality of the accounts. When reviewing the quality of accounts, the four basic principles of accounting should be borne in mind:

a) **objectivity:** everything should be directly measurable and verifiable, not influenced by personal bias or judgement;
b) **matching:** every dollar of revenue has an associated cost, and both must be recorded in the same period;
c) **conservatism:** revenues are recognised only when they are reasonably certain, whereas expenses are recognised as soon as they are reasonably possible;

d) reporting: reporting is done for the benefit of third parties and, therefore, must be prepared according to certain standards.

Key questions to ask in this section are:

a.1. What is the accounting system being used: US, GAAP, IAS, or other?

a.2. Have there been recent regulatory actions or sanctions by regulatory bodies? Have there been recent late or amended filings or restatements and for what reason?

a.3. Has there been a recent change in accounting period?

a.4. What is the impact of recent or upcoming changes in accounting standards?

a.5. Has there been a recent change in external auditors, and if so, why?

a.6. What qualifications and exceptions are there to the auditor's opinion?

a.7. Have there been recent alterations in accounting or estimates, or any reclassifications amongst accounts? Why?

a.8. Have there been notable related-party transactions?

a.9. Has the company grown mainly through internal development or through acquisitions? If through acquisitions, how have these been accounted for?

a.10. Is there a consolidation of all majority-owned subsidiaries?

a.11. What is the nature of equity-method and cost-method affiliates? Are there any non-consolidated affiliates (including joint ventures) where the company has a high degree of control, that are likely to have majority ownership, and/or guarantee debt?

Scholars and practitioners agree that there are some areas that deserve more attention (see Figures 5.1, 5.2, and 5.3) since they are the most commonly used to manipulate earnings. Understanding the quality of earnings is therefore critical.

Quality of Earnings

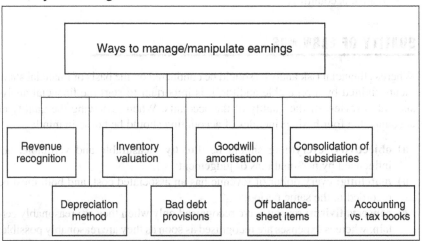

FIGURE 5.1 General key areas of attention in accounting due diligence.

Quality of Earnings – Income Statement

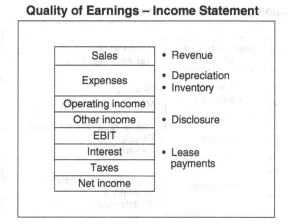

Sales	• Revenue
Expenses	• Depreciation • Inventory
Operating income	
Other income	• Disclosure
EBIT	
Interest	• Lease
Taxes	payments
Net income	

FIGURE 5.2 Profit and loss key areas of attention in accounting due diligence.

Sales Revenue recognition concerns issues regarding the timing and amount of turnover recognised in the income statement. The choice of a particular method of revenue recognition has a different impact on earnings and cash. There are three methods for recognising revenues:

- Recognised based on percentage of completion: recorded incrementally as a product is being produced. This methodology may recognise revenues prematurely, and revenues may never be realised in cash!
- Recognised when shipped: recorded when the product is loaded for delivery. This methodology may recognise revenues prematurely.
- Recognised as title passes: recorded when customer takes possession.

Another area of revenue investigation is long-term contracts: it is in fact important to determine whether revenues are being recognised too early, whether sales around year end are being smoothed, and whether contracted income is being recognised up front. The main issues here concern the timing of recognition of profits (whether at the end of the contract or periodically during the life of the contract), and the method by which profits should be calculated (the basis to be used). The general rule with regard to recognition of cost of goods sold is that costs of sales should match the revenue generated.

Timing recognition is in fact relevant because margins may be affected by different policies. Whether or not today's profit margin provides a solid basis for predicting future margins depends also on the policy of revenue recognition that is used. For contracts which span over an accounting year end, the overall profit margins will not be known until the final year of the contract, and will therefore need to be estimated. Questions to be addressed regarding such estimates include:

- How are the estimates computed?
- How accurate were estimates in the past?

Quality of Earnings – Assets

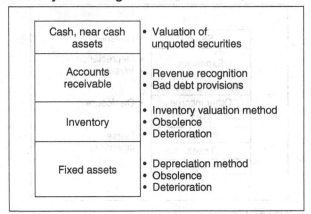

Quality of Earnings – Liabilities

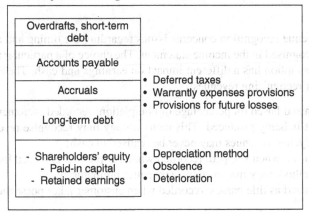

FIGURE 5.3 Balance sheet key areas of attention in accounting due diligence.

- Which are the relevant accounting rules to be applied?
- Are there any penalty clauses (for example, if work is not completed on time)? If so, how are these estimated?
- Out of different estimation methods available to calculate percentage of completion, the key questions to ask are:
  - What are the company's policies?
  - Are these methods used consistently?
  - Why are these particular methods favoured?

Depreciation There are several options for calculating depreciation:

- **Straight-line:** consists of dividing the cost of the asset, less any estimated salvage value, by the number of years of its expected life, to derive the annual depreciation. Often used for reporting purposes, straight-line depreciation results in higher income in the early years of an asset's life than accelerated methods.
- **Production or use (straight-line use):** based on actual production or usage during the period, the depreciation pattern directly relates to the usage pattern. It usually results in the asset depreciating faster than straight-line, because assets are often more heavily used early in their lives.
- **Declining balance:** the net book value (cost less accumulated depreciation but without subtracting salvage value) of the asset at the start of each period is multiplied by a fixed rate. The periodic charge for depreciation declines throughout the asset's life.
- **Sum-of-the-years'-digits:** a fraction, which diminishes from year to year, is applied to the cost, less the estimated salvage value. The numerator of the fraction is the number of years of remaining life at the beginning of the period, while the denominator is the sum of the number of years (5 years = 1 + 2 + 3 + 4 + 5 = 15).

The last three methods are accelerated depreciation methods often used to understate income, and thus reduce taxes, in the early years of an asset's life.

Goodwill amortisation Unless there is or has been an acquisition, goodwill does not appear on the balance sheet. When a merger is accounted for using 'purchase' accounting (rather than 'pooling-of-interests' accounting), a goodwill line item is created on the balance sheet. It is generally amortised as an expense evenly over some time period, just as a fixed asset is depreciated using the straight-line method. Amortisation of goodwill is an expense and therefore reduces earnings: a longer amortisation period (40 vs. 20 years) will decrease expenses and therefore increase earnings.

Provisions Provisions are used when the value of an asset is expected to have failed, or the amount or timing of a liability is not certain. Current and future earnings can be smoothed by increasing or decreasing provisions. Creating and then reversing general provisions permits the smoothing of earnings figures.

Key questions to ask when performing a P&L accounting review are:

b.1. Is the revenue recognition method different from the point of sale?
b.2. How are sales allowances and discounts accounted for?
b.3. Are there any remaining obligations related to revenues?
b.4. How is warranty expense accounted for?
b.5. Are there non-cash transactions?
b.6. Are interest, R&D, and advertising expensed or capitalised?

b.7. Are there any leases? How are they accounted for: operating or capital?

b.8. What is the depreciation method: straight-line, double declining balance, or sum of the digits?

b.9. What is the nature of any non-operating gains or losses?

b.10. Are there any foreign exchange transactions and what are the translation impacts?

b.11. Is there any past impairment and/or restructuring charge?

b.12. Are there any gains or losses on asset sales?

b.13. Are there discontinued operations? Any change in reporting entity?

b.14. Are there extraordinary (unusual nature or infrequent occurrence) items?

b.15. For stock option compensation, is an expense recognised? Using what method of valuation?

Creativity in the balance sheet relates to increasing assets (i.e. deferring expenses in the income statement) and reducing liabilities (hence leverage improved).

Typical areas of investigation are as follows.

Fixed assets: The issue relates to whether these assets are capitalised or expensed: by capitalising and depreciating, current earnings increase.

Research and development: By capitalising and amortising this expenditure, current earnings increase

Inventory valuation: Last in first out (LIFO) and first in first out (FIFO) are two basic inventory valuation methods. Under LIFO, newer, typically more expensive, inventory is recorded as being used before older inventory, with the effect that higher COGS expense depresses earnings. It is more conservative than FIFO. Private companies almost always use LIFO.

Under FIFO, older, typically less expensive, inventory is recorded as being used before newer inventory, with the effect that lower COGS expense increases earnings. It is more aggressive than LIFO

Leasing: Off balance-sheet items can be very important in evaluating the quality of earnings, and therefore should be included in calculations of debt/equity and interest coverage ratios. Leasing is not technically debt but requires fixed payments in the future which resemble interest. If large, the analyst should add lease commitments to interest payments and then calculate earnings/interest.

Associates and joint ventures: It is only the net P&L and balance sheet figures for associates and joint ventures (JVs) that are reflected in consolidated accounts: raising debt in associates/JVs is not reflected in consolidated balance sheet, hence potentially understating liabilities.

Consolidation of subsidiaries: Corporate parents can account for their fully and partially owned subsidiaries in a number of ways:

- less than 20% ownership is usually valued at the lower of cost or market: income is measured as dividends received minus any decreases in market value;
- greater than 20% ownership gives management the option to use an equity method of valuing investment in a subsidiary, as long as the parent has 'significant influence' on the subsidiary's decisions: income is measured as dividends plus pro-rated share of change in subsidiary's retained earnings;
- greater than 50% ownership usually involves a consolidated balance sheet at parent level;
- greater than 80% ownership will usually mandate a consolidated balance at parent level (exceptions are non-financial parents that do not consolidate financial subsidiaries or US parents that do not consolidate foreign subsidiaries). Other shareholders' ownership is recognised as a 'minority interests' balance sheet item, analogous to a negative 'investment' entry.

Key questions to ask when performing a balance sheet accounting review are:

c.1. What is the basis for valuing fixed assets?

c.2. What are the assumptions around economic life of fixed assets?

c.3. What is the method used in depreciation/amortisation of fixed assets?

c.4. Are there any idle fixed assets? Any history of impaired charges of fixed assets?

c.5. What are the origin and nature of intangible assets?

c.6. How are intangibles valued and amortised?

c.7. What is the nature of the investments?

c.8. How is the valuation of investments determined: securities portfolio or market value?

c.9. Are the receivables that have been factored in transferred or securitised?

c.10. What method of valuation of inventory is used – LIFO, FIFO, or average cost? If LIFO, are old inventory layers significant, and what have been the effects of LIFO liquidation credits on reported earnings?

c.11. Are any costs (such as overheads) capitalised to inventory?

c.12. What is the policy with regard to obsolete products?

c.13. What is the method of loss reserve for receivables?

c.14. How adequate are the reserves relative to historical and expected loss experience of receivables?

c.15. Is there a net operating loss position, and what is the valuation allowance against this?

c.16. What is the relationship of P&L expense/credit to actual cash tax paid?

c.17. To what degree does the company engage in aggressive financial transactions for the purpose of avoiding taxation?

c.18. Are there significant tax exposure items, and are there reserves against these? What years are still open for review by tax authorities?

c.19. What is included in 'other liabilities'?

Figure 5.4 summarises the potential effects of some of the accounting policies listed above.

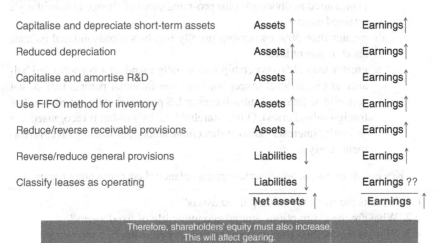

FIGURE 5.4   The effect of some accounting policies on balance sheet and net income.

Finally, other typical questions when performing an accounting review are the following:

d.1. Are there commitments and contingencies? Are there guarantees?

d.2. Are there appropriate assumptions about discount rates, investment earnings, compensation increases, and medical cost inflation of pension benefit obligations?

d.3. What is the gap between balance sheet liability and pension benefit obligation and accumulated pension benefit obligation, and full economic liability?

d.4. Are there take or pay contracts?

d.5. Is there a history of securitisations? What is the nature of the retained risks?

d.6. How is the debt of joint ventures and unconsolidated securities accounted for?

d.7. What is the nature of derivatives and their business purpose?

d.8. Which derivative positions do not qualify for hedge treatment, and why not?

d.8. Are there any positions for trading purposes?

d.10. What is the financial statement impact of the derivatives?

d.11. Are there other significant triggers and obligations linked to derivatives?

RATIO ANALYSIS

Financial ratios are the most common and widespread tools used to analyse a business's financial standing. Ratio analysis is a synthetic way to compare a company over time and several companies across time. Whilst actual ratio levels are quite important, trends and comparisons are more so. In fact, analysis usually takes two forms:

1. **Temporal analysis:** which involves evaluating performance over time. When conducting trend analysis, one should be alert to changes in the company's accounting practices.
2. **Peer analysis:** which involves comparing the company to a set of comparable firms. In order to make useful comparisons, it is important that the companies taken as benchmarks are truly comparable. Accounting differences often arise through incomparability: even companies that are in the same industry may use different accounting policies. However, once accounting differences are identified, it is often possible to make adjustments that put the companies on a level playing field.

The most common financial ratios are: profitability, efficiency, liquidity, and solvency.

■ **Profitability:** profitability ratios show a company's ability to generate profits from its operations. Investors and creditors can use profitability ratios to judge a company's return on investment based on its relative level of resources and assets. In other words, profitability ratios can be used to judge whether companies are making enough operational profit from their assets. In this sense, profitability ratios relate to efficiency ratios because they show how well companies are using their assets to generate profits. The most used ratios are:
   ● Gross margin (Gross Margin / Sales): the gross margin ratio is a profitability ratio that compares the gross margin of a business to the net sales. The gross margin reflects the relationship of price, volume, and cost, and therefore any change in the margin may result from a change in one or more of those variables. The gross profit ratio is essentially the percentage mark up on merchandise from its cost. This is the pure profit from sales that can go toward paying operating expenses.
   ● EBITDA margin (EBITDA / Sales): the EBITDA margin is the most used efficiency ratio since it allows comparison of profitability between different companies by discounting the effects of interest payments from different forms of financing (by ignoring interest payments), political jurisdictions (by ignoring tax payments), tax and accounting policies (by ignoring depreciation of assets), and different M&A histories (by ignoring amortisation often stemming from goodwill). It is quite common to make adjustments to EBITDA to normalise it and allow it to compare the performance of one business to another. Since EBITDA is often used as a quick proxy for cash,

it must be noted that, while a negative EBITDA indicates that a business has fundamental problems with profitability and cash flow, on the other hand a positive EBITDA does not necessarily mean that the business generates cash (since it ignores changes in working capital, capital expenditures, taxes, and interest).

- Return on assets (ROA): (calculated as Net Income / Average Total Assets), this can also be calculated as a product of the profit margin and the total asset turnover. ROA measures how effectively a company can earn a return on its investment in assets. In other words, ROA shows how efficiently a company can convert the money used to purchase assets into net income or profits.
- Return on equity (ROE): (calculated as Net Income / Shareholders' Equity), ROE is a profitability ratio that measures the ability of a firm to generate profits from its shareholders' investments in the company. In other words, the return on equity ratio shows how much profit each dollar of common stockholders' equity generates. Return on equity measures how efficiently a firm can use the money from shareholders to generate profits and grow the company. Unlike other return on investment ratios, ROE is a profitability ratio from the investor's point of view – not the company's.
- **Efficiency (or asset utilisation):** efficiency ratios also measure how well companies utilise their assets to generate income. These ratios are used by management to help improve the company and also by outside investors and creditors looking at the company's operations of profitability. The most used ratios are:
  - Total asset turnover (TATO): (calculated as Sales / Average Total Assets),[1] this is a measure of sales generated per unit of assets available. This indicator suffers from the fact that it does not take into account the different assets (fixed, current), can be distorted by accounting value significantly different from market values, and does not account for multiple product lines with different levels of capital intensity.
  - Fixed asset turnover (FATO): (calculated as Sales / Average Net PP&E), this measures a company's ability to generate net sales from fixed-asset investments.
  - Account receivable turnover (ARTO): [Sales / Average Accounts Receivable and Average Collection Cycle (= 365/ARTO)] are the indicators used to measure how many times a business can collect its average accounts receivable in a year. This ratio shows how efficient a company is at collecting its credit sales from customers. In some ways, the receivables turnover ratio can be viewed as a liquidity ratio as well. Companies are more liquid the faster they can convert their receivables into cash.
  - Inventory turnover (INVTO): [COGS / Average Inventory and Average Holding Period (=365/INVTO)] this shows how many times a company's

---

[1]It is sometimes useful to look at its reciprocal to get a capital intensity ratio.

inventory is sold and replaced over a period. This ratio is important because total turnover depends on two main components. The first component is stock purchasing: if larger amounts of inventory are purchased during the year, the company will have to sell greater amounts of inventory to improve its turnover; if the company can't sell these greater amounts of inventory, it will incur storage costs and other holding costs. The second component is sales: sales have to match inventory purchases otherwise the inventory will not turn over effectively.

- Account payable turnover (APTO): [Purchases[2]/Average Accounts Payable and Days Payable (=365/APTO)], this shows how many times a company can pay off its average accounts payable balance during the course of a year.
- Net trade cycle or cash conversion cycle (NTC): calculated as (Avg. Collection Cycle + Avg. Holding Period − Days Payable), this measures the length of time, in days, that it takes for a company to convert resource inputs into cash flows by looking at the amount of time needed to sell inventory, collect receivables, and pay its payables.

- **Liquidity:** this measures a company's access to cash, from whatever source, in order to meet obligations in the near term. Traditional measures of liquidity focus on the ability of current assets (which are presumed to be readily convertible into cash in the near future) to meet current liabilities (those due within 12 months of the statement date). The most used ratios are:
  - Current ratio: (Current Assets / Current Liabilities). The proportion of current assets available to repay short-term (less than one year) liabilities is a measure of a company's liquidity. All past due or doubtful accounts receivables should be excluded from this ratio. Current liabilities should include the current portion of long-term debt, short-term bank debt, and accrued expenses. Lack of liquidity is often the first sign of difficulty for an operating company and may result in an inability to continue normal operations; it can be the result of money-losing operations, poor cash flow, or diversion of assets into undesirable applications. If a company has to sell off fixed assets to pay for its current liabilities, this usually means the company isn't making enough from operations to support activities. In other words, the company is losing money. Sometimes this is the result of poor collections of accounts receivable. Elements of caution are: 1) slow moving outdated inventory or too many raw materials and dubious sales can overstate assets; and 2) lack of accounts payable should prompt the question of whether the borrower is trusted by its suppliers.
  - Quick ratio (or acid test): [(Current Assets − Inventory) / (Current Liabilities)]. Often, the liquidity of inventory is questionable, and the quick ratio is often preferred to the current ratio. The quick ratio measures the ability of cash, marketable securities, and receivables (debtors) to meet current

---

[2]Purchases = COGS + Δ inventory.

obligations. If a firm has enough quick assets to cover its total current liabilities, the firm will be able to pay off its obligations without having to sell off any long-term or capital assets. Obviously, as the ratio increases, so does the liquidity of the company: this is a good sign for investors, but an even better sign to creditors because creditors want to know they will be paid back on time. It is important to look at these indicators with *granu salis* since, for example, receivables might be high because the company has failed to collect past due obligations, or a high level of inventory may indicate the company has been unable to sell its product; in both cases, the cash that could be realised may be well below the carrying value on the balance sheet.

- **Solvency:** this is an assessment of the degree of financial risk of a company and measures a company's ability to meet its long-term obligations as they fall due and to maintain itself as a viable concern over the long term. In other words, solvency ratios identify going concern issues and a firm's ability to pay its bills in the long term. One should not confuse solvency ratios with liquidity ratios: although they both measure the ability of a company to pay off its obligations, solvency ratios focus on the long-term sustainability of a company instead of the current liability payments. Better solvency ratios indicate a more creditworthy and financially sound company in the long term. Traditional measures of solvency focus on balance sheet and income statement ratios to determine a company's ability to meet its obligations. There are various ratios which can be used to measure the relative amount of funding provided by debt and equity providers to support the business. The most common ratios are:

  - Leverage ratios: a number of ratios, depending on what variables are used, measure the level of debt leverage that is used by a company. The most used are:
    - *Gearing (or debt to equity) ratio*: (Debt[3] / Common Book Equity[4]). The level indicates the ability of a borrower to adequately absorb losses or reductions in earnings without jeopardising the value in the firm available for senior lenders. A high gearing ratio indicates a significant use of leverage: in a business downturn, such companies may have trouble meeting their debt repayment schedules, and could risk bankruptcy. The situation is especially dangerous when a company has engaged in debt arrangements with variable interest rates, where a sudden increase in rates could cause serious interest payment problems; whereas it is less of a concern in a regulated industry, such as a utility, where a business

---

[3]There are two formulas: one uses on balance-sheet debt only, the other also includes off balance-sheet debt.
[4]For listed companies, sometimes an additional version with the market value of equity is considered.

is in a monopoly situation and its regulators are likely to approve rate increases that will guarantee continued survival. Higher levels of leverage are permissible for firms operating in stable, less competitive, or monopolistic markets or industries with fewer fixed assets coupled with highly liquid inventories and receivables (such as retail companies); or those with a high level of diversity in their business and readily liquid or marketable current assets. Lower levels of leverage in the range of 0.5 to 1.0 are appropriate for industries with high fixed costs that operate in cyclical markets (e.g. steel or cement companies). Since lenders are particularly concerned about the gearing ratio, they usually require restrictive covenants that prohibit the payment of dividends, force excess cash flow into debt repayment, impose restrictions on alternative uses of cash, and add a requirement for investors to put more equity into the company. Industries with large and ongoing fixed asset requirements typically have high gearing ratios, whilst companies in a highly cyclical industry tend to have a low gearing ratio (given the inevitable downturn in sales and profits).

o *Debt to capital ratio*: [(Debt) / (Debt + equity)]. This ratio provides an idea of a company's financial structure along with some insight into its financial strength. The higher the debt-to-capital ratio, the more debt the company has compared to its equity. A company with high debt-to-capital ratios, compared to a general or industry average, may show weak financial strength and increase its default risk.

o *Equity ratio*: (Equity / Assets). The lower the equity, the greater the degree of financial risk (i.e. the greater the reliance on external or borrowed funds, respectively, to support the assets and activities of the company). Assets that are stable and of good quality can be leveraged more than assets of uncertain value and cash flow. If a company has different businesses, the quality of the assets for each business will need to be evaluated. However, whilst the ratio gives some indication of the level of financial risk and therefore implies some judgement on the long-term solvency of the company, it does little to measure the ability of a company to repay its obligations. It should be noted that a low equity ratio will produce good results for stockholders as long as the company earns a rate of return on assets that is greater than the interest rate paid to creditors.

o *Leverage ratio*: (Interest Bearing Debt / EBITDA), this may be calculated using total, net, or senior debt. The ratio shows, in theory, how many years it would take for a company to repay its debt based on the current level of EBITDA. Although widely used when structuring LBO facilities, it has several shortcomings: first and foremost, EBITDA is not equal to cash flow and even where it is a good approximation (for example in low-growth companies), the amount of 'cash' generated may not be available to service debt as the company may need to spend money on paying taxes or investing in its business to remain viable. It can overstate repayment capacity since interest expenses are not captured by this ratio.

- **Coverage ratios:** these ratios attempt to measure the ability of the company to meet the debt and/or interest on funds borrowed. Normally, a ratio greater than 1 implies a firm's sound position to pay off the liability or obligation under concern. Different coverage ratios are calculated by different stakeholders of a business. For example, a financial institution or bank extending a loan to the business or firm will calculate the debt service coverage ratio and interest service coverage ratio; and an investor, say an equity shareholder, will look at the dividend coverage ratio. For a lender, the most common ratios are:
  - Interest cover ratio (ICR): (EBITDA / Interest Expense). This may be calculated using total, net, or senior debt, cash interest or total interest. The ratio reveals how many times EBITDA covers interest payments. As said before, EBITDA is rarely a good approximation for cash flow available to service debt. In servicing its debt obligations, a company's obligation is not only to pay interest but also to repay principal – this is not included in the interest cover ratio.
  - Debt service cover ratio (DSCR): (Cash Flow Available for Debt Service[5] / Debt Service[6]). This ratio is a measure of the amount of cash flow available to meet annual interest and principal payments on debt, including sinking fund payments and leases. It therefore provides an indication of the ability of the borrower to repay debt from internally generated cash (and the degree of cash flow reduction that is sustainable before not being able to service debt).

CASH FLOW ANALYSIS

Operating cash flow and free cash flow are fundamental measures of debt-service capacity and firm valuation. Moreover, analysts, investors, and creditors, who can be deceived by fraudulent financial reporting, place their trust in cash flow since cash flow is more substantive and less prone to manipulation by accountants: 'Cash is fact and accounting profit is opinion.'

Change in cash between two accounting periods can be classified into three categories: cash provided or used by:

---

[5]Cash Flows from Operating Activities (as defined by IFRS) + Interest Paid During the Year - Capital Expenditures During the Year. When IFRS statements are not available, cash flows from operating activities shall be defined as: Net Profit After Tax + Depreciation + Non-cash Expense & Amortisation -/+ Change in Working Capital.

[6]Sum of principal (and lease if any), plus interest in the year of calculation of the ratio.

1) **Operating activities:** cash generated through operating activities is the most important source of sustainable cash flow. It provides management with money for discretionary needs, investment, reduction in principal on outstanding debt, stock buybacks, and dividends. Since operating cash flow comes from operations, it can be used to invest in the company's financial needs, to repay creditors, or to return it to investors.

2) **Investing activities:** cash invested or earned by investing in PP&E, acquisition, divestments, and sale of assets.

3) **Financing activities:** cash raised by lenders or equity investors and returned to them.

The cash flow statement is therefore composed of three sections: cash flow from operating, financing, and investing activities.

The cash flow statement can be prepared using either the direct or indirect method: the direct method is a way of creating the cash flow statement in which actual cash flow information from the company's operations is used, instead of accrual accounting values.

The main difference between the direct method and the indirect method involves the cash flows from operating activities, whilst there is in fact no difference in the cash flows reported in the investing and financing activities sections.

Under the direct method, the cash flows from operating activities will include cash received from customers and cash paid to suppliers. In contrast, the indirect method will show net income followed by the adjustments needed to convert the total net income to the cash amount from operating activities. The direct method must also provide a reconciliation of net income to the cash provided by operating activities, whilst this is done automatically under the indirect method. One of the problems with the direct method of preparing the cash flow statement is the level of complexity required. If the company is small, then listing your cash receipts and cash payments is a simple matter. As the company gets larger, the direct method becomes very complex, which is why the majority of companies use the indirect method of developing a cash flow statement.

Table 5.1 shows the typical format of operating cash flow (also 'OpCF'), investing cash flow (also 'InvCF'), and financing cash flow (also 'FinCF') under the direct method.

Because Generally Accepted Accounting Principles (GAAP) requires the net income to be reported using an accrual basis, it therefore requires public companies to calculate operating cash flow using an indirect method by adjusting net income to cash basis using changes in non-cash accounts. Several adjustments to derive operating cash flow are required, as shown in Tables 5.2–5.4.

Once the relevant adjustments have been made, the analyst should derive operating cash flow by following the classification scheme for cash flow effects given here (Table 5.5).

TABLE 5.1 Cash flow statement.

EBITDA
+ (Increase) / Decrease in Net Working Capital
+ (Increase) / Decrease in Other Current Assets / Other Current Liabilities
+ (Increase) / Decrease in Other Long Term Assets / Other Long-Term Liabilities
− Provisions & Leaving Indemnity
− Taxes
= **Operating cash flow (OCF)**

− Capital Expenditures
− Purchase of Leased Assets
− Acquisition of Other Companies
− Purchases of Securities
+ Sales and Maturities of Securities
+ Sale of Assets
+ Proceeds from Sales of Receivables and Leased Investments
= **Investing cash flow (InvCF)**

+ Drawing of New Long-Term Debt
− Repayment of Long-Term Debt
+ Share Capital Increase
+ Dividends
− Share Buyback
= **Financing cash flow (FinCF)**

Source: author.

After deriving operating cash flow, the analyst should derive investing cash flow. Table 5.6 summarises the key items classified as investing cash sources or uses.

After deriving investing cash flow, the analyst should derive financing cash flow. Table 5.7 summarises the key items classified as financing inflows and outflows.

Once the cash flow statement has been derived, both equity investors and creditors seek to find sustainable sources of cash flow (i.e. recurring cash coming from profitable operations). Equity investors make projections of such cash flow and assign an appropriate risk-adjusted discount rate in calculating their present value. This present value is an estimate of a company's intrinsic value. Lenders, who require interest and principal on loans to be repaid, look to sustainable cash flow as a source of repayment. Lenders' claims on cash flow come before those of equity investors.

Sustainable cash flow is cash flow that is recurring and that allocates items in the correct area (i.e. operating, investing, or financing cash flow).

TABLE 5.2 Additions and deductions of key non-cash expense and income.

Additions	Deductions
■ Bad debt expense ■ Deferred tax provision ■ Write-off of fixed assets ■ Loss on disposition of capital assets ■ Non-cash litigation charges ■ Impairment of goodwill ■ Tax benefit from stock options ■ Reserves for returns ■ Cumulative effect of accounting change ■ Amortisation of debt discount ■ Equity in losses of affiliated companies ■ Pension expense, net of contributions ■ Issuance of stock for services and fees ■ Provision for restructuring charges ■ Provision for inventory losses ■ Depreciation and amortisation ■ Minority interest expense ■ Payment in kind (PIK) interest ■ Amortisation of bond premiums	■ Amortised sale and leaseback gains ■ Non-cash pension settlement gain ■ Equity earnings of affiliates, less dividends ■ Foreign currency transaction gains ■ Forgiveness of debt ■ Deferred income tax benefit ■ Interest earned on government bonds ■ Paid-in-kind interest income ■ Amortisation of deferred licensing revenues

TABLE 5.3 Additions and deductions for non-operating gains and losses.

Additions	Deductions
■ Early extinguishment of debt expense ■ Purchased in-process R&D ■ Extraordinary loss on debt extinguishment ■ Loss on derivative instruments	■ Gain on insurance recovery ■ Gain on extinguishment of debt ■ Gain on sale of discontinued units ■ Gain on sale of property and equipment ■ Gain on settlement of interest rate swaps ■ Gain on sales of trading securities

Although there is some debate about the true nature of non-recurring cash flow (it is not defined by GAAP), there is consensus on the following characteristics of non-recurring items of operating cash flow:

■ they do not appear with any regularity;
■ they appear with some regularity, but are very irregular in amount;
■ they are not derived from the central or core operating activities of the firm.

TABLE 5.4 Additions and deductions for changes in operating-related assets and liabilities.

Additions	Deductions
▪ Sale of trading securities ▪ Collections on notes receivable ▪ Decrease in deferred costs ▪ Decrease in accounts receivable ▪ Increase in deferred revenues ▪ Increase in customer deposits ▪ Increase in accrued warranty liability ▪ Decrease in refundable income taxes ▪ Increase in bank overdraft ▪ Accrued interest payable	▪ Purchase of trading securities ▪ Payment on amounts due to related party ▪ Decrease in customer deposits ▪ Additions to trading securities ▪ Capitalised development costs ▪ Decrease in other accrued liabilities ▪ Restructuring costs paid ▪ Cash overdraft ▪ Increase in accounts receivable ▪ Increase in restricted cash ▪ Decrease in unearned income

TABLE 5.5 Operating cash flow.

Addition to net income or loss increases operating cash flow	Deduction from net income or loss decreases operating cash flow
▪ Decrease in operating-related assets ▪ Increase in operating-related liabilities ▪ Non-cash expenses ▪ Non-operating losses	▪ Increase in operating-related assets ▪ Decrease in operating-related liabilities ▪ Non-cash income ▪ Non-operating gains

The development of measures of sustainable cash flow requires that non-recurring items be identified and removed from reported cash flow. Many of these items are commonly non-cash or non-operating in nature. In developing non-GAAP measures, firms do not always include all items that might properly be considered a non-recurring item of operating cash flow – and many diverse items can properly be considered as such. Examples of such items include: litigation proceeds and settlement payments, inventory purchase pre-payment, merger-related charges, operating cash flow of discontinued operations, and restructuring costs payment. There are plenty of other examples.

A large number of non-recurring items of revenue, gain, expense, and loss can be located by examining the income statement and statement of cash flows. Management discussion and analysis (MD&A), especially discussion of comparative operating results, is also a good source of information. Management often discloses non-recurring items of operating cash flow as a part of the process of explaining changes in operating cash flow.

TABLE 5.6   Key items classified as investing cash sources or uses.

Key items classified as Investing cash sources	Key items classified as Investing cash uses
▪ Proceeds from sale of discontinued operations ▪ Net cash received in purchase acquisitions ▪ Proceeds from sale/leaseback transactions ▪ Proceeds from insurance recovery ▪ Decrease in restricted cash ▪ Proceeds from sale of equity securities ▪ Dividends from 50%-owned company ▪ Proceeds from sale of interest rate swaps ▪ Distributions received from investees ▪ Proceeds from sales of trading securities ▪ Proceeds from sale of trademark ▪ Payments received on notes receivable ▪ Payments received on direct finance lease	▪ Cash paid for acquisitions ▪ Purchase of certificates of deposit ▪ Deposits made for equipment purchases ▪ Investment in lease contracts ▪ Purchase of government bonds ▪ Purchases of available-for-sale securities ▪ Brand development costs ▪ Investments in short-term notes receivable ▪ Website development costs ▪ Distributions to holders of minority interest ▪ Capital costs of internal use software ▪ Software development costs ▪ Business acquisitions net of cash acquired ▪ Net increase in restricted cash ▪ Additions to intangible assets ▪ Additions to land

Once non-recurring items of operating cash flow have been identified, it is often necessary to establish if and when cash inflows and outflows occur. This process may be called 'cash flow tracking'. In most cases, a number of steps must be taken to establish that a non-recurring cash flow has occurred. The following steps are suggested for tracking cash flow:

- Identify potential non-recurring items of operating cash flow, usually in the income statement, but possibly in the notes to the financial statements or the MD&A.
- Track these items to the statement of cash flows to see if the potential non-recurring operating cash flow items are adjustments, added to or subtracted from net income or loss, to arrive at operating cash flow. Adjustments may indicate that the item has no associated current cash flow or that it is not an operating cash flow element, or both.
- Track items to the tax note to see whether there are any deferred tax assets or liabilities that may be associated with the potential non-recurring cash flow item. The presence of a deferred tax asset normally indicates that an

TABLE 5.7   Key items classified as financing inflows and outflows.

Key items classified as Financing cash inflows	Key items classified as Financing cash outflows
■ Sale-leaseback transactions ■ Net proceeds from exercise of warrants ■ Contribution of capital ■ Proceeds from initial public offering ■ Proceeds from exercise of stock options ■ Issuance of notes payable ■ Proceeds from terminated interest rate swaps ■ Proceeds from stock subscriptions ■ Tax benefit of stock options exercised ■ Proceeds from short-term debt ■ Issuance of common stock ■ Borrowings on subordinated debt ■ Release of restricted cash	■ Payments for incurred initial public offering (IPO) costs ■ Increase in restricted cash ■ Increase in deferred financing costs ■ Payment of life insurance loans ■ Purchase of treasury shares ■ Repayment of secured note ■ Settlement of forward contract credit ■ Dividends paid ■ Financing fees paid ■ Net cash settlement of put options ■ Payments on line of credit ■ Payments on settlements payable ■ Payments to minority interest stockholders ■ Stock issue costs ■ Payments on capital lease obligations ■ Preferred stock dividends ■ Debt issue costs ■ Purchase of derivative instruments ■ Cash settlement of interest-rate swap ■ Payment of litigation

Source: Mulford and Comiskey (2005). © John Wiley & Sons, Inc. Reproduced with permission.

expense recorded in the income statement has not been paid and therefore is not deductible in the tax return. A deferred tax liability normally indicates that income has been recognised on the books but not in the tax return because cash has not yet been received.

Firms rarely fully revise their reported operating cash flow by removing non-recurring items. However, companies are increasingly making adjustments intended to remove the effects of non-recurring items of operating cash flow. However, information provided by companies on sustainable operating cash flow, is not usually comprehensive, and is not consistent among companies. But, equity investors and creditors need information about stable or recurring cash flow: this information is vital to the valuation of securities, and creditors require it to assess a company's capacity to service debt. Analysts often use a table to derive sustainable cash flow.

Starting from the cash flow statement in the annual report, the analyst can make adjustments (as shown in Table 5.8) to obtain sustainable cash flow.

TABLE 5.8   A guide to obtaining sustainable cash flow.

	Year 1	Year 2	Year 3
Reported operating cash flow source (use)			
Layer 1 Adjustments add (deduct):[a]			
Tax adjustable items[b]			
Litigation settlement, (receipt) payment			
Outsized pension plan contributions			
Restructuring payments			
Cash (provided) used by discontinued operations			
Other			
Subtotal			
Multiply subtotal times (1-marginal tax rate)			
Total tax adjusted items			
Non-tax adjustable items[c]			
One-time working capital (decrease) increase			
Tax (refund) from loss carry backs			
Taxes (avoided) by utilisation of loss carry forwards			
Net increases (decreases) in trading investments[d]			
Income taxes on non-operating gains (losses)			
Stock option tax (benefits)			
Cash (provided) used by discontinued operations			
Net (increase) decrease in overdrafts – in operations			
Accounts receivable securitisation (increase) decrease			
(Capitalised) operating costs in investing section			
(Capitalised) interest			
Other			
Total non-tax adjusted items			
Total adjustments			
Layer 1 sustainable operating cash flow[e]			
Layer 2 Adjustments add (deduct)[f]			
Tax adjustable items			
Litigation settlement (receipt) payment			
Outsized pension plan contributions			
Restructuring payments			
Other			
Subtotal			
Multiply subtotal times (1-marginal tax rate)			
Total tax-adjusted items			

(*continued*)

TABLE 5.8 (*Continued*)

	Year 1	Year 2	Year 3
Non-tax adjustable items			
Other working capital (decreases) increases			
Tax (refund) from loss carry backs			
Taxes (avoided) by utilisation of loss carry forwards			
Net increases (decreases) in trading investments[d]			
Income taxes on non-operating gains (losses)			
Stock option tax (benefits)			
Cash (provided) used by discontinued operations			
Net (increase) decrease in overdrafts – in operations			
Other			
Total non-tax adjusted items			
Total adjustments			
Layer 2 sustainable operating cash flow[g]			
Layer 3 Adjustments add (deduct)[h]			
Tax adjustable items			
Litigation settlement, (receipt) payment			
Outsized pension plan contribution			
Restructuring payments			
Other			
Subtotal			
Multiply subtotal times (1-marginal tax rate)			
Total tax adjusted items			
Non-tax adjustable items			
Other working capital (decreases) increases			
Taxes (avoided) by utilisation of loss carry forward			
Net increases (decreases) in trading investments[d]			
Income taxes on non-operating gains (losses)			
Stock option tax (benefits)			
Cash (provided) used by discontinued operations			
Net (increase) decrease in overdrafts – in operations			

(*continued*)

TABLE 5.8 (*Continued*)

	Year 1	Year 2	Year 3
Other			
Total non-tax adjusted items			
Total adjustments			
Layer 3 sustainable operating cash flow[i]			

[a]The non-operating or non-recurring status is quite compelling. Cash flow is either non-recurring or an amount far greater than normal. Operating cash flow classification is also clear.
[b]The cash flow item has an income statement counterpart that affects the computation of current-period taxable income.
[c]The cash flow item with either no income statement counterpart or an income statement counterpart that has no effect on the computation of current-period taxable income.
[d]Includes only those classified in the operating activities section of the statement of cash flows.
[e]Reported operating cash flow plus level one total adjustments.
[f]The non-operating or non-recurring status is still plausible, but not as compelling as Layer 1 adjustments.
[g]Level 1 SCFO plus level 2 total adjustments.
[h]The non-operating and non-recurring status is more problematic than Layers 1 and 2. Linkage to operating activities is weaker and there may be some overlap of operating and investing or financing characteristics.
[i]Level 2 plus level 3 total adjustments.
Source: Mulford and Comiskey (2005). © John Wiley & Sons, Inc. Reproduced with permission.

CREATIVE ACCOUNTING

Companies may also take advantage of flexibility in accounting systems in order to reflect different figures. Creative accounting refers to actions that deliberately misrepresent a company's reported financial condition. They are used by companies of every size and they can be of different intensity (see Table 5.9): from benign tricks (altering accounting estimates) to extreme fraud (fraudulent claim to false revenue).

Creative accounting is possible by:

1. Adjusting income statements:
   - increasing or decreasing turnover (revenue recognition issues);
   - smoothing costs (provisioning).

The tendency is of course to smooth and/or increase earnings.

TABLE 5.9 Creative accounting tricks by level of intensity.

More benign			Most extreme
1	2	3	4
Change in accounting estimates	Releasing reserves	Capitalising operating costs	Falsifying inventory

Source: Based on data from H.M. Shilit.

2. Reflecting inaccurate asset/liability positions:
- off balance-sheet financing (leases, debt);
- revaluations.

The tendency is of course to reduce liabilities.

Warning signals of improper use of accounting techniques include: 1) a weak monitoring system (e.g. no independent board members or no independent external auditor; 2) management under extreme pressure from competition; 3) management of reputably questionable character. Analysts should take special notice of these indicators in fast-growing companies that are beginning to slow down, in companies that are barely at break-even, and in private companies.

The starting point of analysis are publicly available documents. In particular those in Table 5.10.

We can categorise the main accounting shenanigans according to the area they are applied to. Two basic strategies underlying all accounting tricks are:

a) inflating current-period earnings by inflating current-period income or by deflating current-period expenses;

b) deflating current period earnings by deflating current-period income or by inflating current-period expenses.

Accounting tricks that inflate income are generally more serious than those that affect expenses.

TABLE 5.10 Documents for analysis.

Where to look	What to look for
Auditor's report	Absence of opinion or qualified report
	Reputation of auditor
Proxy statement	Litigation
	Executive compensation
	Related-party transactions
Footnotes	Accounting policies/changes in those policies
	Related-party transactions
	Contingencies or commitments
MD&A	Specific concise disclosure
	Consistency with footnote disclosure
Form 8-K	Disagreements over accounting policies
Registration statement	Past performance
	Quality of management and directors

Revenues

Before reviewing the most common techniques used to overstate revenues, it is important to summarise certain categories that are especially conducive to artificial inflation of revenue.

- **Revenue from long-term construction contracts:** companies normally record revenue after delivery of a product. However, special accounting rules exist where the seller has a contract to deliver a product or a service over a number of years. In these circumstances, a company can wait until the end of the contract to record revenue (completed contract approach) or it can record a part of the revenue each year based on the amount completed (percentage of completion approach). The conservative completion method should be used if there is any significant uncertainty surrounding completion of the contract, or if reliable estimates cannot be obtained. The percentage method is acceptable if completion is likely and if no significant uncertainty exists. However, it is important to consider the risks of companies using the percentage method. This method can be abused by manipulation of estimates or stage-of-completion records because it depends on estimates of future costs and future events. If the company fails to complete the project or fails to complete it in accordance with agreed conditions, recorded revenue will be significantly over-stated. Therefore, the percentage method is considered an aggressive accounting practice.
- **Consignment sales:** with consignment sales, the consignor (seller) delivers the product to a consignee (dealer) but retains ownership of the goods. No revenue should be recorded as the inventory is still on the consignor's books. When the consignee sells the merchandise and receives payment, they earn a commission. The consignor then records a sale and transfers the cost of the merchandise from inventory to cost of goods sold. If the consignee cannot sell the merchandise, it is returned to the consignor and no revenue is recorded. Investors and lenders should be alert to companies that record revenue when they ship goods to a consignee in a consignment sale, as this is an example of recording too soon.
- **Instalment sales:** when important uncertainty surrounding a customer's ability to pay exists, the more conservative instalment method of recognising revenue is called for. In accordance with this method, gross profit from a sale is deferred and recognised as cash is collected.
- **Revenue from leasing assets:** lessors can boost their incomes by using aggressive accounting practices, such as changing from an operating lease to a capital lease and changing capital lease assumptions. It is very important to carefully distinguish between a lease and a disguised sale: a lessor records rental revenue as cash comes in each month, whilst a seller of a product who receives monthly instalments from the customer records the present value of the total amount straightaway.

The most common techniques to over-state revenues are as follows.

- **Recording revenue too soon:** recording revenue too early – before the earning process is completed, or before an unconditional exchange has occurred – is probably the most common trick related to revenue recognition. Accountants use the term front-end loading to describe it. The most common techniques are:
  - Recording revenue when future services are yet to be provided: with this technique, a seller books full revenues although part of the service will be provided in the future.
  - Recording revenue before shipment or before the client has accepted: there are two ways of recording revenue before shipment: 1) using percentage of completion (POC) accounting. Here, revenue is recorded during the production period, before the product is shipped to the customer. This strategy applies only to companies with very long production periods; and 2) using bill and holding accounting. Here, the customer agrees to a future purchase and future payment. The seller keeps the product until the agreed date, and payment is deferred until shipment. The seller records the sale even though the customer has not received the product and has not yet paid for it.
  - Recording revenue even when the client is not obliged to pay: for revenue to be properly recognised, the financial burden must have moved from the seller to the buyer. There may be underlying problems to watch for when the seller provides financing to the buyer, or when the seller offers extended terms of payment, and when customers are unable to pay or their ability to pay is uncertain. Whilst providing financing can be a good selling technique, misuse can be dangerous. In the case of abuse, companies are essentially buying their own products with their own resources, claiming that sales and earnings are growing.
  - Selling to a related party: a company's sale to a vendor, a relative, a corporate director, or a business partner may give cause for concern. One should assess whether the transaction can be considered to be 'at arm's length'.
  - Giving the client something valuable in equal exchange: the revenue recorded becomes dubious if the buyer receives something from the seller, in addition to the product, as a condition for making the sale.
- **Recording fictitious revenues:** good accounting practice dictates that revenue should not be recorded until the earning process has been completed and an exchange has occurred. The following techniques are used to record fictitious revenues.
  - Recording sales with no economic substance: this technique involves fabricating a plan whereby the company sells a product to a customer, but the customer is not obliged to pay for it. Auditors can be deceived into believing the transaction is authentic by having the parties sign a separate, hidden, 'side agreement', in which the sales contract is altered. A side agreement normally modifies key terms in the sales contract. It might, for example, permit the customer to return the goods at any time, for a full refund.

- Recording cash received through borrowing as revenue: a loan received by a company is considered a liability and cannot be considered revenue.
- Recording supplier rebates for future compulsory purchases as revenue: sometimes a company agrees to over-pay for a product, provided the seller rebates the extra charge with a cash payment at a later date. That rebate cannot properly be recorded as revenue. It is merely a modification to the cost of the inventory bought.
- Releasing revenue that was wrongly retained before the merger: this involves instructing the target company to withhold revenue until after the acquisition is closed. In this way, the newly combined company improperly records revenue that was earned by the target company prior to the merger.

■ **Shifting current revenue to a later period:** the aim of this trick is to deflate current profits and move them to a later period when business is going less well. This tactic may be attractive to healthy companies that want a reserve for bad times, and to companies that are about to be acquired and want to defer recording revenue until after the merger. Here are some techniques for doing this.

- Creating reserves and releasing them into income at a later time: when a business is doing very well and earnings exceed estimates, companies may decide to not report all their revenue at once, but to keep some of it back for a time when business is not going as strongly. Moving profits from a strong quarter or year to a future, weaker one helps companies to 'smooth' earnings.
- Non-operating sources of income can be camouflaged as a reduction in expenses: a company may receive a windfall gain from its pension assets and cause the reported pension cost to disappear, or to result in pension income. Alternatively, a company can create a windfall gain by selling an investment and reporting the gain as a reduction in operating expenses.
- Smoothing income: smoothing out high and low periods in business is a fairly common strategy amongst businesses, as a premium is set on solid, reliable growth. However, creating reserves to shift income to a later period, and recording future income in the current period, are accounting tricks used to deceive investors and creditors. Although some would argue that smoothing income is not as grievous as, for example, over-stating profits; investors, lenders, and auditors should watch out for this ploy.
- Inappropriately retaining revenue just before an acquisition closes: watch out for companies that hold back revenue just before being acquired. The months of revenue that are held back may subsequently be released into the income of the merged company, giving an impression of increased revenue.

Costs

■ **Shifting current expenses to a later or earlier period:** the objective is to improperly record a cost as an asset rather than as a cost. Techniques include the following.

- Capitalising normal operating expenses: this technique involves capitalising ordinary operating costs that produce short-term benefits and shifting them to future periods. The costs are improperly recorded as assets (instead of expenses) and the assets are then amortised over future periods. The costs that are most frequently improperly amortised are marketing and solicitation costs, landfill and interest costs, R&D costs, software development costs, store pre-opening costs, and repair and maintenance costs.
- Altering accounting policies and moving current expenses to an earlier period: whilst the previous technique simply moves operating costs into the future, shifting current expenses to an earlier period is a technique that can be used to make expenses evaporate once and for all.
- Amortising costs too slowly: expenditures that provide a company with longer term benefits, like plant and equipment, goodwill, etc., should be expensed over the same period that the benefit is received. Companies can artificially boost earnings by not allocating enough costs to the right period through depreciating fixed assets too slowly, amortising intangible assets or leasehold improvements over too long a period, changing to a longer period to depreciate or amortise an asset, and amortising inventory, marketing, and software costs too slowly. The motivation for writing off assets too slowly are: 1) slow depreciation or amortisation means assets stay on the balance sheet for longer, giving rise to a higher net worth; and 2) expenses are lower and profits are higher with slow amortisation. Investors should be wary when companies write off assets too slowly. This is especially so in industries with rapid technological advancement: companies will be weighed down with outdated equipment if they do not modernise quickly enough. Overly long depreciation or amortisation periods are consistent with aggressive accounting. If a company changes to a longer period, it may be that the company is experiencing difficulty and is seeking to hide a decline. There may be good reason for changing accounting policy, but in general investors should be wary when changes appear motivated by a need to inflate earnings.
- Not writing down or writing off faulty assets: it can be very difficult to decide whether an asset is 'permanently impaired'. An asset is over-valued when its book value exceeds the amount that should be realised through its sale or use. Some assets, like inventory and accounts receivable, will be over-valued if the related reserve account is understated. Failing to establish sufficient reserves or improperly releasing those reserves would under-state expenses and boost earnings. There are two areas to watch out for: receivables that should be written down to their net realisable value (adjusting the receivables to their net realisable value means the company must estimate the amount of defaults and record a reserve that reduces the net receivables by this amount); and investments in stocks, bonds, and real estate that should be written down if their market value goes down and if that decrease is 'other than temporary'.

TABLE 5.11 Summary of asset types and related reserve accounts.

Asset type	Reserve account
Receivables	Allowance for doubtful accounts
Inventory	Allowance for obsolescence
Plant & equipment	Accumulated depreciation
Goodwill	Accumulated amortisation
Deferred taxes	Allowance for decline

- Decreasing asset reserves: companies have to adjust certain assets to reflect customer default and outdated inventory amongst other decreases in asset values. They therefore set up reserves, called contra-accounts, which have to be adjusted in each period. Failing to add to these reserves or reducing them improperly creates artificial earnings. Table 5.11 summarises the asset type and related reserve account.
  Analysts should watch for absence of, or excessive, or very frequent changes in reserves.
- **Shifting future expenses to the current period as a special charge:** when companies are experiencing difficulty, they may move future-period expenses into the current, weak period, thereby removing those burdens from future earnings. There are three techniques used to achieve this.
  - Improperly inflating the amount included in a special charge: special charges are a good way of artificially inflating operating profits. A company can announce a special charge and increase the amount to include future operating expenses. Profits in future periods will be higher because those periods' expenses formed part of an earlier period's charge.
  - Improperly writing off in-process R&D costs from an acquisition: the trick used in this technique is to write off as much of the purchase price of an acquisition as possible, whilst claiming to be 'conservative'. Such write offs effectively reduce operating expenses in the current and future periods, and thereby inflate reported operating and net income.
  - Bringing forward discretionary costs into the current period: if a company's income expectations for the current period have already been met, it may try to move next year's expenses into that period. Watch out for prepayment of operating expenses, decreases in depreciation or amortisation periods, and acceleration of depreciation expense by changing accounting estimates.

Other income

- **Boosting income with one-time gains:**
  - Elevating profits by selling assets: one way to boost profits is to sell assets that have appreciated at prices above their cost or book value. Gains from their sale will be high if the assets are on the books at improbably low

prices. Investors and lenders should watch out for one-off gains resulting from the sale of undervalued assets, particularly if the sale lacks a business rationale (e.g. selling crown jewels that are part of the core business) or financial sense.

- Recording investment income or gains as part of revenue: GAAP requires that one-time gains be recorded separately from income arising out of normal operational activities. Analysts should be wary when non-operational gains appear as sales revenue or as a reduction of operating costs.
- Recording investment income or gains as a decrease in operating costs: non-operating sources of income can be camouflaged as a reduction in expenses: a company may receive a gain from its pension assets or by selling an investment and report the gain as a reduction in operating expenses.
- Creating revenue by reclassifying balance sheet accounts: appreciation in an investment normally results in income only when the investment is sold at a gain. However, companies can sometimes record income arising from appreciation in value of investments that have not been sold. This technique is often used by companies with an active trading portfolio.

- **Liabilities:** some companies prefer to record as little as possible regarding litigation, long-term purchase agreements, and other commitments. In addition to those obligations that should be recorded on the balance sheet, there are other commitments that should be recorded in the footnotes. Investors and lenders ought to read the financial statements, the footnotes, and the proxy statements to uncover all of the company's obligations.

  - Failing to record or improperly reducing liabilities: income can be inflated by failing to record expenses and related liabilities. Existing obligations that have arisen from past transactions must obviously be reported as liabilities. If obligations are significant and the company may be unfavourably affected by terms in the agreement, the company is required to provide a detailed footnote.
  - Not recording costs and related liabilities when there are future obligations: losses should be accrued for expected payments relating to matters such as litigation and tax disputes. GAAP require that companies accrue a loss when: 1) there is a probable loss; and 2) the amount of the loss can be estimated.
  - Changing accounting assumptions to reduce liabilities: companies that provide pensions and other post-retirement benefits to employees can modify their accounting assumptions so as to reduce the recorded liability and related expense. Companies that lease equipment can make estimates regarding residual value and interest rates that will affect reported liability and expense. Airlines make estimates of unearned income related to frequent flyer points given. Liabilities can be reduced and earnings inflated by altering accounting or actuarial assumptions.
  - Placing dubious reserves into income: earnings can be boosted by taking a special charge because future costs will already have been

written off through the charge. Moreover, the liability resulting from the charge becomes a reserve that can be released into earnings at a later time. Various reserves appear on the balance sheet. Failing to maintain a sufficient amount of reserves or releasing reserves artificially boosts earnings.

- Creating false rebates: fake rebates from suppliers can also be used to artificially reduce costs and boost profits. This trick obviously needs the suppliers to cooperate. The company tells the supplier that it will agree to buy a certain large amount of inventory over the next year. In exchange for this substantial order, the supplier agrees to pay a 'rebate' on signing the agreement. The company then records this rebate as a reduction of expense.
- Reporting income when cash is received, even though there are future obligations: many companies receive cash before they have earned it. Financial statements are misleading and profits are over-stated when companies such as this fail to defer revenue and record liability until it has been earned. A liability should be recorded if the risks or benefits have not passed to the buyer (just as a liability should be established for companies that earn revenue over time). When significant contingencies exist, no revenue should be recorded.

REFERENCES AND FURTHER READING

C.W. Mulford and E. Comiskey. 2005. *Creative Cash Flow Reporting: Uncovering Sustainable Financial Performance*. John Wiley & Sons.

H.M. Shilit. 2002. *Financial Shenanigans: How to Detect Accounting Gimmicks & Fraud in Financial Reports*. McGraw Hill.

SUGGESTED CASES

R.S. Kaplan and D. Kiron. 2004. 'Accounting Fraud at WorldCom.' Harvard Business School Case 104-071.

S. Srinivasan and I. McKown Cornell. 2013. 'First Solar: CFRA's Accounting Quality Concerns.' Harvard Business School Case 113-044.

S. Srinivasan and M. Norris. 2012. 'Trouble Brewing for Green Mountain Coffee Roasters.' Harvard Business School Case 113-035.

CHAPTER 6

Business Plan

INTRODUCTION

Private equity and private debt funds mainly base their financing decisions on projected cash flow. To this end, it is essential to prepare a financial model (so called pro-forma) to forecast cash flows and produce all relevant ratios. Key industry drivers and company specific success factors (influencing sales, profitability, asset base, and liabilities profile) are translated as key drivers in a worksheet. Pro-forma financials provide a logical, structured, and comprehensive approach that allow us to clearly evaluate the reasonableness of the assumptions.

Whilst we do not deal with this topic in great detail in this book, it is important to provide a concise outline of the key steps in financial projection.

PRO-FORMA FINANCIALS

The starting point of the financial forecasting process is the acknowledgement that profit and loss (P&L) and balance sheet (BS) are intrinsically linked.

Another essential building block is the fundamental accounting identity:

$$Assets = Liabilities + Equity.$$

The income statement records the performance in a given year, whilst the balance sheet is a picture of the situation at the beginning of and at the end of the year.

The first link between P&L and BS is:

$$Net\ Income - Dividends = Change\ in\ Retained\ Earnings.$$

The second link between P&L and BS is:

$$Interest\ Expense = Interest\ Rate \times Interest\ Bearing\ Debt.$$

The above relations, together with the fundamental accounting equation, tie the income statement directly to the balance sheet and vice versa.

In other words, there is an element of circularity since

1. interest expense comes from the amount of interest-bearing debt;
2. interest expense affects net income;
3. which affects changes in retained earnings;
4. which, through the equality requirement for the balance sheet, affects the amount of interest-bearing debt that is necessary.

Since interest-bearing debt is the unknown in each equation, we have to solve them simultaneously to find the external debt financing required.

The first two steps in building pro-forma financials are to:

1. **Determine a forecast horizon:** ideally, the time horizon for a financial forecast should reflect the tenor of the loan or the holding period of the equity investment. For a stable firm, a relatively short forecast horizon may be sufficient (e.g. five to seven years). However, for many firms, a longer horizon is necessary. In general, we need to forecast out to the point that the firm reaches a steady state. A steady state implies the following:
   a. common-size ratios (e.g. gross margins, expense ratios) do not change from year to year;
   b. asset turnovers are constant from year to year;
   c. sales growth is constant from year to year.
2. **Establish assumptions and business 'drivers' and develop financial projections:** starting from key business drivers, build a financial model.

PROFIT AND LOSS PROJECTIONS

- **Sales:** different sales components are often forecast separately and then combined to arrive at a final figure. Separating sales by line of business and/or geographic region is a natural starting point. It may be helpful to further separate sales along the lines of price and quantity. Evaluating past trends may also be useful: if the firm is stable, and analysis suggests that little has changed, determining a trend may be viable. Even where there is no stability, past trends can provide a good starting point in the forecasting process. Examples of other information to consider may include management's plans for expansion, the firm's circumstances (product quality, marketing, etc.), industry circumstances (competition, regulation, etc.), and economy-wide factors (business cycle, disposable income, inflation, etc.). It is important to note that:
  - in mature sectors, past performance should provide a good foundation for a base-case scenario;
  - in cyclical industries, a credit analyst should use sector information to identify price points in the cycle and run appropriate scenarios;
  - in very competitive or fast-growing industries, assumption can vary greatly from industry to industry;
  - in niche sectors, assumptions will vary from company to company.

- **Cost of goods sold:** once the sales forecast has been developed, forecasting operating expenses before depreciation and amortisation can begin. Common size income statements can be very helpful in this. In particular, once common size ratios have been developed, they can be converted to value by combination with the sales forecast. It may not always be reasonable to assume common size ratios will be a constant percentage of sales. Rather, it is possible that certain activities contain both a fixed and variable component. Therefore, as sales rise or fall, the cost of the activity as a percentage of sales will decline or increase. A simple way to estimate fixed and variable costs is through a regression of total cost on sales.
- **Other sundry items:** especially if not material and there is no other indication (e.g. fixed cost, trend linked to a specific variable), they are usually projected as a percentage of revenues.
- **Depreciation and amortisation:** see capex and long-term asset below.
- **Interest expense:** determined analytically for existing long-term and short-term facilities topped up with the interest cost of the short-term debt 'plug' (see below) equal to the interest rate multiplied by the average balance of the short-term debt 'plug'.
- **Tax:** tax rate multiplied by taxable income.

BALANCE SHEET PROJECTIONS

- **Assets:**
  - Determine capital expenditures and fixed assets: when forecasting PP&E, the equations below may provide a useful guide.

$$\text{Gross PP\&E}_t = \text{CAPX}_t - \text{Gross Disposals}_t + \text{Gross PP\&E}_{t-1}$$
$$\text{Accum DEPX}_t = \text{DEPX}_t - \text{Accum DEPX Disposals}_t + \text{Accum DEPX}_{t-1}$$
$$\text{Net PP\&E}_t = \text{CAPX}_t - \text{DEPX}_t - \text{Net Disposals}_t + \text{Net PP\&E}_{t-1}$$

Information from the company's management of capex plans and industry are the most used drivers.
  - determine account receivables: projected by multiplying the Average Collection Cycle (= 365/ARTO) by Sales and dividing by 365. The Average Collection Cycle is usually the average of the last three years, eventually adjusted for specific unusual circumstances or industry:

$$Acct.\ Rec._{t+\tau} = \frac{Days\ Rec._{t+\tau} \times Sales_{t+\tau} \times 2}{365} - Acct.\ Rec._{t+\tau}$$

$$Inventory_{t+\tau} = \frac{Inv.\ Holding\ Period_{t+\tau} \times COGS_{t+\tau} \times 2}{365} - Inventory_{t+\tau-1}$$

$$Acct.\ Pay._{t+\tau} = \frac{Days\ Pay._{t+\tau} \times Purchases_{t+\tau} \times 2}{365} - Acct.\ Pay_{t+\tau-1}$$

- determine inventory: projected by multiplying Average Holding Period (= 365/INVTO) by COGS and dividing by 365. The Average Holding Period is usually the average of the last three years, eventually adjusted for specific unusual circumstances or industry.
- Bring forward sundry items: usually projected as a percentage of sales.

- **Project liabilities:**
  - Determine account payables: projected by multiplying Days Payable (= 365/ARTO) by Purchase and dividing by 365. Days Payable is usually the average of the last three years, eventually adjusted for specific unusual circumstances or industry.
  - Determine long-term debt and leasing run off: use the amortisation plan agreed with banks and lessors.
  - Other debt-like obligations (e.g. leases and pension liabilities): use leasing amortisation and projected benefit obligations (net of the fair value of plan assets).
  - Bring forward sundry liabilities: usually projected as a percentage of sales.
  - Shareholder's equity: this is equal to the Equity of the Previous Year + the Net Income of the Current Year - Dividends (here assumed as an exogenous financing decision).

PUTTING IT ALL TOGETHER: MODELLING CASH, SHORT-TERM DEBT, NET INCOME, AND SHAREHOLDERS' EQUITY

At this point of the forecasting exercise:

- assets and liabilities do not match;
- cash on the asset side of the balance sheet has not been modelled;
- short-term debt of the balance sheet has not been modelled;
- net income (equal to the difference between revenues and costs) will be impacted by the interest (positive or negative) derived by the cash or short-term balance;
- shareholder's equity will be impacted by modification as per above in net income.

Given the basic accounting equation (*Assests = Liabilities + Equity*), use cash (if liabilities are bigger than assets) or short-term debt (if liabilities are smaller than assets) as a plug to make to make the basic accounting equation hold.

Since this involves circularity (iteration), remember to use the Excel feature Tools–Options–Calculation and tick the Iteration feature.

SENSITIVITY ANALYSIS

A sensitivity analysis is a business case in which the base case assumptions are revised to account for probable variances in critical performance drivers. The purpose is to test the robustness of cash flow to service principal and interest in unexpected conditions. A sound business will be able to absorb a worst-case scenario without triggering covenants or undermining the going concern of the company. The variables chosen for the sensitivity analysis will depend on the industry to which the company belongs, but these must be significant for the success of the company (e.g. a raw material business is likely to be sensitive to input prices and production costs, a service business is likely to be affected by changes in wage rates and sales volumes, etc.). Factors should be looked at jointly as would logically occur. It is also useful to test the standard variables (as a matter of due diligence), such as sales or gross revenues, operating costs, borrowing costs, foreign exchange rate (resulting from a devaluation of the currency in excess of that produced by foreign and local inflation rate differentials), local inflation rate, price per unit sold, working capital, and interest rate (in the event of a floating rate loan). As a general guideline:

- A worst-case model should select one to three variables and assume each is worse by 10–20% relative to the base case. A best-case model should be based on one to three variables and assume each is better by 10, 15, and 20%. A scenario in which debt service can just be met (break-even) should also be included.
- Companies:
  - with high business risk or heavy debt are usually stressed for revenues that are weakening quickly (10–30% decline), with relatively high costs (no reduction in the first 18–24 months);
  - with strong credit can be tested by unforeseen events such as environmental accidents, strikes, and litigation settlements;
  - in competitive industries usually need to invest significantly in their business to maintain their competitive edge.

The final outcome of the business plan (P&L, BS, cash flow (CF)) should therefore include the following different scenarios (to measure the financial effects of changes in key drivers of the business plan):

- base case: provided by the firm based on assumptions about the future made on the basis of the past;
- stress case: with assumptions of harsh economic and business conditions;
- default case: with assumptions of default on payment by the company.

CONSISTENCY CHECKS

Checks for consistency should include:

- operating margins consistent with industry trends;
- sales growth consistent with market share and market size assumptions;
- operating profit growth consistent with margin and sales volume growth (adjusted for improvements in scale operating costs);
- debt service obligations consistent with realistic interest rates.

Business Plan

Profit & Loss Key input	2014A	2015A	2016A	2017A	2018A	2019E	2020E	2021E	2022E	2023E	2024E
Sales YoY growth		12.5%	10.4%	11.9%	12.2%	11.0%	11.0%	11.0%	11.0%	11.0%	11.0%
Operating Costs / Sales (%)	(50.0%)	(49.1%)	(49.6%)	(46.9%)	(46.6%)	(47.0%)	(47.0%)	(47.0%)	(47.0%)	(47.0%)	(47.0%)
Personnel Costs / Sales (%)	(19.5%)	(20.3%)	(20.5%)	(21.1%)	(20.8%)	(21.0%)	(21.0%)	(21.0%)	(21.0%)	(21.0%)	(21.0%)
D&A / Sales (%)	(2.5%)	(2.7%)	(2.4%)	(2.3%)	(4.0%)	(4.0%)	(4.0%)	(4.0%)	(4.0%)	(4.0%)	(4.0%)
Tax rate	(26.0%)	(26.0%)	(26.0%)	(24.0%)	(24.0%)	(24.0%)	(24.0%)	(24.0%)	(24.0%)	(24.0%)	(24.0%)
Interest rate on cash balance	3.4%	1.1%	1.5%	1.1%	1.2%	1.0%	0.8%	0.6%	0.4%	0.4%	0.3%

(€M)	2014A	2015A	2016A	2017A	2018A	2019E	2020E	2021E	2022E	2023E	2024E
Total Sales	**40.0**	**45.0**	**49.7**	**55.6**	**62.4**	**69.3**	**76.9**	**85.3**	**94.7**	**105.1**	**116.7**
Cost of materials	(15.0)	(16.8)	(18.1)	(18.2)	(20.1)						
Cost of service	(3.0)	(3.3)	(4.3)	(5.6)	(6.6)						
Rents and leasing	(2.0)	(2.0)	(2.2)	(2.3)	(2.4)						
Total Operating Cost	**(20.0)**	**(22.1)**	**(24.6)**	**(26.1)**	**(29.1)**	**(32.6)**	**(36.1)**	**(40.1)**	**(44.5)**	**(49.4)**	**(54.9)**
Salaries	(5.4)	(6.3)	(7.3)	(8.2)	(9.0)						
Social contributions	(1.6)	(2.0)	(1.9)	(2.4)	(2.6)						
Other personnel costs	(0.8)	(0.9)	(1.0)	(1.1)	(1.4)						
Total Personnel Costs	**(7.8)**	**(9.2)**	**(10.2)**	**(11.7)**	**(13.0)**	**(14.5)**	**(16.1)**	**(17.9)**	**(19.9)**	**(22.1)**	**(24.5)**
Other operating costs	(1.8)	(1.2)	(0.7)	(0.8)	(0.6)	(0.7)	(0.7)	(0.7)	(0.7)	(0.7)	(0.7)
EBITDA	**10.4**	**12.6**	**14.2**	**17.0**	**19.7**	**21.5**	**23.9**	**26.6**	**29.6**	**32.9**	**36.6**
% Sales	26.0%	27.9%	28.5%	30.6%	31.6%	31.0%	31.1%	31.2%	31.3%	31.3%	31.4%
Depreciation & Amortisation	**(1.0)**	**(1.2)**	**(1.2)**	**(1.3)**	**(2.5)**	**(2.8)**	**(3.1)**	**(3.4)**	**(3.8)**	**(4.2)**	**(4.7)**
EBIT	**9.4**	**11.4**	**13.0**	**15.7**	**17.2**	**18.7**	**20.8**	**23.2**	**25.8**	**28.7**	**32.0**
(Interest expense) / income	0.2	0.1	0.2	0.2	0.2	0.2	0.2	0.2	0.2	0.2	0.2
Non-op income						0.2	0.2	0.2	0.2	0.2	0.2
Pretax Profit	**9.6**	**11.5**	**13.2**	**15.8**	**17.4**	**18.9**	**21.0**	**23.4**	**26.0**	**28.9**	**32.2**
Taxes	(2.5)	(3.0)	(3.4)	(3.8)	(4.2)	(4.5)	(5.0)	(5.6)	(6.2)	(6.9)	(7.7)
Net Income	**7.1**	**8.5**	**9.7**	**12.0**	**13.2**	**14.3**	**16.0**	**17.8**	**19.8**	**22.0**	**24.4**
% Sales	17.8%	18.8%	19.6%	21.7%	21.2%	20.7%	20.8%	20.8%	20.9%	20.9%	20.9%

FIGURE 6.1 A modelling example of a business plan.

Balance Sheet

Key input	2014A	2015A	2016A	2017A	2018A	2019E	2020E	2021E	2022E	2023E	2024E
Days receivables	207.7	194.5	163.2	159.5	150.3	150.0	145.0	130.0	120.0	120.0	120.0
Days payables	91.3	85.9	88.9	93.7	91.6	100.0	110.0	120.0	120.0	120.0	120.0
Days inventories	58.4	52.7	48.5	43.3	46.8	45.0	45.0	45.0	45.0	45.0	45.0
Dividend payout ratio		41%	69%	83%	62%	50%	50%	50%	50%	50%	50%

(€M)	2014A	2015A	2016A	2017A	2018A	2019E	2020E	2021E	2022E	2023E	2024E
Trade receivables	22.8	24.0	22.2	24.3	25.7	28.5	30.5	30.4	31.1	34.6	38.4
Inventories	6.4	6.5	6.6	6.6	8.0	8.5	9.5	10.5	11.7	13.0	14.4
Trade payables	(5.0)	(5.2)	(6.0)	(6.7)	(7.3)	(8.9)	(10.9)	(13.2)	(14.6)	(16.2)	(18.0)
NWC	24.2	25.3	22.8	24.2	26.4	28.1	29.1	27.7	28.2	31.3	34.7
Tangible fixed assets	17.0	15.5	16.0	16.5	19.0	21.2	23.7	25.8	28.1	28.8	29.2
Intangible fixed assets	10.0	12.0	12.5	12.0	12.0	12.0	12.0	12.0	12.0	12.0	12.0
Financial fixed assets	-	-	-	-	-	-	-	-	-	-	-
FIXED ASSETS	27.0	27.5	28.5	28.5	31.0	33.2	35.7	37.8	40.1	40.8	41.2
TOTAL ASSETS	**51.2**	**52.8**	**51.3**	**52.7**	**57.4**	**61.3**	**64.8**	**65.6**	**68.2**	**72.1**	**75.9**
Cash and equivalents	(5.8)	(9.2)	(13.7)	(14.8)	(15.6)	(17.8)	(23.1)	(32.1)	(40.4)	(48.6)	(58.2)
Financial debts	-	-	-	-	-	-	-	-	-	-	-
Net debt	(5.8)	(9.2)	(13.7)	(14.8)	(15.6)	(17.8)	(23.1)	(32.1)	(40.4)	(48.6)	(58.2)
Provisions	2.0	2.0	2.0	2.5	3.0	3.0	3.0	3.0	3.0	3.0	3.0
Net equity	55.0	60.0	63.0	65.0	70.0	76.1	84.9	94.7	105.6	117.7	131.1
TOTAL LIABILITIES	**51.2**	**52.8**	**51.3**	**52.7**	**57.4**	**61.3**	**64.8**	**65.6**	**68.2**	**72.1**	**75.9**

check

Cash flow statement

(€M)	2014A	2015A	2016A	2017A	2018A	2019E	2020E	2021E	2022E	2023E	2024E
EBITDA	10.4	12.6	14.2	17.0	19.7	21.5	23.9	26.6	29.6	32.9	36.6
Taxes	(2.5)	(3.0)	(3.4)	(3.8)	(4.2)	(4.5)	(5.0)	(5.6)	(6.2)	(6.9)	(7.7)
Change in provisions				0.5	0.5	-	-	-	-	-	-
Change in NWC		(1.1)	2.5	(1.4)	(2.2)	(1.7)	(1.0)	1.4	(0.5)	(3.1)	(3.4)

FIGURE 6.1 (Continued)

	2014A	2015A	2016A	2017A	2018A	2019E	2020E	2021E	2022E	2023E	2024E
Cash flow from operating activities		8.5	13.2	12.3	13.8	15.2	17.8	22.4	22.9	22.9	25.5
Capex		(1.7)	(2.2)	(1.3)	(5.0)	(5.0)	(5.5)	(5.6)	(6.0)	(5.0)	(5.0)
FCFF		6.7	11.0	11.0	8.8	10.2	12.3	16.8	16.9	17.9	20.5
(Interest expenses) / Income		0.1	0.2	0.2	0.2	0.2	0.2	0.2	0.2	0.2	0.2
New debts / (Reimbursements)		-	-	-	-	-	-	-	-	-	-
FCFE		6.8	11.2	11.2	9.0	10.4	12.5	17.0	17.1	18.1	20.7
Equity injections / (Distributions)		(3.5)	(6.7)	(10.0)	(8.2)	(8.2)	(7.2)	(8.0)	(8.9)	(9.9)	(11.0)
Net Cash Flow		3.4	4.5	1.1	0.8	2.2	5.3	9.0	8.2	8.2	9.7
Cash beginning of period	5.8	5.8	9.2	13.7	14.8	15.6	17.8	23.1	32.1	40.4	48.6
Cash end of period	5.8	9.2	13.7	14.8	15.6	17.8	23.1	32.1	40.4	48.6	58.2

Ratios	2014A	2015A	2016A	2017A	2018A	2019E	2020E	2021E	2022E	2023E	2024E
Profitability											
ROE	13%	14%	15%	19%	19%	19%	19%	19%	19%	19%	19%
ROA (on NOPAT)	11%	12%	13%	16%	16%	16%	16%	16%	16%	16%	16%
Profit Margin (NOPAT)	17%	19%	19%	21%	21%	20%	21%	21%	21%	21%	21%
Total Asset Turnover	0.65	0.67	0.70	0.75	0.78	0.79	0.78	0.77	0.77	0.77	0.77
A/R Turnover	1.76	1.88	2.24	2.29	2.43	2.43	2.52	2.81	3.04	3.04	3.04
A/R collection period (Days Receivables)	207.68	194.51	163.19	159.52	150.33	150.00	145.00	130.00	120.00	120.00	120.00
Inventory Turnover (on sales)	6.25	6.92	7.53	8.42	7.80	8.11	8.11	8.11	8.11	8.11	8.11
Inventory Holding Period (Days Inventories)	58.40	52.72	48.47	43.33	46.79	45.00	45.00	45.00	45.00	45.00	45.00
Earnings Quality											
Avg. useful life of fixed assets	27.00	22.94	23.75	21.92	12.40	11.99	11.59	11.09	10.57	9.71	8.82
Effective tax rate	26%	26%	26%	24%	24%	24%	24%	24%	24%	24%	24%
Capex / Gross PPE	26%	11%	14%	8%	26%	24%	23%	22%	21%	17%	17%
Liquidity											
Current Ratio	5.00	5.51	5.31	4.97	4.79	4.60	4.55	4.51	4.72	4.99	5.28
Quick Ratio	4.09	4.61	4.49	4.25	4.01	3.88	3.87	3.86	4.05	4.32	4.59
A/R collection period (Days Receivables)	207.68	194.51	163.19	159.52	150.33	150.00	145.00	130.00	120.00	120.00	120.00
Inventory Holding Period (Days Inventories)	58.40	52.72	48.47	43.33	46.79	45.00	45.00	45.00	45.00	45.00	45.00
Operating Cycle	266.08	247.23	211.66	202.85	197.12	195.00	190.00	175.00	165.00	165.00	165.00
Solvency											
Total Debt / Total Assets	-9.42%	-13.68%	-19.27%	-19.95%	-19.43%	-20.24%	-23.42%	-28.98%	-32.75%	-35.46%	-38.27%
LT Debt / Total Assets	0%	0%	0%	0%	0%	0%	0%	0%	0%	0%	0%
Total Debt / Shareholders' Equity	0%	0%	0%	0%	0%	0%	0%	0%	0%	0%	0%
LT Debt / Shareholders' Equity	0%	0%	0%	0%	0%	0%	0%	0%	0%	0%	0%
Times Interest Earned	-47.00	-113.50	-64.83	-98.05	-95.56	-103.86	-115.71	-128.86	-143.47	-159.67	-177.67

FIGURE 6.1 (Continued)

Areas that should attract particular attention are: ensure that the financing plan shown in the base case shows a credible repayment schedule for the loan; avoid unrealistic scenarios, such as the build-up of large cash balances during the life of the loan; assess the impact of exchange rate, interest rate, and commodity price fluctuations (if applicable) upon the financial viability of the business jointly and severally, as well as the impact of delays, reduced volumes, and lower prices.

Business plan: a modelling example

Figure 6.1 shows a modelling example for a business (the related Excel file can be found on the companion website).

REFERENCES AND FURTHER READING

P. Pignataro. 2013. *Financial Modeling & Valuation: A Practical Guide to Investment Banking and Private Equity*. Wiley.

J.K. Smith, R.L. Smith, and R.T. Bliss. 2011. *Entrepreneurial Finance: Strategy, Valuation, and Deal Structure*. Stanford University Press.

SUGGESTED CASES

M. Hart and J.M. Dror. 2000. 'TruckitNow.com Business Plan.' Harvard Business School Case 801-151.

J.B. Lassiter III and M.J. Roberts. 1998. 'Business Plan for Room For Dessert: Adding Unique Ingredients to Life's Balancing Act.' Harvard Business School Case 899-008.

CHAPTER 7

Valuation

INTRODUCTION

Valuation aims to provide a value to the economic capital of a company. We can categorise the various methodologies as based in the asset side and equity side. In the first case, the value of the economic capital is estimated indirectly by estimating the current value of the company and then subtracting its net financial indebtedness. From the equity-side perspective, the market value of the shares is instead determined directly. The two perspectives of analysis should in any case lead to an equivalent result in terms of estimation of the value of economic capital, if the evaluation parameters and assumptions have been chosen consistently.

The following present the most used valuation methods in private capital:

1. financial approach: the method of discounted cash flows (DCF) asset side, and the method of the adjusted present value (APV);
2. comparative approach: the method of market multiples and multiples of transactions.

While we do not deal with this topic in great detail in this book, it is important to provide a concise outline of the different techniques since the determination of a price is at the basis of a private equity transaction.

FUNDAMENTALS #1: PRICE AND VALUE

There is a significant difference between the value and price of a company. Value represents a quantification of target per se and does not consider external elements such as potential buyers. Price is the amount of money that a buyer is willing to pay in a transaction.

As part of the acquisition of a majority stake in a company, the difference between value and price represents the control premium that the purchaser is willing to pay. This derives from several factors:

1. The owner of a company can manage the assets as desired and obtain direct access to cash flows, whilst a minority shareholder must rely on management and Board of Directors for the realisation of its future cash flows.
2. A strategic buyer of a company is able to extract synergies by combining the reference activity with that of another company, generating additional value for the purchaser's shareholders. How much of the value of these synergies will be passed on to the seller, as part of the purchase price, will depend on the parties' negotiating power.

   In practice, control premiums are 20–50% higher than traded values (if listed) or valuation.

FUNDAMENTALS #2: ENTERPRISE VALUE AND EQUITY VALUE

Two other key concepts are equity value and enterprise value (EV).

They depend on the type of approach used by the analyst, who can opt for the 'asset-side' or 'equity-side' perspective.

With the asset-side perspective, the value of the equity is estimated indirectly, by first assessing the company's operating capital and deducting the net financial position from it. Conversely, according to the equity side, the value of the equity is estimated directly.

Equity value is the value of the share capital and is defined as:

$$EQUITY\ VALUE = ENTERPRISE\ VALUE - NET\ DEBT.$$

Enterprise value is the 'total value' of a company, with reference not only to shareholders but also to lenders. It is therefore composed of two parts: the value referred to the risk capital (shareholders) and the value referred to the debt capital (lenders). On the asset side, it is equal to the sum of the total value generated by the operating and investment activities of an enterprise and must be divided between the various bearers of capital (whether by way of debt or by way of risk).

Depending on the valuation method, the enterprise value can be obtained as the result of:

- market multiples or comparable transactions (the most used are the multiples EV / EBIT and EV / EBITDA);
- valuation method for Discounted Cash Flow (DCF) and Economic Value Added (EVA).

Depending on the company's level of indebtedness, equity value may be higher or lower than enterprise value (see Figure 7.1):

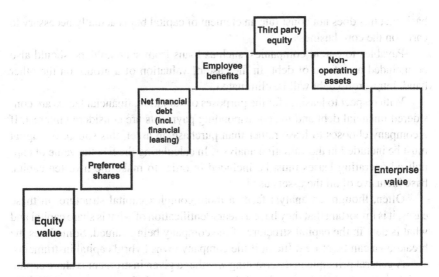

FIGURE 7.1 From equity value to enterprise value.

- if there are more financial debts than cash, the equity value will be lower than the enterprise value;
- if the liquid assets are higher than the financial debts, the equity value will be higher than the enterprise value.

It is important to note that there are situations (e.g. listed companies or equity multiples such as P/E) in which the equity value is determined directly, whilst the value of the assets is calculated indirectly.

Net financial debt included in the EV calculation generally refers to the interest-bearing capital due to third parties. It includes all debt financing (short-term and long-term), including bank loans, current account overdrafts, capitalised bonds, and finance leases, but does not include liabilities that do not generate interest, such as trade payables, accrued expenses, and deferred income or tax payables of an ordinary nature. Where possible, debt instruments should be valued at their market value. In most cases, this will simply be equal to the carrying amount indicated in the financial statements, but for companies with long-term bonds issued in a different interest rate environment and for companies in financial difficulty, an adjustment to the market value should be made.

Net financial debt is shown net of:

- balances of cash and cash equivalents;
- negotiable securities (generally investments included amongst the circulating assets, which are readily liquidated).

If there is a minimum level of operating cash that must be maintained for the management of the activity, this is typically excluded from the calculation on the basis that this does not constitute an element of capital but is actually necessary to carry on the core business.

Payables to parent companies, such as loans from shareholders, should also be included as a form of debt. In the case of valuation of a group, on the other hand, intra-group debt will be eliminated.

With respect to leasing, for the purposes of valuation, financial leases are considered financial debt and the corresponding payments are considered interest. If a company chooses to lease rather than purchase an asset, this source of capital must be included in the valuation analysis. In calculating the EV, the value of capitalised operating leases must be included in order to make the invested capital base inclusive of all the assets used.

Often, though, an analyst faces a more complex capital structure: in these cases, it is important that they have a clear identification of what is share capital and what is debt in the capital structure of the company being valued. Sometimes the breakdown can be more difficult if the company owns hybrid capital instruments.

A general principle in determining whether a given instrument is share capital or debt is to establish the priority of the company's cash flows on a going concern basis. For example, risk capital has a subordinated position on cash flows compared to the amount owed to financial creditors: dividends and repayment of share capital are only disbursed after interest and principal payments have been paid to creditors.

The most frequent changes to the formula above include:

- **Options, warrants, and convertible debt securities or convertible preference shares:** fully diluted capital considers the worst-case scenario for investors, which assumes that all potentially dilutive securities are converted. Share options and warrants are dilutive only when their strike price is lower than the current market price of the security. If this is the case, they are said to be in the money (ITM) as opposed to out of the money (OTM) if the strike price is higher than the current market value. Options on dilutive shares, warrants, and convertible bonds increase the number of ordinary shares outstanding.
- **Preferred shares:** preferred shareholders of a company have priority over ordinary shareholders when profits are distributed. The preference dividend is usually an amount per share that is fixed at the time of issue. The preference shares must be considered as subordinated debt. However, if a preferred share is convertible, it should be treated in the same way as a convertible bond. It is also possible to consider the preference shares as equity if they are perpetual and have the characteristics of deferring ordinary dividends.
- **Employee benefits:** the pension systems in force in different countries can be divided into two major types: defined benefit schemes and defined contribution schemes. Well-defined benefit schemes (DBs), once common in industrial companies in the United Kingdom and the United States, began to fade out

with the realisation that they were bearing all the risks associated with performance of the assets in the pension scheme (since the liabilities are fixed in relation to the salaries of the pensioners). More recently, defined contribution schemes (DCs) have become the norm, by which the employee assumes the risk of return on assets, whilst the company provides fixed contributions to its employees. For calculation of the value of the company, the DB type bonds are considered a 'debt-like' element; in other words, a loan provided by the employees to the company that will be repaid upon retirement. Moreover, like pension debts, they are recorded at present value, and this therefore implies an implicit cost of annual financial interest. This, together with the long-term nature of pensions, makes us consider these obligations as financing in kind. Some legal systems require companies to finance these debts by allocating a part of their assets or liquid assets to the service of reimbursement of employee benefits. An unpaid pension obligation is included in the value of the company. This difference is defined as surplus (or over-financing) if the assets exceed the obligation, and deficit (or under-funding) if these are lower. This deficit may vary depending on whether accounting estimates or actuarial estimates of the liability are used.

- **Third-party equity:** if a company owns the majority, but not the whole, of a subsidiary, the interest of third parties emerges in its liabilities; i.e. the share of total shareholders' equity pertaining to minority shareholders of the subsidiaries. The minorities therefore have rights on the total value of the company that are separate from ordinary shareholders. The value pertaining to them should therefore be considered as other third-party liabilities. Where possible, it would be better to evaluate a subsidiary as an independent entity and then assign the proportional share of its value to the main group (rather than simply taking the book value of minorities); if the subsidiary is quoted, one should use market capitalisation. Alternatively, in the case in which less information is available, it is possible to consider the application of a multiple P/E to the net profit attributable to third parties in the income statement.
- **Non-operational activities:** the balance sheet of a company could include assets (or liabilities) not strictly related to its core business, and which therefore do not generate an operating cash flow (or do not contribute to the generation of generic operating cash flows) on which the valuation is carried out. This may be the case for non-instrumental real estate, funds for risks and charges of specific and non-recurring nature, or in the case of subsidiaries outside the consolidation perimeter (in this case, if they were instrumental in nature, the business plan could not bring out their income and financial contribution). The current value of these items must therefore be separately added to the value of the target company rather than a simple discount from the OpCF (in the case of DCF asset side or APV). The logic is also valid in the opposite direction, where the analyst aims to estimate the enterprise value starting from the market capitalisation.

- **Off balance-sheet debt:** ideally, off balance-sheet finance which is material to EV would be included in its calculation. However, this is often difficult because of a lack of detailed disclosure.

FUNDAMENTALS #3: MARKET VALUES VS. BOOK VALUES

When calculating EV, market values should be used for its components. While this is relatively straightforward for the equity component of listed companies (in fact, one can use equity market capitalisation), this is often not the case for debt, since few companies have quoted debt.

The investing focus of private equity and private debt is investment in private (i.e. non-listed) companies, thus book values for both equity and debt are used.

DISCOUNTED CASH VALUATION METHOD

There are several steps in a DCF valuation, as shown in Figure 7.2.

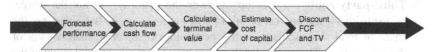

FIGURE 7.2 Steps in a DCF valuation.

DISCOUNTED CASH VALUATION: WACC APPROACH

The weighted average cost of capital (WACC) approach is composed of the following steps:

1. **Step 1:** Select a forecast horizon.

    The duration of the flow projection period depends on various requirements:
    - describes the dynamics in sectors characterised by cyclical behaviour;
    - represents the cash flow dynamics in the presence of extraordinary capex cycles or business restructurings;
    - complies with the duration of contract renewals or concessions.

    The time horizon can greatly influence the evaluation: the use of a horizon that is too short risks 'cutting' considerable financial results, whilst the horizon that is too long increases the unreliability of the most distant values. It is therefore important to evaluate the type of company with the market in which it operates. In particular:
    - for highly volatile sectors: an extended horizon risks altering the valuation;

- for stable sectors: results are appreciable after a certain number of years. From a theoretical point of view, the forecast period should be that of the company's competitive advantage.

  From a practical point of view, the most used period is eight to ten years.
2. **Step 2:** Forecast free cash flows (FCF) for each year of the forecast horizon. Where FCF = cash flows from operating activities that are 'freely available' to suppliers of capital, such as creditors and stockholders (before interest, dividends, or any other cash payments are made to lenders and stockholders). It is important to emphasise here that FCF is the so-called *enterprise free cash flow* (also called free cash flow to the firm), which is the cash available to the financiers. It may be used to pay interest or repay debt, to build cash balances or other investments, or to pay dividends or buy-back shares.

  In a formula:[1]

EBIT

− cash taxes on EBIT[2]

= NOPLAT (net operating profit less adjusted taxes)

+ depreciation (and other non-cash expenses)

= Gross cash flow

− increase in operating working capital

− capital expenditures (net of disposals)

− net expenditures for acquisitions and intangible assets

= Free cash flow (FCF)

  In most cases, five to ten years of projected results are used for a DCF analysis. It is important to make sensible assumptions for years beyond the company-provided range. If there aren't solid sector analysis and company positioning for making projections, some good guidelines are:

- grow sales at a rate consistent with the historical information and the company's own projections;

---

[1]Rather than starting with EBIT, an alternative formulation derives FCF starting from cash from operations. In this case: FCF = Operating Cash Flow − Increase in Operating Cash Balance + Interest Expense × (1- Marginal Tax Rate) − Non-operating Income × (1- Marginal Tax Rate) − Capital Expenditures (net of disposals) − Net Expenditures for Acquisitions and Intangible Assets. The two methodologies provide approximately the same result, except when non-operating cash flows are materially different from non-operating expenses and revenues or when tax rates on non-operating revenues and expenses differ from statutory tax rates.

[2]Cash taxes on EBIT = Tax Expense on EBIT (equal to Total Income Tax Expense + Interest Expense × Marginal Tax Rate − Non-operating Income × Marginal Tax Rate) − Net Increase in Deferred Tax Liability.

- project EBITDA holding the EBITDA margin (EBITDA as a percentage of sales) constant at a rate consistent with historical information and company projections;
- hold working capital items constant as a percentage of sales;
- set capital expenditures at an annual rate that grows slowly with inflation;
- remember that in the long run depreciation should resemble capital expenditures.

When finished, the analyst should ask the following questions:

- o do they seem unreasonable or over-optimistic?
- o do they display any 'hockey-stick' characteristics (unusually large jumps in sales or EBITDA that exceed those seen historically)?
- o does the company operate in a cyclical market segment? If so, consistently growing operating numbers are probably not correct.
- o is the company in a rapidly expanding segment? If so, relatively aggressive growth rates are appropriate.

3. **Step 3:** Estimate WACC.

In a formula:

$$\textbf{WACC} = [\textbf{Wd} \times \textbf{Rd} \times (\textbf{1} - \textbf{tr})] + [\textbf{We} \times \textbf{Re}]$$

where

Wd = targeted proportion of debt in capital structure (based on market values) = $D/(D+E)$

We = targeted proportion of common stock in capital structure (based on market values) = $E/(D+E)$ = $1 - Wd$

tr = marginal corporate tax rate

Rd = expected cost of debt capital (pre-tax)

Re = expected cost of equity capital = $Rf + [\beta*(E(Rm) - Rf)]$ (if using Capital Asset Pricing Model, for which see below)

Rf = 'riskless' return

$E(Rm) - Rf$ = expected risk premium on the market portfolio

β = beta of common stock.

A few points are worth mentioning:

- *We* (and its reciprocal *Wd*) indicates the objective financial structure (optimal and not the current one) of the company;
- *Rd* is determined as: free risk + spread rate, where
  - o free risk = yield of government bonds;
  - o spread = weighted average of the differential interest rates that the company supports on short and long-term debt.
- if a new target capital structure is adopted, the WACC should reflect the new structure (i.e., new *Rd, Re, Wd,* and *We*).

With regard to *Re*, the model most commonly used to estimate it is the capital asset pricing model (CAPM). CAPM is heavily criticised, but is widely used and is the most generally accepted basis for estimating the cost of equity.

Alternative models (although less used in practice) to the CAPM are the arbitrage pricing theory (APT) of Ross (1976) and the three factor model of Fama and French (1993).

When calculating Rf + [β * (E(Rm) − Rf)], it is worth noting that:

- *Rf* (risk-free rate): typically government bonds with medium/long term maturities
- *(E(Rm) − Rf)*: represents the risk premium. Investment in equities involves two risk profiles: the specific risk, which can be eliminated through a diversification process, and the systematic risk, which depends on the general economic trends and which cannot be eliminated. The CAPM estimates this component; in particular, it estimates the corporate risk in terms of the variability of the company's historical returns with respect to market returns; the more the company returns are different from those of the market, the higher the risk, and the higher the premium required by the investor to invest in the company.
- β: measures how the return on capital of the company being valued reacts to changes in market performance and represents a non-diversifiable systemic risk coefficient. Formally

$$\beta = \frac{COV(R_A; R_m)}{VAR(R_m)}$$

where

- $COV\,(R_A; Rm)$, is the covariance between the returns of the target company and those of the market
- $VAR\,(Rm)$, is the variance of market return
  β is affected by the following factors:
- reference sector: the more the sector the company belongs to is sensitive to market trends in general, the higher the beta;
- operational leverage: greater operational leverage results in greater variability in company results, which translates into greater beta;
- financial leverage: a greater level of leverage corresponds to a higher beta.

When estimating the beta of private (i.e., unlisted companies), average beta are used, determined with reference to a sample of companies belonging to the same sector. When the financial risk of the company being valued is very different from the average financial risk of the companies that compose the comparables sample, it is necessary to redefine the company's beta. In this case, beta should be separated from the financial component (beta unlevered or βu) and recalculated considering the specific financial risk of the company (beta levered or βL) through the following formula:

i. unlevering: $\beta_u = \beta_L / \left(1 + D/E\right)$

ii. relevering: $\beta_L = \beta_u \times \left(1 + D/E\right)$.

Several sources regularly publish the beta of listed securities (Morgan Stanley Beta Book, Merrill Lynch Beta Book, Bloomberg, Barra, Ibbotson).

4. **Step 4**: Discount FCF of the forecast horizon using WACC as discount rate. In formula:

$$PV(FCFH) = FCF_1/(1 + WACC)^1 + FCF_2/(1 + WACC)^2$$
$$+ \ldots + FCF_T/(1 + WACC)^T$$

where

$PV(FCFH)$ = present value of FCF during the forecast horizon,
T = # of years in forecast horizon.

5. **Step 5**: Estimate the terminal value (TV) and discount it back to the current period to obtain the present value of the terminal value PV(TV).

The TV expresses the value of the operating cash flows forecast for the period following the explicit projection time horizon. Great care must be taken to estimate the terminal value, as this can have a significant impact (70–80%) on the total value. The most common methodologies to calculate the TV are:

Constant growth method:

$$[FCT_{T+1}/(WACC - g)]/(1 + WACC)^T$$

where
$$FCT_{T+1} = FCF_T {}^* (1 + g)$$

g = expected constant growth rate in FCF.
Perpetuity method:

$$[FCT_{T+1}/g]/(1 + WACC)^T.$$

6. **Step 6**: Sum PV(FCFH) and PV(TV).

7. **Step 7**: From the above result, subtract the value of net debt (as illustrated previously) to obtain

EQUITY VALUE = TOTAL VALUE OF FCF − NET DEBT.

DISCOUNTED CASH FLOW VALUATION: ADJUSTER PRESENT VALUE METHOD

One of the advantages of adjusted present value (APV) over WACC is that:

- it can accommodate a changing capital structure;
- it clearly distinguishes the value of the firm from financing 'side-effects'.

The APV approach is composed of the following steps:

1. **Step 1**: Same as WACC approach.
2. **Step 2**: Same as WACC approach.
3. **Step 3**: Estimate the unlevered cost of equity capital (Ru).
   Where

$$\textbf{Ru} = \textbf{Rf} + \boldsymbol{\beta}\textbf{u}^{*}\, [\textbf{E(Rm)} - \textbf{Rf}]$$

where βu = unlevered beta (i.e., for an all equity financed firm), also called asset beta.

There are two main formulas to estimate the unlevered beta as a function of the assumed risk of the interest tax shield.

Method A (assumes the risk of the tax shield on interest is the same as the risk of the assets):[3]

$$\boldsymbol{\beta}\textbf{u} = [\boldsymbol{\beta}\textbf{e} + (\boldsymbol{\beta}\textbf{d})(\textbf{D}/\textbf{E})]/[1 + (\textbf{D}/\textbf{E})]$$

where

βe = levered beta on common equity
βd = beta on debt[4]
D/E = capital structure (in market value terms).

Note: if $\beta d = 0$ (i.e., debt is risk-free), then the formula becomes

$$\boldsymbol{\beta}\textbf{u} = \boldsymbol{\beta}\textbf{e}/[1 + (\textbf{D}/\textbf{E})].$$

Method B (assumes the risk of the tax shield is the same as the risk on the debt):

$$\boldsymbol{\beta}\textbf{u} = [\boldsymbol{\beta}\textbf{e} + (\boldsymbol{\beta}\textbf{d})(1 - \textbf{tr})(\textbf{D}/\textbf{E})]/[1 + (1 - \textbf{tr})(\textbf{D}/\textbf{E})]$$

where

βe = levered beta on common equity
βd = beta on debt
D/E = capital structure (in market value terms).

Note: if $\beta d = 0$ (i.e., debt and tax shield are risk-free), then the formula becomes

$$\boldsymbol{\beta}\textbf{u} = \boldsymbol{\beta}\textbf{e} + /[1 + (1 - \textbf{tr})(\textbf{D}/\textbf{E})].$$

4. **Step 4:** Use Ru to discount the FCF during the forecast horizon (same as WACC approach but for the different discount rate, i.e., Ru instead of WACC).

---

[3]Used when capital structure is expected to remain stable while cash flow is volatile/highly uncertain.
[4]For investment grade debt, $\beta d \approx 0.2$; for junk debt $\beta d \approx 0.5$.

In a formula:

$$PV(FCFH) = FCF_1/(1 + Ru)^1 + FCF_2/(1 + Ru)^2 + \ldots + FCF_T/(1 + Ru)^T$$

where

PV(FCFH) = present value of FCF during the forecast horizon

T = number of years in forecast horizon.

5. **Step 5**: Estimate the terminal value (TV) and discount it back to the current period to obtain the present value of the terminal value PV(TV). This step is the same as WACC approach but for the different discount rate (i.e., *Ru* instead of WACC).

Constant growth method:

$$[FCF_{T+1}/(Ru - g)]/(1 + Ru)^T$$

where

$$FCF_{T+1} = FCF_T{}^* (1 + g)$$

g = expected constant growth rate in FCF.

Perpetuity method:

$$[FCF_{T+1}/g]/(1 + Ru)^T.$$

6. **Step 6**: Add present value of total interest tax shield PV(TS). This is equal to the sum of the tax shield during the forecast horizon [PV(TSFH)] and after the forecast horizon [PV(TSAFH)].

a. During the forecast horizon

     Two alternative methodologies:

     ○ Using the discount rate derived under Method A above (i.e., assumes the risk of the tax shield on interest is the same as the risk of the assets):

$$PV(TSFH) = [tr \times int\ exp_1]/(1 + Ru)^1$$
$$+ \ldots + [tr \times int\ exp_T]/(1 + Ru)^T.$$

     ○ Using the discount rate derived under Method B above (i.e., assumes the risk of the tax shield is the same as the risk on the debt):

$$PV(TSFH) = [tr \times int\ exp_1]/(1 + Rd)^1$$
$$+ \ldots + [tr \times int\ exp_T]/(1 + Rd)^T.$$

b. After the forecast horizon

     Two alternative methodologies:

     ○ Assuming D_{T+1} (debt outstanding at $T + 1$) will grow forever at growth rate g.

         Under Method A:

$$PV(TSAFH) = [tr \times Rd \times D_{T+1}]/(Ru - g)/(1 + Ru)^T.$$

Under Method B:

$$PV(TSAFH) = [tr \times Rd \times D_{T+1}]/(Rd - g)/(1 + Rd)^T.$$

○ Assuming D_{T+1} (debt outstanding at $T + 1$) stays equal (in amount) to D_T

$$PV(TSAFH) = [tr \times Rd \times D_{T+1}]/R/(1 + R)^T.$$

7. **Step 7**: Sum PV(FCFH) and PV(TV) and PV(TSFH) and PV(TSAFH)
8. **Step 8**: From the above result, subtract the value of net debt[5] (same as illustrated previously) to obtain

EQUITY VALUE = TOTAL VALUE OF FCF − NET DEBT.

COMPARABLES VALUATION METHOD

A valuation multiple is an expression of a company's value relative to a key statistic that is assumed to be linked to that value. A multiple is a relationship between a numerator (enterprise value or equity value) and a denominator (a variable that can summarise a company's ability to produce 'income').[6] The aim of this approach is to determine a 'reasonable price' that is in line with other companies.

There are two basic types of multiple: enterprise value and equity.

- **Enterprise multiples:** express the value of an entire enterprise (i.e. the value of all claims on a business) relative to a statistic that relates to the entire enterprise, such as sales, EBITDA, or EBIT. Typical enterprise multiples used are:
  - Sales
  - EBITDA
  - EBIT
  - NOPLAT
  - Operating free cash flow
  - Enterprise cash flow
  - Total capital employed
  - Other business activity measures.
- **Equity multiples:** express the value of shareholders' claims on the assets and equity cash flow of the business. An equity multiple therefore expresses the value of this claim relative to a statistic that applies to shareholders only, such as earnings. Typical equity multiples used are
  - Earnings (per share)
  - Cash earnings (per share)
  - Equity free cash flow (per share)
  - Debt adjusted equity free cash flow (per share)

---

[5]In theory, the analyst should subtract the cost of financial distress. Given that it is difficult to calculate this, in practice it is always ignored.
[6]These can be accounting quantities (sales, EBITDA, EBIT, profit, book equity) or physical entities (number of subscribers, hotel rooms, contacts, users).

- Dividends (per share)
- Net assets (per share).

The merits of the multiples method as an evaluation criterion can be summarised as follows.

- **Simplicity:** it is an evaluation mechanism based on the observation of analogies with other companies that requires few simple operations (multiplication/division; addition/subtraction).
- **Comparability:** the value of a company cannot differ significantly from the value expressed by the market (stock exchange or transactions) for companies of similar size, in the same sector and operating on the same geographical markets.
- **Convergence:** any significant differences with respect to the sample tend to be filled sooner or later.
- **Ordinability:** with the same historical results, companies present multiples that are as much higher as the future opportunities for value creation are greater.

Amongst the disadvantages of multiples:

- **Simplistic:** a multiple incorporates a great deal of information into a single number. By combining many value drivers into a single number, it may be difficult to disaggregate the effect of different drivers (e.g., growth) on value.
- **Static:** a multiple represents a snapshot of where a firm is at a point in time, but fails to capture the dynamic nature of business and competition.
- **Difficult to compare:** multiples are primarily used to make comparisons of relative value.

Depending on the reference sample, the multiples are distinguished as:

- **Market multiple:** expresses the relationship between the stock market values and the equity values of a company. This methodology compares the income trend of the target company being valued to that of its listed peers. The economic rationale behind this method is the theory of efficient markets, which infers that similar activities should have comparable value (i.e. they should be exchanged for similar multiples). The valuation by multiples of comparable companies is widely used in practice, both by investors and by consultants. It has the advantage of using market-derived data and should ensure that trading values reflect the latest information on industry trends, industrial risk, and market growth taking into account the estimates of the results future. The main disadvantage is that really comparable companies are rare and the differences can be difficult to explain. It does not define a fundamental value but rather a price that is probable that the market is willing to pay.
- **Multiple of comparable transactions:** expresses the relationship between implicit values in a transaction and the value of a company. The analysis

of comparable transactions is a methodology that compares the multiples implied by the selected M&A operations involving companies exhibiting characteristics similar to the company in question, in order to derive a value of the implicit transaction for that company. Transaction multiples give an indication of the recent market prices paid by other buyers and accepted by other sellers. When choosing transactions, the goal must be to find offers that have assets and financial characteristics similar to the transaction under consideration:

- same sector of the reference business;
- nearby geographic areas;
- acquired quota (majority or minority);
- transaction rationale and financial profile of acquired companies: economies of scale, growth, synergies, diversification;
- timing: the more recent the data, the more relevant the multiple, especially in cyclical industries;
- size: transactions of similar size to the company being evaluated are generally more relevant.

Depending on the temporal data used, multiples are distinguished between:

- **historical:** use the data presented in the last published annual report;
- **trailing:** use the sum of data for the last four quarters;
- **leading:** use prospective data.

The multiple valuation process is composed of the following phases:

1. **Choice of significant multiples:** asset side vs. equity side. Attention should be paid to the fact that multiples built using accounting values are more influenced by tax policies, but at the same time tend to highlight with greater significance of the ability of a company to generate wealth from the operational point of view.
2. **Determination of the sample of comparable companies:** stock exchange or transactions. The selection of comparable companies is the most delicate but necessary phase in order to constitute a homogeneous sample with respect to the target company to be evaluated. If the number of sample components is – from a statistical point of view – important, the 'similarity' (sector, size, profitability, product mix, etc.) of the sample is even more important.
3. **Calculation of selected multiples for the companies represented in the sample.**
4. **Identification of the range of values of the multiples to be applied to the target company being evaluated.**
5. **Application of multiples to the company being valued.**

Table 7.1 illustrates some key characteristics of the most common multiples.

TABLE 7.1 Comparison of the most used multiples.

Multiple	Features	Application areas	Frequency of use
EV / sales	▪ never expresses negative values (always calculable) ▪ less influenced by accounting policies	▪ start-up ▪ companies with low operating leverage	Medium–low
EV / EBITDA	▪ able to express the ability of a company to generate value through the operating activity ▪ not very influenced by accounting and tax aspects	▪ companies operating in stable and mature sectors ▪ very used in manufacturing ▪ always inserted inside a basket of multiples	Very high
EV / EBIT	▪ alternative to the multiple of EBITDA for companies whose assets are characterised by the predominant presence of fixed assets (materials) ▪ takes into account the amortisation policies, but is more affected by accounting rules	▪ company with a stable and mature business, with high capital invested ▪ may be distorted by different amortisation policies amongst countries	High
P / E	▪ simplicity of calculation ▪ multiple most used for listed companies	▪ heavily influenced by accounting, tax, and extraordinary policies ▪ indiscriminately in all sectors	High
P / BV	▪ immediate interpretation (represents the premium that an investor is willing to pay compared to the simple asset value of the company) ▪ often flanked by other methods	▪ used for companies characterised by a high level of equity ▪ very common for the evaluation of banks, insurance companies, and financial companies	Average

Weighted average cost of capital

SUMMARY OF WEIGHTED AVERAGE COST OF CAPITAL CALCULATION – BASED ON CAPM (CAPITAL ASSET PRICING MODEL)

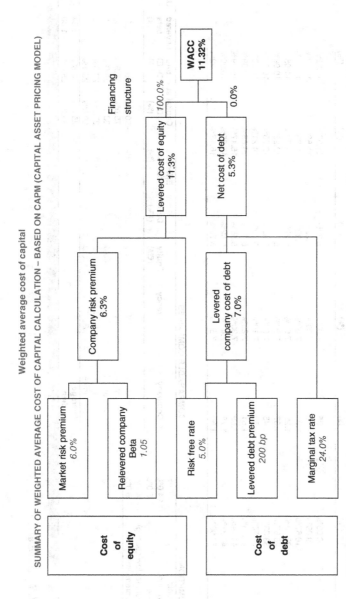

FIGURE 7.3 Valuation methodologies: a modelling example.

WACC – SENSITIVITY ANALYSIS

| Capital structure | | Relevered | Cost of debt | | Cost of equity | Cost of capital |
D/E (%)	D/(D+E) (%)	beta (x)	Pre-tax (%)	Post-tax (%)	(%)	(%)
0.00%	0.00%	1.05	7.00%	5.32%	11.32%	11.32%
10.00%	9.09%	1.13	7.00%	5.32%	11.80%	11.22%
20.00%	16.67%	1.21	7.00%	5.32%	12.29%	11.12%
30.00%	23.08%	1.29	7.00%	5.32%	12.77%	11.05%
40.00%	28.57%	1.37	7.00%	5.32%	13.25%	10.98%
50.00%	33.33%	1.45	7.00%	5.32%	13.73%	10.93%
60.00%	37.50%	1.53	7.10%	5.40%	14.21%	10.90%
70.00%	41.18%	1.61	7.20%	5.47%	14.69%	10.89%
80.00%	44.44%	1.69	7.30%	5.55%	15.17%	10.89%
90.00%	47.37%	1.78	7.40%	5.62%	15.65%	10.90%
100.00%	50.00%	1.86	7.50%	5.70%	16.13%	10.92%

KEY ASSUMPTIONS

Unlevered beta	1.05
Marginal tax rate	24.0%
Risk free rate	5.0%
Debt premium (at low gearing)	200 bp
Market risk premium	6.0%

COMPARABLE COMPANIES

Company	Currency	Equity (€M)	Debt (€M)	Effective tax rate (%)	Capital structure D/E (%)	D/(D+E) (%)	Levered beta (x)	Unlevd. beta (x)
Company A	EUR	100.0	(50.0)	30.0%	-50.0%	-100.0%	1.50	2.31
Company B	EUR	200.0	150.0	30.0%	75.0%	42.9%	1.40	0.92
Company C	EUR	300.0	100.0	30.0%	33.3%	25.0%	1.30	1.05
Company D	EUR	400.0	150.0	28.0%	37.5%	27.3%	1.20	0.94
Company E	EUR	500.0	150.0	28.0%	30.0%	23.1%	1.30	1.07
Average					25.2%	3.6%	1.34	1.26
Median					33.3%	25.0%	1.30	1.05

FIGURE 7.3 (*Continued*)

Valuation – DCF

Key Assumptions:

WACC	11.32%
Valuation date	31/12/18
Perpetual growth rate	2.00%

DCF Valuation output

Present Value FCFF – years (1–6)	72.38
Present Value of Terminal Value	117.68
Enterprise Value	**190.06**
Net Debt @ Valuation Date	–15.6
Equity Value	**205.66**

Present value of years 1–6 free cash flow

	31/12/2018 A	31/12/2019 E	31/12/2020 E	31/12/2021 E	31/12/2022 E	31/12/2023 E	31/12/2024 E
FCFF	**8.83**	**10.25**	**12.31**	**16.80**	**16.92**	**17.91**	**20.49**
Discount factor	1.00	0.90	0.81	0.72	0.65	0.58	0.53
Unlevered free cash flow	**8.83**	**9.21**	**9.93**	**12.17**	**11.01**	**10.47**	**10.76**

Present value of FCFF – years (1–6) €M	**72.38**

Present value of terminal free cash flow

	31/12/2024 E	Adjustments	Normalised 2024 E	TV (Y7)
EBIT	**31.98**	-	**31.98**	**32.62**
- Cash taxes	(7.7)	-	(7.7)	(7.9)
NOPAT	**24.26**	-	**24.26**	**24.75**
+ D&A	4.7	-	4.7	4.8
- Capex	(5.0)	-	(5.0)	(5.1)
- Delta NWC	(3.4)	-	(3.4)	(3.5)
- Delta provisions	-	-	-	-
FCFF	**20.49**		**20.49**	**20.90**
Discount factor	0.53		0.53	5.63
Unlevered free cash flow	**10.76**		**10.76**	**117.68**

Net Present Value of Terminal Value	**117.68**

FIGURE 7.3 (*Continued*)

Valuation – APV

Key Assumptions:

Valuation date	31/12/18
Tax rate	24%
Market premium	6%
Book value of debt	70 *hypothesis – not linked to BP case as debt free company*
Book value of equity	100
Market value of equity	
b_{equity}^{L} (historical)	1.30
Risk free rate	5%
Long-term debt interest rate	7%
Long-term growth rate	2%

APV	
β_{equity}^{U}	1.1
k_{equity}^{U}	**11.8%**

WACC	
Target D/E (MV)	40%
Target Debt	40
β_{equity}^{U}	1.1
β_{equity}^{L}	1.70
k_{equity}^{L}	15.2%
WACC	**11.2%**

		31/12/2018 A	31/12/2019 E	31/12/2020 E	31/12/2021 E	31/12/2022 E	31/12/2023 E	31/12/2024 E
	FCFF	8.83	10.25	12.31	16.80	16.92	17.91	20.49
DCF/WACC	Terminal value (WACC)							225.96
	FCF to all equity firm (WACC)	8.83	10.25	12.31	16.80	16.92	17.91	246.45
	Discount factor	1.00	0.90	0.81	0.73	0.65	0.59	0.53
	NPV^{L}	**191.66**						
	Terminal value (APV)							213.89
	FCF to all equity firm (APV)	8.83	10.25	12.31	16.80	16.92	17.91	234.38
	Discount factor	1.00	0.89	0.80	0.72	0.64	0.57	0.51
	NPV^{U}	**181.12**						
APV	Interest Expenses	2.80	2.80	2.80	2.80	2.80	2.80	2.80
	ITS	0.67	0.67	0.67	0.67	0.67	0.67	0.67
	Terminal value of ITS							7.02
	Discount factor	1.00	0.89	0.80	0.72	0.64	0.57	0.51
	NPV (ITS)	**3.60**						
	NPV^{L} = NPV^{U} + NPV (ITS)	**184.71**						

FIGURE 7.3 (*Continued*)

Valuation – Multiples (precedent transactions)

Precedent transactions analysis:

Date	Target	Bidder	Business of Target	Sales of Target	EBITDA of Target	Net Profit of Target	Net Debt of Target	Price paid	Acquired Stake	Implied equity value	P/E	Implied EV	EV/EBITDA	EV/Sales
06/05/18	Alpha	Aries	pharma	52	15.6	10.4	-10	80	50%	160	15.4	150.0	9.6	2.9
30/07/18	Beta	Taurus	pharma	43	15.1	645	-15	108.4	80%	135.5	0.2	120.5	8.0	2.8
20/08/18	Gamma	Gemini	supplements	67	14.7	6.7	-10	51	40%	127.5	19.0	137.5	9.3	2.1
01/09/18	Delta	Cancer	pharma	71	21.3	14.2	-13	150	70%	214.2857143	15.1	201.3	9.5	2.8
15/09/18	Epsilon	Leo	pharma	84	25.2	16.8	-11	174.5	75%	232.6666667	13.8	221.7	8.8	2.6
01/10/18	Zeta	Virgo	supplements	250	42.5	20	15	240	100%	240	12.0	255.0	6.0	1.0
30/11/18	Eta	Libra	pharma	58	19.7	11.6	3	164.62	100%	164.62	14.2	167.6	8.5	2.89

Comparable	
Not Comparable	

	P/E	EV/EBITDA	EV/Sales
Average (excl. not comparable)	13.0	8.9	2.7
Median (excl.not comparable)	14.6	9.1	2.8

Multiples valuation output

Indicators	Target Values (€M)	Enterprise Value	Equity Value
Valuation Sales	62.40	175.88	191.48
Valuation EBITDA	19.70	178.53	194.13
Valuation Net Profit	13.21	177.79	193.39
Valuation Net Debt	-15.6		

Equity Value from	to
190	200

Enterprise Value from	to
174.4	184.4

FIGURE 7.3 (*Continued*)

It is also important to note the following:

- **H-growth businesses have higher multiples:** the market is usually willing to pay more for these company shares in anticipation of earnings growth.
- **Multiples for growth businesses will get smaller each year:** as earnings for the business increase (and expected growth is realised), the multiple will decrease.
- **EBIT multiple > EBITDA multiple > revenue multiple:** because the numerator (enterprise value or levered market capitalisation for public companies) is the same for each of these multiples, the larger the denominator, the smaller the multiple.

Valuation methodologies: a modeling example

An example of a valuation is reproduced in Figure 7.3 (the accompanying Excel file is downloadable from the companion website).

REFERENCES AND FURTHER READING

A. Damodaran. 2012. *Investment Valuation: Tools and Techniques for Determining the Value of Any Asset*. Wiley Finance.

J. Pearl and J. Rosenbaum. 2015. *Investment Banking: Valuation Leveraged Buyouts And Mergers And Acquisitions*. Wiley.

S. Pratt., R. Reilly, and R. Schweihs. 2008. *Valuing A Business: The Analysis and Appraisal of Closely Held Companies*. McGraw Hill.

SUGGESTED CASES

R.G. Hamermesh. 2010. 'Shurgard Self-Storage: Expansion to Europe.' Harvard Business School Case 810-102.

E. Stafford and J.L. Heilprin. 2011. 'Valuation of Air Thread Connections.' Harvard Business School Case 114-263.

CHAPTER 8

Growth Equity

INTRODUCTION

Growth equity (also called growth or expansion capital) is one of three asset classes comprising the private equity industry, the other two being venture capital (not part of this book) and leveraged buyout (or LBO, for which see the relevant chapter). Growth equity is usually a minority private equity investment in which investment returns are generated by investing in companies that create value through profitable EBITDA growth.

Companies that seek growth capital will often do so in order to finance a transformational event in their lifecycle. These companies are likely to be more mature than venture capital funded companies, able to generate revenue and profit, but unable to generate sufficient cash to fund major expansions, acquisitions, or other investments.

Typical growth equity situations are:

- new markets/products/distribution channels
- consolidation
- operating efficiencies
- capacity/production increase
- improvement of management
- multiple expansion.

Growth capital is often structured as preferred equity, although certain investors will use various hybrid securities (such as mezzanine) that include a contractual return (i.e. interest payments) in addition to ordinary equity.

DIFFERENCES BETWEEN VENTURE CAPITAL, GROWTH EQUITY, AND LBO

The differences between venture capital and growth equity (see also Table 8.1) are to do with the stage of target companies in which they invest: venture capitalists

TABLE 8.1 Differences between venture capital and growth equity.

Venture capital	Growth equity
Invests in early-stage operating companies with unproven business model	Invests in later-stage companies with proven business models
Typically has an industry focus (e.g. TMT, biotech, etc.)	Generally industry agnostic
Investment thesis based on revenue growth	Investment thesis based on profitability (EBITDA) growth
Invests in companies with future capital requirements, part of which are still undefined	Invests in companies with limited future capital requirements to achieve profitability target

invest in small, early-stage, emerging firms (or even in ideas and a team, although revenues still lag behind), whilst growth equities invest in later stage companies with proven business models, substantial organic revenue growth (usually in excess of 10%, and often more than 20%), and positive EBITDA.

The differences between growth equity and LBO capital (see Table 8.2) are obvious in the names: growth capital is typically invested to foster growth via a minority equity investment (effected through a share capital increase), whilst LBO involves the takeover of a majority stake (through a combination of debt and equity, both of which are used to pay the exiting shareholder).

Growth equity therefore resides on the continuum of private equity investing and at the intersection of venture capital and control buyouts.

TABLE 8.2 Key differences between growth equity and LBO.

Growth equity	LBO
Buys a minority position via share capital increase	Buys a majority position via a share acquisition of a control or whole stake
Invests in companies with limited free cash flow	Invests in companies with consistent free cash flow
Limited or no use of debt financing to leverage the investment	Significant use of debt financing to leverage the investment
Invests at inflection point where growth opportunities can boost revenues and profitability	Invests at a plateau where revenues and profitability are projected to remain stable or grow moderately steady

TABLE 8.3 Key differences between venture capital, growth equity, and LBO.

	Venture capital	Growth equity	LBO
Target company sales	€0–5m	€5–50m	€20m+
Target company profitability	Not profitable	Generally profitable	Profitable, with a history of positive EBITDA and cash flow
Fund's stake	Minority	Minority	Control
Fund's holding period	5–10 years	3–7 years	2–5 years
Fund's target IRR	35–50%+	30–40%	20–35%
Fund's target cash on cash (or money multiple)	5–10x	3–7x	2–5x
Sources of returns	Revenue growth	Revenue and profitability growth	Debt repayment and EBITDA growth
Product risk	Yes, high	No	No
Market risk	Yes, high	No	No
Entrepreneur/ management risk	Yes, high	Yes	Yes, but limited
Execution risk	Yes	Yes	Yes
Debt default risk	No	No/very limited	Yes
Risk of losing capital	High	Moderate	Low

Table 8.3 summarises the key differences among the three types of private equity investing.

INSTRUMENTS

Figure 8.1 breaks down the different products of the capital structure by debt and equity as a function of their use by private equity, private debt, and hybrid capital funds.

Typical product uses in growth equity deal structures are: ordinary shares, preferred shares, shareholders' loans, options and warrants, and convertible loans. Please refer to Chapter 2 for product descriptions and modelling examples.

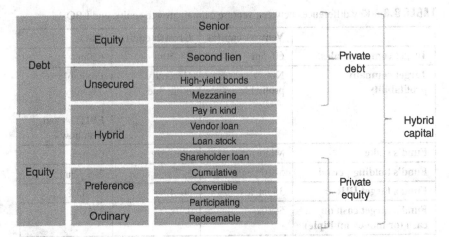

FIGURE 8.1 Products used by private capital funds in deal structuring.

FUNDAMENTALS #1: PRE-MONEY AND POST-MONEY VALUATION

The concept of pre-money and post-money valuation is always present in any growth equity deal. In essence, a growth equity transaction consists of a cash infusion in a company in return for newly issued shares of that company.

- pre-money value is the valuation of a company immediately before an injection of capital occurs;
- post-money value is the valuation of a company including the capital provided by the current round of financing.

Pre-money and post-money valuations are implied valuations since they are not an input to decide the purchase of a company but rather calculated as a result of a financing event.

In particular:

- pre-money: price paid per share in the financing round multiplied by the number of shares before the financing event;

$$Pre\text{-}money\ Valuation = Share\ Price * Pre\text{-}money\ Shares$$

$$(i.e.\ Share\ Price * Number\ of\ old\ Shares);$$

- post-money: price paid per share in the financing round multiplied by the number of shares after the financing event (i.e. includes old and new); it is obtained by dividing the cash infusion by the stake acquired:

$$Post\text{-}money\ Valutaion = Investment/Percent\ Ownership\ Acquired.$$

The total amount invested is just the share price times the number of shares issued. Thus:

$$Investment = Share\ Price\ *\ Shares\ Issued$$

(therefore *Share Price = Investment/Number of New Shares Issued*).

Unlike when one buys existing shares, the shares purchased in a growth equity (via share capital increase) investment are new shares, leading to a change in the number of shares outstanding. Thus:

$$Post\text{-}money\ Shares = Pre\text{-}money\ Shares + Shares\ Issued.$$

And because the only immediate effect of the transaction on the value of the company is to increase the amount of cash it has, the valuation after the transaction is just increased by the amount of that cash. Thus:

$$Post\text{-}money\ Valuation = Pre\text{-}money\ Valuation + Investment$$

therefore:

$$Pre\text{-}money\ Valuation = Post\text{-}money\ Value - Investment$$

and

$$Post\text{-}money\ Valuation = Total\ Shares\ (includes\ old\ and\ new)$$
$$*\ Share\ Price.$$

The portion of the company owned by the investors after the deal will just be the number of shares they purchased divided by the total shares outstanding. Thus:

$$Fraction\ Owned = Shares\ Issued/Post\text{-}money\ Shares.$$

Solving algebraically, we find that:

$$Fraction\ Owned = Investment/Post\text{-}money\ Valuation$$
$$= Investment/(Pre\text{-}money\ Valuation + Investment).$$

It should be noted that:

- if there are multiple investors, they must be treated as one in the calculations above;
- to determine an individual ownership fraction, divide the individual investment by the post-money valuation for the entire deal.

Since the above definitions and calculations are the bread and butter of a private equity investor, it is simple to remember that share price is easier to calculate with pre-money numbers, whilst fraction of ownership is easier to calculate with post-money numbers. To switch back and forth from pre-money to post-money valuations, one adds or subtracts the amount of the investment.

Let's now look at a simple example to review the concepts above.

A private equity fund proposes an investment of $2 million at $3 million pre money valuation). Therefore, since

Fraction Owned = Investment/Post-money Valuation

= Investment/(Pre-money Valuation + Investment)

the fund will own 40% of the company [$2m / ($3m + $2m)].

Assuming that there are 1.5 million shares outstanding prior to the investment, since

Share Price = Pre-money Valuation/Pre-money Shares

the price per share will be equal to $2.00 ($3m / 1.5m).

Therefore:

Shares Issued = Investment/Share Price

the number of shares issued is equal to 1m ($2m / $2.00).

In the case of multiple rounds of equity financing, equity owners look at the price step up, which is defined as the increase in share price from one round to the next. The formula to calculate the step-up is:

Step-up = New Round Share Price/Previous Round Share Price

Step-up = New Round Pre-money Valuation/

Previous Round Post-money Valuation.

In the example above, if we assume that the price per share pre-money was $1.5, then since

Step-up = New Round Share Price/Previous Round Share Price

the step-up would be 1.3 ($2 / $1.5); or

Step-up = New Round Pre-money Valuation/
Previous Round Post-money Valuation

the step-up would be 1.3 (3m / 2.25m).

Some express the step-up not as a multiple increase but as the percentage increase in share price or equity value. The formula then becomes:

*Step-up = [(New Round Share Price/Previous Round Share Price) – 1] * 100*

Step-up = [(New Round Pre-Money Valuation/

*Previous Round Post-Money Valuation) – 1] * 100.*

In this case:
the step-up would be 33% [($2 / $1.5) – 1] * 100; or

Step-up = New Round Pre-money Valuation/

Previous Round Post-money Valuation

the step-up would be 33% [(3m / 2.25m) – 1] * 100.

TABLE 8.4   Example of a capitalisation table with no price dilution.

	Founders' round		Round 1: $1.5m		Round 2: $2.5m	
	Shares	**% owned**	**Shares**	**% owned**	**Shares**	**% owned**
Private equity fund			1 500 000	48.0	1 500 000	26.7
Private equity fund - 2nd round					2 500 000	44.4
Option pool						
Subtotal			1 500 000	48.0	4 000 000	71.1
Private equity fund			1 500 000	48.0	4 000 000	71.1
Founders	1 625 000	100	1 625 000	52.0	1 625 000	28.9
TOTAL SHARES	**1 625 000**		**3 125 000**	**100.0**	**5 625 000**	**100.0**

Price per share (Cash in / New shares issued)		1.00	1.00	
Pre-money valuation	1 625 000	1 625 000	3 125 000	
Cash infusion	-	1 500 000	2 500 000	
Post-money valuation	1 625 000	3 125 000	5 625 000	

TABLE 8.5 Example of capitalisation table with option pool (issue option with no cash infusion).

	Founders' round		Round 1: $1.5 mln		Round 2: $2.5 mln		Option pool	
	Shares	% owned	Shares	% owned	Shares	% owned	Shares	% owned
Private equity fund			1 500 000	48.0	1 500 000	26.7	1 500 000	23.5
Private equity fund - 2nd round					2 500 000	44.4	2 500 000	39.2
Option pool							750 000	11.8
Subtotal			1 500 000	48.0	4 000 000	71.1	4 750 000	74.5
Private equity fund			1 500 000	48.0	4 000 000	71.1	4 000 000	62.7
Founders	1 625 000	100	1 625 000	52.0	1 625 000	28.9	1 625 000	25.5
TOTAL SHARES	1 625 000		3 125 000	100.0	5 625 000	100.0	6 375 000	

Price per share (Cash in / New shares issued)	1.00	1.00	1.00	1.00
Pre-money valuation	1 625 000	1 625 000	3 125 000	5 625 000
Cash infusion	-	1 500 000	2 500 000	-
Post-money valuation	1 625 000	3 125 000	5 625 000	6 375 000

FUNDAMENTALS #2: CAPITALISATION TABLE

A capitalisation table is a spreadsheet that shows ownership stakes in a company (including equity shares, preferred shares, and options) and the various prices paid by stakeholders for these securities on a fully diluted basis.

Let's now look (refer to Table. 8.4) at a simple case where a private equity fund invests $4m in two rounds ($1.5m in the first round and $2.5m in the second round) at the same share price of $1 where the founders do not invest alongside the fund and therefore their stake is diluted.

Growth equity investors will almost always require that the company set aside additional shares for a stock option plan for managers and key employees and these shares are set aside prior to the investment, diluting the founders/existing shareholders. Options are rights to purchase or sell shares of stock at a specific price within a specific period of time. Stock purchase options are commonly used as long-term incentive compensation for employees and management.

Assuming an option pool of 750 000 that converts into an equal amount of shares and without cash infusion, the capitalisation table would be the one represented in Table 8.5.

FUNDAMENTALS #3: DILUTION AND EQUITY STAKE CALCULATION

Dilution occurs when the private equity ownership is reduced by the issue of new shares (due to multiple equity rounds, exercise of options, mergers, etc.).

Defining:

PE post: stake held post cash infusion

PE prior: stake held pre cash infusion

x: stake acquired in round after 1st.

The cumulative stake of the private equity fund is equal to the prior cumulative stake multiplied by the percentage it has been diluted plus the percentage it has purchased in the equity round.

$$PEpost = PEprior \ (1-x) + x.$$

Therefore:

$$x = (PEpost - PEprior)/(1 - PEprior).$$

The following example (Table 8.6) illustrates three rounds of financing ($1m in Round 1, $1.5m in Round 2, and $2.5m in Round 3) at different prices ($1.22 in Round 1, $3.71 in Round 2, and $1.41 in Round 3). The stake owned at the end of each round and the step-up (-down) in value are calculated using the formulas above.

TABLE 8.6 Example of a capitalisation table with different share prices and step-up/-down in price.

	Founder round		Round 1		Round 2		Round 3	
	Shares	% owned	Shares	% owned	Shares	% owned	Shares	% owned
Private equity fund								
Round 1			818 182	45.0	818 182	36.8	818 182	20.5
Round 2					404 040	18.2	404 040	10.1
Round 3							1 777 778	44.4
Subtotal			818 182	45.0	1 222 222	55.0	3 000 000	75.0
Founders & others	1 000 000	100	1 000 000	55.0	1 000 000	45.0	1 000 000	25.0
TOTAL SHARES	1 000 000		1 818 182	100.0	2 222 222	100.0	4 000 000	100.0

	Round 1	Round 2	Round 3
Share price (=cash infusion/shares issued)	1.22	3.71	1.41
Step-up in value		204	-62
Pre-money valuation	1 222 222	6 750 000	3 125 000
Cash infusion	1 000 000	1 500 000	2 500 000
Post-money valuation	2 222 222	8 250 000	5 625 000

FUNDAMENTALS #4: ANTI-DILUTION PROVISIONS

Private equity funds are concerned with down rounds (financing rounds that value the company's stock at a lower price per share than previous rounds); therefore, they usually negotiate anti-dilution provisions to protect their investment.

The anti-dilution provision protects investors from dilution caused by new stock issues at a price that is lower than the investor's original investment. Such dilutions are common for companies with capitalisation tables that have a large number of options and convertible securities.

The two most common mechanisms are full ratchets and weighted average ratchets.

A 'full ratchet' provision is the simplest type of anti-dilution provision but it is the most burdensome on the common stockholders and it can have significant negative effects on later stock issuances. Full ratchet works by simply reducing the conversion price of the existing options or preferred to the price at which new shares are issued in a later round. Full-ratchet anti-dilution protection therefore allows an investor to have his percentage ownership remain the same as the initial investment and has the effect of protecting the ratchet holder's investment by automatically increasing his number of shares. Of course, this occurs at the expense of any stockholders who do not also enjoy full ratchet protection.

Weighted average provisions are considered to be less harsh than full ratchets. In general, the weighted average method adjusts the investor's conversion price downward based on the number of shares in the new (dilutive) issue. If relatively few new shares are issued, then the conversion price will not drop too much and common stockholders will not be rammed down as severely as with a full ratchet. If there are several new shares and the new issue price is highly dilutive to earlier investors, then the conversion price will drop more.

Let's look at a full ratchet example starting with the initial ownership situation depicted in Table 8.7.

The company seeks funding from an outside investor (Private Equity Fund #2), who is willing to invest $1 million at $0.10 per share.

TABLE 8.7 Initial ownership structure with two shareholders and two instruments.

Initial situation					
Investor	Instrument	Investment	Shares	Share price	Stake owned (%)
Founders	Ordinary shares	50 000	5 000 000	0.0100	56
Private Equity Fund #1	Convertible preferred	2 000 000	4 000 000	0.5000	44
TOTAL			**9 000 000**		**100**

TABLE 8.8 Ownership situation with full ratchet of one investor and entry of a second investor.

Full ratchet for Private Equity Fund #1					
Investor	Instrument	Investment	Shares	Share price	Stake owned (%)
Founders	Ordinary shares	50 000	5 000 000	0.0100	14
Private Equity Fund #1	Convertible preferred	2 000 000	20 000 000	0.1000	57
Private equity fund #2	Convertible preferred	1 000 000	10 000 000	0.1000	29
TOTAL			35 000 000		100

Assuming that Private Equity Fund #1's convertible preferred shares carry a full ratchet (see Table 8.8b), the ratchet reprices the Private Equity Fund #1 convertible preferred stock at $0.10 per share, giving Private Equity Fund #1 a total of 20m total shares [$2m (original investment) / $0.10 (new share price)].

Note that Private Equity Fund #1 now owns 57% of the company, Private Equity Fund #2 owns 29%, and the founders have been rounded down to only 14%.

The valuation is calculated as follows:

Post-money = $1m (Investment) / 29% (Ownership Acquired) = $3.5m

Post-money = 35m (New Total Shares) * $0.10 (Price Per Share) = $3.5m

Pre-money = 25m (Previous Total Shares, applying ratchet but excluding new shares) * $0.10 (Share Price) = $2.5m

Pre-money = $3.5m (Post-money Valuation) − $1m (Investment) = $2.5m.

Let's look now at the weighted average ratchet. A typical form is the following.

Assuming:

A^1 = number of shares outstanding before the dilutive event (i.e. new issue)

C = number of shares that would have been issued at the old conversion price for the investment in the dilutive round

D = number of shares actually issued in the dilutive round

The new conversion price = $(A + C) / (A + D)$ * old conversion price.

---

[1]The number of shares can be on a fully-diluted basis or simply taking into account only preferred stock (hence omitting options outstanding).

TABLE 8.9 Ownership situation with weighted ratchet of one investor and entry of a second investor.

Weighted average ratchet for Private Equity Fund #1					
Investor	Instrument	Investment	Shares	Share price	Stake owned (%)
Founders	Ordinary shares	50 000	5 000 000	0.0100	23
Private Equity Fund #1	Convertible preferred	2 000 000	6 909 091	0.289	32
Private Equity Fund #2	Convertible preferred	1 000 000	10 000 000	0.1000	46
TOTAL			21 909 091		

The initial ownership structure is the same as in Table 8.7.

The company seeks funding from an outside investor (Private Equity Fund #2), who is willing to invest $1 million at $0.10 per share. Assuming that Private Equity Fund #1 convertible preferred shares carry a weighted average ratchet (see Table 8.9), applying the weighted average formula:

A = 9m (Number of Shares before the B Round)

C = $1m (New Investment) / $0.50 (Old Conversion Price) = 2m (Number of Shares that would have been issued at the old conversion price)

D = 10 000 000 (New Shares actually issued)

New conversion price = (11m / 19m) * $0.50 per share = $0.289 per share.

Therefore, Private Equity Fund #1 receives 2 909 091 new shares ($2m / $0.289 – 4m).

Note that Private Equity Fund #1 now owns 32% of the company, Private Equity Fund #2 owns 46%, and the founders have been rounded down to only 23%.

FUNDAMENTALS #5: STRUCTURING FOR EXIT (ORDINARY SHARES VS. OTHER INSTRUMENTS)

Although a technical description of the financial instruments used in an equity transaction has already been given in Chapter 3, we focus in this section on a practical example to show the impact of financial structuring in a growth equity transaction.

Let's start by looking at ordinary shares (Table 8.10).

TABLE 8.10 Exit example in presence of private equity fund owning ordinary shares.

Scenario 1: ordinary shares					
Investor	**Instrument**	**Investment**	**Shares**	**Share price**	**Stake owned (%)**
Entrepreneur	Ordinary shares	50 000	6 000 000	0.0083	67
Private Equity Fund #1	Ordinary shares	2 000 000	3 000 000	0,6667	33
TOTAL			9 000 000		

Sale of the company for		4 000 000			
Proceeds to entrepreneur		2 666 667			
Proceeds to Private Equity Fund #1		1 333 333			
Capital gain/(loss) for entrepreneur		2 616 667			
Capital gain/(loss) for Private Equity Fund #1		(666 667)			

It is of course unlikely that a wise investor would accept being forced to sell at any price, and so potentially incur a loss. Typically, a growth equity investor would use an instrument to protect their investment against a sale at a price below the investment cost (so called downside protection).

Let's look at the outcome with convertible preferred shares (Table 8.11).

In this case, the fund – unlike in Scenario 1 – would not incur a loss. The fund would not convert its instrument until the sale price (pro quota) allows recovery of investment. For prices above its investment cost, the fund would have the incentive to convert.

Let's look at the outcome with participating preferred (Table 8.12). Participating preferred shares are composed of two elements: preferred and ordinary shares. The preferred share element entitles the fund to receive a pre-determined sum of cash (usually the original investment plus any accrued dividends) when

TABLE 8.11 Exit example in presence of private equity fund owning convertible preferred.

Scenario 2: convertible preferred					
Investor	Instrument	Investment	Shares	Share price	Stake owned (%)
Entrepreneur	Ordinary shares	50 000	6 000 000	0.0083	67
Private Equity Fund #1	Convertible Preferred	2 000 000	3 000 000	0,6667	33
TOTAL			9 000 000		

Sale of the company for		4 000 000			
Proceeds to entrepreneur		2 000 000			
Proceeds to Private Equity Fund #1		2 000 000			
Capital gain/(loss) for entrepreneur		1 950 000			
Capital gain/(loss) for Private Equity Fund #1		–			

the company is sold or liquidated, whilst the ordinary share continues to enjoy any remaining proceeds available to the common shareholder class.

Both convertible preferred and participating preferred shares usually convert to ordinary shares (without triggering the participating feature) if the company goes public (IPO).

Let's look (see Table 8.13) at the outcome with a liquidation preference that provides preferred shareholders a multiple (2x, 3x, or above) of their original investment if the company is sold or liquidated. A multiple liquidation preference still allows the investor to convert to common stock if the company does well, and it provides a higher return (assuming the selling price is sufficient to cover the multiple) if an IPO is unlikely.

TABLE 8.12 Exit example in presence of private equity fund owning participating preferred.

Scenario 3: participating preferred					
Investor	Instrument	Investment	Shares	Share price	Stake owned (%)
Entrepreneur	Ordinary shares	50 000	6 000 000	0.0083	67
Private Equity Fund #1	Participating Preferred	2 000 000	3 000 000	0,6667	33
TOTAL			9 000 000		

Sale of the company for		4 000 000			
Proceeds to entrepreneur		1 333 333			
Proceeds to Private Equity Fund #1		2 666 667			
Capital gain/(loss) for entrepreneur		1 283 333			
Capital gain/(loss) for Private Equity Fund #1		666 667			

FUNDAMENTALS #6: REDEMPTION

In addition to the traditional exit strategies, growth equity investors often offer the entrepreneur an additional exit route: redemption. In this strategy, investors have the right to require the company to purchase or redeem their shares after a negotiated period of time if no liquidity event has occurred. This feature is subject to statutory or law limitations that preclude redemptions unless the company can make the purchase out of its equity reserves.

TABLE 8.13   Exit example in presence of private equity fund owning, participating preferred.

Scenario 4: liquidation preference at 2x of the orginal investment of the fund					
Investor	Instrument	Investment	Shares	Share price	Stake owned (%)
Entrepreneur	Ordinary shares	50 000	6 000 000	0.0083	67
Private Equity Fund #1	Convertible Preferred	2 000 000	3 000 000	0,6667	33
TOTAL			**9 000 000**		

Sale of the company for		4 000 000			
Proceeds to entrepreneur		0			
Proceeds to Private Equity Fund #1		4 000 000			
Capital gain/(loss) for entrepreneur		−50 000			
Capital gain/(loss) for Private Equity Fund #1		2 000 000			

FUNDAMENTALS #7: THE GROWTH CAPITAL METHOD (ADAPTED FROM THE VENTURE CAPITAL METHOD)

The starting point here is to understand how a growth equity fund thinks. In essence:

- it intends to invest the least amount possible at the minimum pre-money valuation;
- it wants to sell the company at the highest possible price in the shortest possible time;
- it identifies the inherent risks in a transaction and its mitigants.

In practice, a growth equity fund performs the following steps:

1. development of a business plan (income statement, balance sheet, and pre-money cash flow statement);
2. determination of share capital increase needed to achieve the objectives of the business plan;
3. calculation of the return (in monetary terms) required by the fund (on the basis of the IRR target of the fund and of the expected holding period) at the end of the expected holding period;
4. determination of the post-money value of the company (typically using the multiples method);
5. calculation of the shareholding stake to be held to achieve the IRR objective.

In formulas this can be written as follows.
Let's define:

R = the return (in monetary terms) required by the fund at the end of the expected holding period

I = investment (i.e. share capital increase) required to achieve the objectives of the business plan

IRR = the IRR required by the Fund

t = expected holding period

V = equity value of the whole Target at exit

S = shareholding stake to be held by the Fund in order to achieve the IRR objective

PRE = pre-money value of the Target

$POST$ = post-money value of the Target

y = number of shares required by the Fund to achieve its target IRR

x = number of existing shares

p = price per share.

The steps are:

1) Calculate the return (in monetary terms) required by the Fund at the end of the expected holding period to achieve its required return (in terms of IRR):

$$R = I * (1 + IRR)^t.$$

2) Calculate the post-money equity value of the company at exit (typically using the multiples method): V.

3) Determine the share of ownership S required by the Fund to achieve its target IRR:

$$S = R/V.$$

4) Calculate the number of shares required by the Fund to achieve its required ownership stake:

$$y = x * [S/(1 - S)].$$

5) Determine the price per share:

$$p = I/y.$$

Therefore, we obtain:

$$POST = I/S \text{ [or } POST = p * (x + y)]$$
$$PRE = POST - I \text{ (or } PRE = p * x).$$

In the case that during the holding period of the Fund there are more than one share capital increases and there is a dilution of the initial stake owned by the Fund, the share of ownership S should be adjusted for the dilution. For example, let's assume two rounds in which 25% and 30% respectively are underwritten by a third party and an S equal to 10%: the shareholding stake S of the formula above should be adjusted as follows: $S/(1 + 0.25)/(1 + 0.3) = 6.15\%$.

In general terms, let's define:

$D1$ = expected dilution in round 1 (subsequent to round 0 when the Fund has become shareholder);

$D2$ = expected dilution in round 2 (subsequent to round 1 and round 0).

$$Sadj = S/(1 + D1)/(1 + D2).$$

RR = $Sadj/S$ as the retention ratio, whereby $Sadj$ is the final stake owned by the Fund after the dilution effect (in the example above $RR = 6.15\% / 10\% = 61.5\%$).

The formula under step 3 above would therefore be modified by using Sadj instead of S as:

$$Sadj = S/V.$$

Determine the share of ownership S required by the Fund to achieve its target IRR:

$$S = R/V.$$

Table 8.14 illustrates a simple growth capital method case with one financing round.

TABLE 8.14   Growth capital method with one financing round.

Investment ($m) required – input from business plan (*a*):	2.0
Target IRR of the Fund % (*b*):	30.0
Holding period (years) of the investee from the Fund (*c*):	5
EBITDA ($m) at Exit (i.e. after 5 years) – input from business plan (*d*):	2.6
EBITDA multiple (x) at Exit (*e*):	6.0
Cash ($m) at Exit – input from business plan (*f*):	2.4
Debt ($m) at Exit – input from business plan (*g*):	5.0

On the basis of the above, we obtain

Return ($m) required by the Fund [$h = (a*(1 + b)^c)$]:	7.4
Enterprise ($m) Value at Exit [$i = d*e$]:	15.5
Equity ($m) Value at Exit [$j = (i + f - g)$]:	12.9
Ownership stake needed to achieve the required return [$k = h/j$]:	57.6%

Given the above, we obtain the valuation today of the Target above which the Fund would jeopardise its returns:

Equity ($m) post-money value [$l = a/k$]:	3.47

FUNDAMENTALS #8: CALCULATION OF THE PRICE PER SHARE

In order to obtain the price per share that the Fund shall have to pay to acquire the stake, the analyst should divide pre-money valuation of the company by the number of shares before the round of financing.

In other words:

$$p1 = PRE/x.$$

FUNDAMENTALS #9: PUT AND CALL OPTIONS

An option is a legal instrument which – in exchange for a payment made or value given – conveys the legal right but not the obligation to buy or sell an asset at a future date or during a future period at an agreed price or using an agreed formula.

A put option entitles the holder of an asset to sell it for the agreed price, whilst a call option entitles the holder of the option to acquire an asset for the agreed price. By its nature, an option entitles the holder to exercise discretion at a later date. The ability to defer a decision has a value, as does the price of entry vs. current estimate of future value.

The value is normally a function of:

- the value of the underlying asset;
- the price at which the option can be exercised (the strike price);
- the length of time during which the option can be exercised;
- the uncertainty over the future value of the underlying asset (i.e. volatility).

The option only has value if the counterparty can be expected to fulfil its obligations.

As well as a value, an option generally has a cost (the 'premium'). The premium can be paid through:

- the simultaneous granting of a call option;
- a lower debt margin than without the option;
- willingness to put more capital at risk;
- payment of a higher entry price (due to security of exit route);
- being prepared to stay committed for longer.

Options are used for the following.

a) To become further/more deeply involved in a transaction by deferring an equity entry decision. In this case, the call is used to obtain a right to purchase equity at a pre-agreed value or by a pre-agreed formula as part of a convertible loan/equity instrument or a loan.

b) To achieve an exit from a transaction where the exit options are limited. In this case, the put option is used to establish both a time and a price or a formula under which a price is established. There are two reasons to use put options to make exits:

a. to identify an exit counterparty and achieve a hedge due to uncertainty about performance outcome;

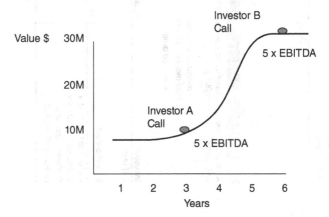

FIGURE 8.2 Example of two investors with a call option at the same valuation price but different timing exercise.

Initial situation

Shareholders	Equity		%	Equity Value
	Share capital	Share premium		
A (Founder)	4.50	0.00	60.00%	6.00
B (Founder)	3.00	0.00	40.00%	4.00
Total	7.50	0.00	100.00%	10.00

NFP	4.00
EV	14.00
EBITDA	2.50
EV/EBITDA	5.60 X

Step 1 (Y1)

A Financial Investor subscribes to a share capital increase for USD 3M, o/w USD 2M qualified in ordinary equity and USD 1M qualified in preferred equity (return 20%).

Pre-money EqValue	10.00
Post-money EqValue	13.00
Preferred dividend	20%

Investor	Invested ordinary	% total share capital	Invested preferred	% total share capital
C (Fund)	2.00	15.38%	1.00	7.69%

Shareholders	Equity		%	Preferred dividend	Proportional Equity Value	Total Equity Value
	Share capital	Share premium				
A (Founder) - Ordinary	4.50	0.00	46.15%		6.00	6.00
B (Founder) - Ordinary	3.00	0.00	30.77%		4.00	4.00
C (Fund) - Ordinary	1.50	0.50	15.38%		2.00	2.00
C (Fund) - Preferred	0.75	0.25	7.69%	0.00	1.00	1.00
Total	9.75	0.75	100.00%		13.00	13.00

NFP	1.00
EV	14.00
EBITDA	2.50
EV/EBITDA	5.60 X

Dilution Founders	-23.08%

FIGURE 8.3 Growth equity structuring: a modelling example.

Step 2 (Y2)

The Fund subscribes to a share capital increase for USD 5M. The number of new shares to be issued is calculated based on required return method.

Investment amount	5.00	Assumed Exit EBITDA	8.50
Target Annual Return (%)	18.0%	Assumed Exit EV/EBITDA	5.60 X
Assumed Exit Timing (Y)	5	Assumed Exit NFP	6.00
Target Ownership Value at Exit	11.44	Assumed Exit EqValue	41.60
Target Ownership % at Exit	**28.23%**	o/w preferred dividend	1.07
Implied post-money valuation	17.71	o/w to equity	40.53
Implied pre-money valuation	12.71		

Investor	Invested ordinary	% ordinary
C (Fund)	5.00	28.23%

	Equity						
Shareholders	Share capital	Share premium	%	Preferred dividend	Proportional equity value	Total equity value
A (Founder) - Ordinary	4.50	0.00	33.13%		5.80	5.80
B (Founder) - Ordinary	3.00	0.00	22.08%		3.87	3.87
C (Fund) - Ordinary - Y1 investment	1.50	0.50	11.04%		1.93	1.93
C (Fund) - Ordinary - Y2 investment	3.83	1.17	28.23%		4.94	4.94
C (Fund) - Preferred	0.75	0.25	5.52%	0.20	0.97	1.17
Total	13.58	1.92	100.00%		17.51	17.71

NFP	1.50
EV	19.21
EBITDA	3.50
EV/EBITDA	5.49 X

Dilution Previous Investments	-28.23%

FIGURE 8.3 (Continued)

Step 3 (Y3)

A, B and C subscribe to a pro-rata (calculated on share capital, ordinary and preferred) convertible bond for USD 2M, convertible after 1 year in shares (1,3 share: 1 bond).

Investment amount	2.00	Assumed pre-money EqValue	20.00
Conversion ratio	1.30	Assumed post-money EqValue	20.00
Conversion timing	4		

Shareholders	Equity Share capital	Share premium	%	Preferred dividend	Proportional equity value	Total equity value
A (Founder) - Ordinary	4.50	0.00	33.13%		6.48	6.48
B (Founder) - Ordinary	3.00	0.00	22.08%		4.32	4.32
C (Fund) - Ordinary - Y1 investment	1.50	0.50	11.04%		2.16	2.16
C (Fund) - Ordinary - Y2 investment	3.83	1.17	28.23%		5.52	5.52
C (Fund) - Preferred	0.75	0.25	5.52%	0.44	1.08	1.52
Total	13.58	1.92	100.00%		19.56	20.00

NFP	3.00
EV	23.00
EBITDA	4.00
EV/EBITDA	5.75 X

Convertible bondholders	Bond amount	%
A (Founder)	0.66	33.13%
B (Founder)	0.44	22.08%
C (Fund)	0.90	44.79%
Total	2.00	100.00%

Dilution Previous Investments	0.00%

FIGURE 8.3 (Continued)

Step 4 (Y4)

Convertible bond is converted and it is exercised an Option Pool by the CEO.

Assumed Y4 EBITDA	7.00
Assumed Y4 EV/EBITDA	5.60 X
Assumed Y4 NFP	2.00
EqV pre-money	37.20
o/w preferred dividend	0.73
o/w to equity	36.47
EqV post-money	39.20 >> + bond amount converted, as not anymore in NFP

Share capital increase by conversion of the bonds	2.60
CEO Option Pool (%)	3% >> pre conversion of the bonds
Capital increase for Option Pool	0.42

Shareholders	Equity Share capital	Share premium	Preferred dividend	%	Proportional equity value	Total equity value
A (Founder) - Ordinary	5.36	0.00		32.29%	12.42	12.42
B (Founder) - Ordinary	3.57	0.00		21.53%	8.28	8.28
C (Fund) - Ordinary - Y1 investment	1.50	0.50		9.03%	3.48	3.48
C (Fund) - Ordinary - Y2 investment	3.83	1.17		23.09%	8.88	8.88
C (Fund) - Ordinary - conversion bond	1.16			7.01%	2.70	2.70
C (Fund) - Preferred	0.75	0.25	0.73	4.52%	1.74	2.47
CEO	0.42			2.53%	0.97	0.97
Total	16.60	1.92		100.00%	38.47	39.20

NFP	0.00
EV	39.20
EBITDA	7.00
EV/EBITDA	5.60 X

FIGURE 8.3 (*Continued*)

Step 5 (Y5)

Exit from the investment.

Assumed Exit EBITDA	8.50
Assumed Exit EV/EBITDA	5.60 X
Assumed Exit NFP	6.00
Assumed Exit EqValue	41.60

Return Sensitivity

A (Founder)

	Exit EqValue		
	40	45	50
Implied EV/EBITDA	5.41 X	6.00 X	6.59 X
IRR	26.46%	30.51%	34.22%
MoM	2.43	2.75	3.06

B (Founder)

	Exit EqValue		
	40	45	50
Implied EV/EBITDA	5.41 X	6.00 X	6.59 X
IRR	26.46%	30.51%	34.22%
MoM	2.43	2.75	3.06

C (Fund)

	Exit EqValue		
	40	45	50
Implied EV/EBITDA	5.41 X	6.00 X	6.59 X
IRR	24.13%	28.47%	32.47%
MoM	2.03	2.28	2.52

FIGURE 8.3 (Continued)

A payout timeline

EqV	1	2	3	4	5
40	−4.50	0.00	−0.66	0.00	12.57
45	−4.50	0.00	−0.66	0.00	14.18
50	−4.50	0.00	−0.66	0.00	15.80

B payout timeline

EqV	1	2	3	4	5
40	−3.00	0.00	−0.44	0.00	8.38
45	−3.00	0.00	−0.44	0.00	9.46
50	−3.00	0.00	−0.44	0.00	10.53

C payout timeline

EqV	1	2	3	4	5
40	−3.00	−5.00	−0.90	0.00	18.07
45	−3.00	−5.00	−0.90	0.00	20.25
50	−3.00	−5.00	−0.90	0.00	22.43

FIGURE 8.3 (*Continued*)

b. to identify an exit counterparty but still take performance risk. Performance risk is taken when the formula includes the 'fair market value', multiples of EBITDA, net asset value, independent appraisal, etc.

In many transactions, there are a combination of puts and calls. Multiple puts and calls will have a variety of potential outcomes, some of them inter-related. A symmetrical put and call arrangement is very unlikely to have a symmetrical financial outcome (see Figure 8.2 for an example).

If Investor B has a put at a value of 5 × EBITDA between Years 3 and 6, the rational choice would be for Investor B to exercise the option at the end of Year 6. However, they will only receive 1/3 of value (or €20m less) if there is a symmetrical call for Investor A to purchase Investor B's shares at 5 × EBITDA in the same period. The value of Investor B's put has been compromised. Asymmetrical options in terms of periods, multiples, and formulas need to be used to conserve the value to Investor B.

Growth Equity structuring: a modelling example

An example of growth equity structuring is reproduced in Figure 8.3 (the accompanying Excel file is downloadable from the book's companion website).

REFERENCES AND FURTHER READING

C. Blaydon and F. Wainwright. 2001. *Note on Securities and Deal Structure*. Tuck Business School.

L.A. Cyr. 2002. 'A Note on Pre-Money and Post-Money Valuation.' Harvard Business School Note 9-801-446.

J. Levin. 2001. *Structuring Venture Capital, Private Equity and Entrepreneurial Transactions*. Aspen Publishers.

SUGGESTED CASES

Malcom Baker. 2015. 'Corning, 2002.' Harvard Business School Case 216-037.

P.A. Gompers, J.D. Kim, and V. Mukharlyamov. 2012. 'United Capital Partners (A).' Harvard Business School Case 213-044.

H. Kent Bowen and R. Bradley Staats. 2005. 'Bayside Motion Group (A).' Harvard Business School Case 605-040.

C. Rymbrandt. 2014. *Palamon Capital Partners/TeamSystem*. Darden Business Publishing, UVA-F-1331.

William A. Sahlman, Joseph B. Lassiter III, and Liz Kind. 2011. 'Verengo Solar Plus!' Harvard Business School Case 812-049.

CHAPTER 9

Leveraged Buyout

INTRODUCTION

A leveraged buyout (LBO) is the acquisition of a whole company or a division thereof (the 'Target') financed with an above average level of debt (usually secured). Debt is provided by one or more 'acquisition finance' houses (usually banks), is repaid by the Target's cash flow (and sometimes also upon the sale of selected Target's assets), and is secured against the Target's assets. Equity is provided by a private equity fund (the 'Sponsor'), which takes a relatively small equity investment risk; the Sponsor's objective is to realise an adequate return on its equity investment upon exit (typically through a sale or IPO of the Target). Management usually retains a shareholding that is often incentivised.

There are various types of buyout:

- **management/leveraged buyout, also referred to as (M)LBO:** managers acquire a business they have been managing and voting control after the buy-out lies with the management team;
- **management buy-in (MBI):** the management does not already work for the target company, but is taken on by the Sponsor, and will co-invest alongside;
- **leveraged build up/platform buyout/roll on:** buyout with the intention of making further synergistic acquisitions;
- **sponsored spin out:** a new company is owned by the previous owners;
- **leveraged recap(italisation):** a company borrows money in order to make a cash payout to existing shareholders.

In general narrative terms the elements of a typical LBO can be summarised as follows: the first stage involves raising the necessary funds (debt and equity) and establishing a management incentive system. Normally the investor group (led by the Sponsor and the company's top management) provides 30–50% of the price paid (also called the 'Transaction Value'), while the remainder is provided by the lenders (banks, specialised debt providers, and/or capital market). At the second stage, the Sponsor purchases all (or the vast majority) of the outstanding shares of the Target or the assets of the company. At the third stage, the management implements operating efficiencies (cost cutting, asset optimisation) and executes eventual growth strategies (mainly via acquisitions) so as to increase profits and cash flow. In the last stage (after the majority or whole acquisition/LBO debt has been repaid), the Sponsor sells the Target. Financial sponsors generally seek to exit in three to five years. There must be a clear route to exit, to be established before the close of the deal: potential exit routes include IPO, trade sale, leveraged recapitalisation, and break-up.

An LBO falls therefore in the category of acquisition financing (money lent by a group of banks for the purpose of M&A). There are, though, a number of transaction features that distinguish an LBO from acquisition financing, including:

- principal is a private equity financier (financial sponsor) usually acting with elements of an existing or new management team;
- usually, a Special Purpose Vehicle ('NewCo') is established to purchase the target for limited liability reasons; i.e. to prevent lenders against the newly acquired assets from having any claim on other (existing) assets of the buyer;
- capital structure of the 'NewCo' will be geared with an above average level of debt;
- any gap between what banks will lend as senior debt and what financial sponsors and management will provide as equity can be filled with intermediate or mezzanine capital, such as subordinated debt with warrants; alternatively, the 'NewCo' can issue a high-yield bond, typically providing a layer of subordinated capital that may continue well after the sponsor has exited the investment;
- sometimes, management participation is extended to all employees of the target ('employee buyout'), which can bring significant tax advantages.

From a historical perspective, LBOs saw massive popularity in the 1980s when sleeping, public, large corporations with established market position and massive cash generation were poorly managed (e.g. not focused on core, highly inefficient, overly diversified) by overpaid managers. In this context, some private equity players (e.g. KKR) took leadership in the large ticket LBO market, often via hostile and aggressive takeover. This first LBO phase was dominated by the 'break-up' model, where a large amount of debt was repaid shortly after the LBO via sale of non-core assets. In the 1990s, strategic LBOs emerged, where lower debt levels prevailed in order not to depress earnings per share (EPS), to allow the company's growth and allow an exit via an IPO. In the mid-2000s, the LBO level was largely driven by low interest rates, availability of debt financing, and easy lending policies. Over the last decades, the LBO demand has been driven by the development of innovative financing techniques (e.g. securitisation) and markets (e.g. junk bonds/high-yield) and fund dry powder, whilst LBO supply has been mostly represented by hostile takeovers, sale of non-core/marginal business, sale of family businesses, and need for cash by parent.

LBO: KEY CONCEPTS

A typical LBO candidate

The typical LBO candidate is an established company that has the following characteristics.

- **Stable operating cash flow:** the ability to generate significant, resilient, and predictable cash flow is the key element of any LBO candidate. Therefore, companies operating in regulated or mature or niche sectors with high barriers to entry, established and recurring customer base, and long-term sales contracts are typical LBO candidates. Limited maintenance capex companies are also usually sought as LBO candidates.

- **Established position:** financing buyouts by way of additional leverage is easier in established firms. Monitoring use of financial resources is less difficult in firms with limited resources and capital expenditure requirements. Moreover, it is unlikely there will be any moral hazard toward debtors as established firms with stable cash flows have limited opportunity or motivation to redeploy assets so as to increase risk. Additionally, in established industries, the company assets have greater market value because secondary markets for corporate assets are more efficient. This increases the ability to raise secured debt.

- **Leading market share:** high (relative) market share usually implies an established customer base (in relationships driven industries), a strong brand (in premium category sectors), and a better relative cost positioning (in commodity style industries). All these key success factors increase the stability and predictability of a company's cash flow.

- **Significant assets:** a strong asset base can be used as a collateral to the benefit of lenders, thus reducing their risk of losses in the event of default. The combination of cash flow stability and predictability with a significant target's asset base is particularly important in an LBO, because the value of the assets is used to calculate both the debt capacity and the recovery of each debt instrument in a distressed scenario. Furthermore, a strong asset base usually implies high barriers to entry because of the substantial capital investment required, which serves as a deterrent to new entrants.

- **Management team with a proven track record:** industry experience and the capability to manage a highly leveraged capital structure and reach ambitious performance targets are the key requirements for a successful LBO management team. Prior successful experience in operating under such conditions, as well as M&A and post-integration skills, are highly sought after by sponsors. It is a market standard in LBO transactions that the management retain/invest a meaningful amount ('skin in the game') as well as be granted an equity stake to align incentives with the Sponsor.

■ **Operating improvements:** companies with cost-cutting improvements (e.g. cutting corporate overhead, streamlining operations, reducing head-count, etc.), asset optimisation (disposal of non-core business units, sale of non-instrumental real estate, etc.), and other efficiencies (improvement in terms with customers and suppliers, rationalising the supply chain, etc.) that increase EBITDA and improve cash generation are interesting LBO candidates.

Other desirable characteristics for an LBO target are companies operating in mature industries with no rapid technological change within the industry, limited technological threats from adjacent sectors, and quality customers.

A final point on companies with growth potential/opportunities: histori-cally these were seen as second-best candidates since rapid growth typically requires increased investment in plant and equipment and requires additional working capital to finance increasing levels of accounts receivable and inventory (thus consuming too much cash to be able to take on more debt); slow-growth companies, on the other hand, can reduce their weighted average costs of capital and increase returns on equity by replacing equity with debt. However, over the years (also in coincidence with global competition coming from low-cost countries that has reduced low hanging fruit LBO candidates with strong market position and cash flow generation), Sponsors are increas-ingly looking for companies with growth potential, both organically and through acquisitions. Consolidation strategies (whereby a Sponsor, starting from an LBO target, creates a larger player via acquisitions) are very often used to create larger companies, with increased size, scale, and efficiency: all these attributes generate higher amounts of cash (available for debt repayment), higher EBITDA (hence enterprise value), and might accelerate exit timing.

In this sense, the capital structure of LBOs has changed over the years: the Sponsor decides in fact not to maximise the amount of LBO debt financing (hence lower acquisition debt levels at closing) and requests either committed (capex or acquisition) facilities to pursue growth or flexibility in the legal document, or covenants to accommodate for further debt facilities.

LBOs normally occur as a result of one of three scenarios:

a) a going-private transaction
b) a corporate divestiture
c) a sale of a private company.

The common characteristics of these three LBO scenarios are as follows:

a) **Going-private transaction (stock transaction):**
  • book value of assets is at historical levels as opposed to replacement cost;
  • market value of equity is attractive vis-à-vis current market multiples of comparable public companies;

- buyer can accumulate or tender for shares at a reasonable premium to market price;
- opportunity to de-conglomerate at good business-unit sale values;
- company is managed by corporate stewards rather than by owner-entrepreneurs;
- alternative to leveraged recapitalisation.

b) **Corporate divestiture (stock or asset transaction):**
- book value of assets is at historical levels as opposed to replacement cost;
- not 'core' business of parent company;
- corporate over-management, bureaucracy, and excessive corporate over-head allocations or corporate carelessness and insufficient funding;
- alternative to spin-off, IPO, leveraged recapitalisation, or liquidation;
- opportunity for seller financing, reinvestment, or earn-out.

c) **Private sale (stock or asset transaction):**
- book value of assets is at historical levels as opposed to replacement cost;
- inflated owner expenses represent cost-cutting opportunity;
- insufficient financing in the past;
- opportunity for negotiated purchase price and ability to acquire particular assets;
- company management retiring or lacking depth, new owner can take to 'next level'.

Step by step construction of an LBO

The basic concept of an LBO structure can be summarised as follows.

PHASE 1

1) Sponsor sets up NewCo with €/$33.3m.
2) NewCo receives a bridge loan from short-term lenders of €/$66.7m.
3) NewCo pays €/$97.0m for shares of the Target.
4) NewCo gives Target's shares as a pledge to short-term lenders.
5) Sponsor gives NewCo's shares as a pledge to short-term lenders.
6) NewCo pays €/$3.0m to consultants.
7) Very often there is outstanding debt in the Target (mostly for working capital needs). The Target's working capital debt before acquisition may appear in various forms:
   - a secured revolving credit loan from an outside lender;
   - a parent's inter-company transfers, either with or without interest;
   - bank letters of credit or guarantees to secure purchases from suppliers.
      The first three types of debt will probably have to be refinanced at the closing of the deal, due to covenants on existing debt. Both secured and unsecured revolvers will tie up assets and obstruct plans for secured acquisition financing.

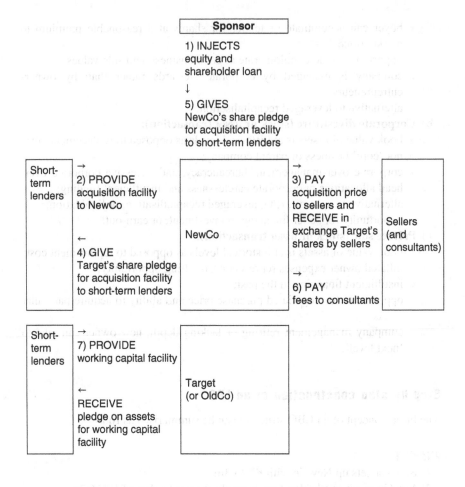

Assuming a very simple balance sheet of the Target (assets of €/\$20m, liabilities of €/\$10m, equity of €/\$10m), at the end of steps 1 and 2 above we would have:

NewCo

| Cash 100.0 | Equity 33.3 |
| | Financial debt 66.7 |

Target

| Assets 20.0 | Equity 10.0 |
| | Liabilities 10.0 |

At the end of step 6, and assuming that transaction costs are capitalised (thus increasing the acquisition cost of the Target), we would have:

NewCo

Target's shares 100.0	Equity 33.3
	Financial debt 66.7

Target

Assets 20.0	Equity 10.0
	Liabilities 10.0

PHASE 2

8) NewCo and Target merge.
9) The bridge loan of Phase 1 to NewCo is fully repaid via a new long-term facility (for the same amount and by the same lenders) and receives a full security package (assets, shares) over Target's assets and shares.
10) The medium/long-term loan is repaid over time by the cash flow of MergeCo.

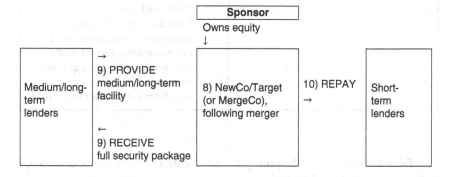

At the end of step 8, as a result of the merger, the Target's shares (€/$100m in NewCo's balance sheet) disappear as well as the Target's equity (€/$10m). The merger deficit[1] (€/$90m) is allocated to goodwill.

MergeCo

Target's assets 20.0	Equity 33.3
Goodwill 90.0	Financial debt 66.7
	Target's liabilities 10.0

---

[1]Difference between the purchase price (€/$100m) and the Target's equity (€/$10m).

TABLE 9.1 Sources and uses table of an LBO.

Sources	Uses

■ Equity
   ● New equity from LBO sponsor
   ● Potential equity contribution from existing management
   ● Potential continuing investment by existing shareholders
   ● Strategic equity
	■ Purchase equity of the target company
	   ● Pay existing equity owners
	   ● If public, current share price plus tender premium (driven by leverage and general market conditions)
	   ● Include cost of options, convertibles, and other potentially dilutive securities (i.e. ESOPs)

■ Debt
   ● Senior debt (bank)
   ● Subordinated debt (high-yield)
	■ Retire existing debt
	   ● Existing covenants typically prohibit post-LBO debt levels
	   ● May call existing debt at premium
	   ● Bank debt can be repaid

■ Mezzanine securities	■ Transaction expenses
	   ● Bank debt fees
	   ● High-yield fees
	   ● Consultants fees (lawyers, management consultants, etc.)
	   ● Fee percentages depend on the company's credit rating and deal structure
	   ● May be amortised over life of deal

Table 9.1 summarises the principal components and factors to be considered in the 'sources and uses' analysis.

A typical capital structure of an LBO

A typical capital LBO comprises senior debt (representing usually 50% of the total structure), subordinated debt (25% of total transaction), and equity (remaining 25%). Over the last 40 years, conservative and aggressive structures have followed one another as a function of risk appetite and overall liquidity. In more conservative years, total debt totals up to 3.5x, subordinated debt disappears from the capital structure, and equity represents up to 60% of the total amount, Tranche B (bullet) on senior loans virtually disappears, and the spread on senior debt ramps up to 400–500 bps. Table 9.2 represents a generalisation for 'normal' years.

Although a detailed explanation of the debt and equity instruments has been presented in the credit and equity chapters, it is worth noting the following.

TABLE 9.2 A typical LBO capital structure.

Financing source	Costs	Lending parameters	Likely sources
Senior debt (50–60%)	■ Arranging / underwriting fee: 200–250 bps ■ Floating: LIBOR / EURIBOR + 250–275 bps (Tranche A). Tranche B is usually 50 bps higher than Tranche A to compensate for longer tenor ■ Pre-payable at par	■ Senior debt leverage = 3.5x to 4.0x LTM EBITDA ■ 6-year tenor (Tranche A, amortising) / 7-year tenor (Tranche B, bullet) (sometimes also Tranche C, bullet, tenor of 8 years)	■ Commercial banks ■ Credit companies ■ Insurance companies ■ Public market
Subordinated debt/mezzanine debt (25–35%)	■ Arranging/ underwriting fee: 250–325 bps ■ High-yield: 700–900 bps ■ Mezzanine: LIBOR/EURIBOR + 500 bps cash (+ 500 bps PIK) ■ Callability: non-call or pre-payable above par (103-102-01) in the first three years	■ Total leverage = 4.5x to 5.5x EBITDA (in other words, subordinated debt attracts 1.0–1.5X EBITDA of additional debt) ■ EBITDA coverage above 1.8x ■ 7-year bullet	■ Public market ■ Insurance companies
Equity (typically 20–25%)	■ 25–30%	■ 4–6 year exit strategy	■ Management investors ■ LBO funds ■ Investment banks ■ Merchant banking

■ **Senior debt:** senior debt is often 50% or more of the capital structure. Therefore, the senior lender should be brought into the deal as soon as possible, since they represent the single largest amount of cash needed for the transaction. MergeCo is the borrower. The advantage of senior debt is that there are lower financing costs. The disadvantages are that the company is burdened with more limiting financial covenants. These covenants restrict the company's ability to make further acquisitions, raise additional debt, or pay dividends to equity holders. Moreover, they require that there be full amortisation over a period of seven years, which means the company will be bound to use a substantial amount of its cash flow to make repayments.

- Acquisition debt: usually senior term debt is made of a Tranche A (amortising repayment structure, tenor 6 years) and a Tranche B (bullet repayment, tenor 7 years), more rarely of Tranche C. Senior debt is secured by a first claim on fixed assets, a first or second claim on current assets, and claims on the intangibles and stock of the company and subsidiaries. Commercial banks usually provide it together with senior revolving debt; other commercial lenders and insurance companies can also provide it.
- Senior revolving debt: is secured by a first claim on current assets. It is usually provided by commercial banks or similar institutional lenders, and typically provides working capital.

- **Subordinated debt:** typically public high-yield debt, subordinated debt is often 25–30% of the capital structure. MergeCo is usually the borrower, although it can be the holding company ('HoldCo') controlling MergeCo; thus, subordinated debt can be either contractually (when MergeCo is the borrower) or structurally subordinated (when HoldCo is the borrower) to senior debt. The advantage of subordinated debt is that the company retains greater flexibility through less restrictive covenants and a bullet structure (no amortisation). The disadvantage is that the financing costs are higher. Subordinated debt can often be repaid, at the company's discretion, any time after Year 3.
- **Mezzanine financing:** mezzanine financing is subordinated debt (sometimes combined with preferred stock) with warrants or some other equity kicker. MergeCo is usually the borrower, thus making mezzanine contractually (via an inter-creditor agreement) subordinated to senior debt. Mezzanine usually enjoys second ranking security, has covenants that track senior ones (although with headroom), and has moderate pre-payment penalties. Targeted returns tend to be 15–20%. Mezzanine financing enables investors to receive:
  - a cash coupon (4–6% annually);
  - a payment-in-kind, also referred as PIK, coupon (4–6% annually) which does not normally pay an annual coupon but is accrued and paid at loan maturity;
  - plus the chance to be included in the upside (via warrants or options to acquire common stock) if the company increases equity value.
- **Equity:** equity investments are usually made by LBO investors or private equity investors. Equity often represents 20% or more of the capital structure. Banks and other lenders frequently require that the equity holders contribute at least 20% equity in order to obtain a loan. Since there is a high level of risk to the equity holders, expected returns are often over 30%.

Other potential instruments (although less frequently seen) can be used to finance an LBO:

- **PIK loan:** a loan issued at a discount to par. It does not normally pay a semi-annual cash coupon but pays a dividend by way of common stock or preferred stock. This form of debt is appealing in situations where cash flow is limited, such as in the years immediately following the close of a deal. HoldCo is usually the borrower.
- **Seller's subordinated note:** unsecured, possibly convertible to stock.
- **Seller's preferred stock:** usually appearing as an alternative to a vendor note, possibly exchangeable for a subordinated note.

Table 9.3 summarises the advantages, disadvantages, documentation, and due diligence requirements of the main debt instruments used in an LBO transaction.

Differences between LBO and recapitalisation

A leveraged recapitalisation (also known as leveraged recap or simply recap) is a monetisation or exit strategy whereby the existing equity holders change the existing capital structure by re-leveraging the Target. Shareholders are paid a large cash dividend by utilising a high amount of leverage or repurchase of stock. In an LBO, shareholders are bought out and the company (or part of it) changes ownership and eventually (if public) goes private. In a leveraged recap (also known as leveraged cash out, or LCO), a company raises cash (through increased leverage) that is distributed to existing shareholders by way of a dividend. Unlike LBOs, in a leveraged recap shareholders continue to hold shares (also known as 'stub 2 shares') in the company: they are worth less per share, owing to the large cash payout (shareholders could receive debt securities or preferred stock, although the use of cash is most common).

Recap analysis is used to:

- measure the impact on a public company's Earning Per Share (EPS);
- determine the effect (and related credit ratios and rating impact) of replacing equity with more debt.

Table 9.4 compares different recap structures.

A couple of final points should be considered – in case the form of consideration is stock (instead of cash) – when comparing LBOs and recaps.

- Stock may be issued in an LBO; however, this is rare. In a recap, selling shareholders could receive the consideration in the form of NewCo stock. Additional NewCo stock may also be issued to finance the acquisition/repurchase of OldCo stock.
- The issuance of shares dilutes the net income per share in a recap. In an LBO, issuing additional stock reduces initial equity returns.

TABLE 9.3 Comparison of different debt products used in an LBO.

	Advantages	Disadvantages	Documentation	Due diligence

Senior	■ Lowest cost
	■ High certainty of execution
	■ Limited pre-payment penalties
	■ No SEC reporting
		■ Amortisation schedule
		■ Shorter maturity
		■ Security
		■ Restrictive maintenance covenants
		■ Floating rate funding
			■ Required for signing of the sale and purchase agreement:
			  ■ commitment letter
			  ■ term sheet
			■ Required at closing:
			  ■ loan agreement
			  ■ security documents
			  ■ inter-creditor agreement (if any subordinate debt is used)
				■ Accounting and tax
				■ Legal
				■ Business
				■ Environmental (if applicable)

Mezzanine	■ Coupon has a mix of cash and non-cash components ■ Limited pre-payment costs ■ Likely to have a smaller lender group ■ No regulator reporting ■ No credit rating required	■ Uncertainty of execution ■ High target return ■ Equity dilution ■ Maintenance covenants	■ Similar to senior bank debt documentation	■ Similar to senior bank due diligence

High-yield	■ Fixed rate
	■ High certainty of execution
	■ Less restrictive incurrence-based covenants
	■ No amortisation requirement
	■ Longer maturity
	■ Unsecured
		■ Relevant regulator (e.g. SEC) reporting requirements
		■ Listing
		■ Call protection
		■ Credit rating required
		■ Incurrence covenants
			■ Required at signing of the sale and purchase agreement:
			  ■ highly confident letter
			  ■ term sheet
			■ Required at closing of the high-yield:
			  ■ prospectus
			  ■ purchase agreement
			  ■ indenture
			  ■ registration rights agreement
				■ Legal
				■ Business

TABLE 9.4 Three alternative leveraged recapitalisation structures.

Modest recap	Leveraged recap	Leveraged recap with financial sponsor
▪ Bank debt ▪ Debt/EBITDA: 2.0x	▪ Bank and subordinated debt ▪ Debt/EBITDA: 2.0–3.0x	▪ Bank and subordinated debt, other securities issued ▪ Debt/EBITDA: up to 5.0–6.0x (but may vary over time as a function of general risk appetite, liquidity, etc.)
▪ Cash used to pay a dividend to existing shareholders and/or to repurchase shares	▪ Cash used to pay a dividend to existing shareholders and/or to repurchase a material amount of shares	▪ NewCo merged with OldCo (or tender offer followed by merger) ▪ Majority of shares sold/tendered for cash ▪ Financial sponsor receives the majority of shares
▪ No equity sold to third party ▪ Equity can be repurchased by the company ▪ Taxes paid by shareholders on cash dividend received or share tendered	▪ No equity sold to third party ▪ Equity can be repurchased by the company ▪ Taxes paid by shareholders on cash dividend received or gain on share tendered	▪ Equity sold to third party ▪ Change of control Taxes paid by shareholders on gain on shares sold or tendered

Value creation in LBOs

Financial sponsors usually want a return (IRR) on their equity investment of between 25% and 35%, over a three to four year period. In order to increase returns, financial sponsors minimise equity investments by using leveraged capital structures: 25–35% of transaction value funded by equity. The primary way in which value is created in an LBO is in fact through the use of borrowing to finance the acquisition. A key driver behind the outsized returns generated in a successful LBO is reducing the weighted-average cost of capital (WACC) by employing more debt (cheaper than the cost of the equity). As the debt is paid down, the value of the equity increases. The simple example below shows that the value of equity has increased from 30 (the initial equity investment) to 90 (value of equity at the time of exit of the private equity fund) by simply paying down debt with Target cash flow.

Target		MergeCo (at entry)			MergeCo (at exit)	
			Liabilities			**Liabilities**
Assets	**Equity**	**Assets**	70		**Assets**	10
100	100	100	**Equity**	$\Rightarrow$	100	**Equity**
			30			90

Returns are also increased through growth, value extraction, and operation efficiencies. This can be seen in the example in Table 9.5 of two LBOs with the same enterprise value at entry (5000) and exit (7500), but different capital structure (a gearing ratio of 0.33 in Example 1 and a gearing of 3 in Example 2).

TABLE 9.5   Value creation in an LBO with the same entry and exit values but different capital structures.

Example 1:	
Enterprise value (at entry)	5000
Enterprise value (at exit)	7500
Debt	25.0%
Equity	75.0%

	Year 0	Year 1	Year 2	Year 3	Year 4	Year 5
Debt (beginning balance)		1250	1000	750	500	250
Cash flow available for debt service		250	250	250	250	250
Debt (end balance)	1250	1000	750	500	250	0
Equity	−3750	0	0	0	0	7500
IRR (%)						14.9
CoC (x)						2.0

Example 2:	
Enterprise value (at entry)	5000
Enterprise value (at exit)	7500
Debt	75.0%
Equity	25.0%

	Year 0	Year 1	Year 2	Year 3	Year 4	Year 5
Debt (beginning balance)		3750	3620	3496	3378	3266
Cash flow available for debt service		130	124	118	112	105
Debt (end balance)	3750	3620	3496	3378	3266	3161
Equity	−1250	0	0	0	0	4339
IRR (%)						28.3
CoC (x)						3.5

In other words, financial sponsors look for growth to increase company value and strengthen the case for investment (increase enterprise value), or increase the repayment of debt to increase equity value (retain enterprise value but reduce debt).

LBO ANALYSIS

Back-of-the-envelope LBO analysis

Before using the LBO model, it is a good idea to obtain a rough estimate of what the purchase price should be. A back-of-the-envelope calculation will enable the determination of reasonable initial inputs. The following steps should be effected:

- Obtain the company's projected EBITDA.
- Determine the maximum amount of annual interest expense the cash flow could support:
- EBITDA ÷ Predetermined Interest Coverage Ratio
- Deals generally done at 1.8x to 2.0x Coverage Ratios

$$\frac{Implied\ Total\ Debt\ the\ Company}{Can\ Support} = \frac{Implied\ Annual\ Interest\ Expense}{Average\ or\ 'Blended'\ Interest\ Rate}$$

- Assume a capitalisation structure (e.g. 80% debt and 20% equity)
- Determine the purchase price: Total Capitalisation – Cash Plus Marketable Securities - Existing Debt & Estimated Transaction Costs.

Before debt amortisation (€/$m)

LTM EBITDA (€/$)		200.0
Assumed Pro Forma Interest Coverage (x) (EBITDA ÷ Interest)	÷	2.0
Implied Maximum Annual Pretax Interest Expense ($)	=	100.0
Assumed Pro Forma Blended Interest Rate[2]	÷	9.0
Implied Maximum Total Debt ($)	=	**1111.1**
	÷	0.80
Implied Total Capitalisation ($)[3]		**1388.9**

LBO model in a nutshell

LBO analysis is a modelling technique that has several typical uses, such as: 1) obtaining an LBO value for a company; 2) determining the type of equity

---

[2] This would be the blended interest rate assuming that debt is split equally between senior secured (8.0%) and subordinated debt (10.0%).

[3] Assumes capital structure comprised of 80% debt and 20% equity.

returns that can be achieved; and 3) establishing how much debt the company can afford to take on. On the sell side, LBO analysis (an essential component of the M&A toolkit) involves identifying and selecting the best buyers and determining which prices they might be willing to pay (including what amounts will be debt or equity). It also involves determining which companies have complementary businesses.

On the buy side, it involves determining how much a buyer can pay in an acquisition, in addition to analysing the capital structure impact of potential acquisitions.

The main steps for an LBO analysis (Steps 1, 2, and 3 have been already thoroughly explained in the credit chapter and are therefore only mentioned here) are:

1 Analyse the business profile of the company:
  i) identify the main drivers of the business and its cashflows;
  ii) identify the main risks associated with the business;
  iii) identify important dependencies on products, suppliers, customers, and so forth;
  iv) identify important opportunities and threats;
  v) identify sources of growth – i.e. top line versus margin growth;
  vi) consider stability and sustainability;
  vii) consider reliance on the occurrence of major events such as asset disposals, restructuring, and product launches
  viii) identify major sensitivities.

2 Develop a pre-LBO financial model of the Target:
  i) build a 7–10 years profit and loss (until EBIT) forecast;
  ii) build a 7–10 years balance sheet forecast;
  iii) build a 7–10 years cash flow (until investment activities) forecast.

3 Input the transaction structure:
  i) input purchase price assumptions;
  ii) input LBO capital structure into sources and uses;
  iii) make adjustments to bridge the opening balance sheet of MergeCo to the pro forma closing balance sheet.

4 Calibrate an appropriate capital structure:
  i) input (senior, subordinated, etc.) debt schedule;
  ii) finalise P&L, BS, and CF.

5 Perform LBO analysis:
  i) assess the resulting LBO capital structure and critically review the output;
  ii) evaluate equity returns;
  iii) determine valuation.

A deep dive on the last three steps is presented in the following paragraphs.

Input the transaction structure

Purchase Price The purchase price is the key starting point. We can get to the equity purchase price (see Figure 9.1a):

a) starting from enterprise value comparables (mostly used for private companies).

The most common methodology used is the comparable company one. Starting from public market EV/EBITDA comparables (to which an illiquidity discount of 20–30% is applied) or from transaction EV/EBITDA comparables, we multiply the selected EV/EBITDA by the EBITDA of the Target company and obtain the EV of the Target. We then subtract the net financial position (total debt minus cash) to obtain the equity purchase price (or ES).

b) starting (Figure 9.1b) from share price (commonly used for listed companies).

VALUATION MULTIPLES		EV/EBITDA		
		2012A (x)	2013A (x)	2014A (x)
Comparable 1	Country X	12.8x	11.5x	10.7x
Comparable 2	Country Y	11.8x	10.9x	10.2x
Comparable 3	Country Z	6.8x	6.2x	5.9x
.....	....			
High		12.8x	11.5x	10.7x
Low		6.8x	6.2x	5.9x
Mean		10.5x	9.6x	**9.0x**
Median		11.8x	10.9x	10.2x
Target EBITDA (€/$ m)				200
Target Enterprise Value				**1.800**
Less: Total Debt				100
Plus: Cash				20
Net Financial Position				**80**
Equity Purchase Price				**1.720**

FIGURE 9.1a Determination of equity value starting from purchase price.

Current Share Price (€)	30
Premium (Discount) to Market Price (%)	16.61%
Share Purchase Price ($)	34
Number of Shares Outstanding	50 000 000
Amount of Equity Purchased (%)	100%
Equity Purchase Price (€m)	**1.720**
Plus: Total Debt	100
Less: Cash	20
Net Financial Position	**80**
Enterprise Value	**1.800**

FIGURE 9.1b Determination of equity value starting from share price.

With respect to the shares outstanding, often the number reported is the 'fully diluted amount of shares outstanding'. It is important to note that in several publicly traded industries, companies have set up relatively complex capital structures in which options and other potentially dilutive securities (e.g. warrants and convertible bonds) may significantly impact the calculation of EPS and the consideration paid in a transaction. All decisions regarding the treatment of outstanding options and convertible securities depend on the aims and circumstances of the Target and buyer. In an LBO, the Target's stock options are usually liquidated or rolled over, whilst the Target's convertible securities are converted, liquidated, or rolled over.

When options or convertibles are liquidated, the option or convertible security holders receive cash from the acquiring company in exchange for tendering the security. The cash payment is payment for in-the-money options (options for which the offer price is greater than the exercise price). The payment provides value only to the in-money amount, and not to the residual option value. Therefore, option holders typically prefer to roll over the options if permitted to do so.

A convertible security holder is not permitted to roll over the interest in the transaction prior to the transaction itself. The holder must decide whether to cash out as a debt holder or as an equity holder: the decision depends whether the convertible bonds are:

- **In-the-money:** the holder of the convertible security usually converts the bond into the underlying stock, receiving the same consideration and treatment as a normal equity holder does (in some cases, the redemption value is greater than face value of the bond if there are early call protection features).
- **Out-of-the-money:** the holder will not convert and will receive the redemption value of the bond. The bond should be treated as normal debt and should be included in the overall target company enterprise value, not in the equity consideration.

LBO Capital Structure The next step is to build a sources and uses table: this is a separate Excel tab where initial LBO capital structure assumptions are input. Figure 9.2 replicates a typical LBO structure (for a Target with a €300m EBITDA).

Make Adjustments to Bridge the Opening Balance Sheet of MergeCo to the Pro-forma Closing Balance Sheet This step represents an important phase of building an LBO model. Key assumptions and adjustments are the following.

- **Closing date:** the assumed closing date is not usually an issue as pro forma, full year results are typically modelled. The analysis will show the closing date as having taken place on the first day of the financial year.
- **Balance Sheet:**
  - Assets:
    - ○ *Cash*: cash on the Target's balance sheet before the LBO is usually distributed to the Target's sellers (and hence must be eliminated from the pro-forma).
    - ○ *Goodwill:* goodwill is a component of a purchase accounting transaction (and hence must be added to the pro-forma). It is the difference between the equity consideration (and not the enterprise value) or purchase price (equity + other dilutive securities) that the buyer is willing to pay, and the book value (a proxy for fair market value) of the Target. It is important to note that existing goodwill dissipates (the fair market value is written up from tangible book value, i.e. book equity minus existing goodwill) and that goodwill calculations are not affected by the form of payment (in fact, irrespective of the amount of stock being used as payment, with purchase accounting goodwill is calculated off the total equity consideration).
    - ○ *Transaction costs (incl. fees on debt facilities):* these are usually capitalised (and hence must be added to the pro-forma). LBO relates that fees and expenses that cannot be capitalised must be deducted from the Sponsor's equity contribution.
  - Liabilities:
    - ○ *Debt:* NewCo's debt is added to the Target's existing debt (and hence must be added to the pro-forma), whilst existing debt is usually refinanced (and hence must be eliminated from the pro-forma).
    - ○ *Equity:* in an LBO, any stock issued as part of the consideration is added to NewCo's stockholders' equity: therefore, existing equity of the Target must be eliminated while the Sponsor's equity contribution (net of fees and expenses not capitalised) should be added to the pro-forma. In a recap, the stockholders' equity of the target is immediately reduced by the value of the cash dividend or the value of the stock repurchased.

USES (€m)	Amount
Cash on Balance Sheet	20
Existing Debt	100
Acquisition Price	1720
Transaction costs	50
Capex	110
Total uses at Closing	**2000**

SOURCES (€m)	Amount	% total	EBITDA x
Cash on Balance Sheet	0	0%	0.0
Existing Debt	0	0%	0.0
Senior Tranche A	650	33%	2.2
Senior Tranche B	300	15%	1.0
Senior Tranche C	0	0%	0.0
Invoice financing (drawn)	100	5%	0.3
Total Net Senior Drawn	**1050**	**53%**	**3.5**
Second lien	0	0%	0.0
Mezzanine	350	18%	1.2
Total Net Debt Drawn	**1400**	**70%**	**4.7**
Vendor loan	0	0%	0.0
New Cash Equity	600	30%	2.0
Total Funded Sources	**2000**	**100%**	**6.7**

FIGURE 9.2 Sources and uses of an LBO.

- **P&L:**
  - Goodwill amortisation: amortised over the years (depending on jurisdiction, accounting rules, and tax reasons), and hence must be added to the pro-forma.
  - Transaction costs: amortised over the years (depending on jurisdiction, accounting rules, and tax reasons), and hence must be added to the pro-forma.

Calibrate an appropriate capital structure

Whereas the LBO financing structure is quite standard in terms of 'debt layers', the level of total (and senior) debt, the tenor, the repayment profile, the breakdown across the 'alphabet' loans (Term A, B, C), the cost (fees and interest), and the subordination type (contractual, structural) can vary significantly across time, geographies, and industries.

The debt schedule is typically constructed in accordance with:

- cash flow generation
- security package and seniority
- market appetite
- securities, and other debt instruments in the capital structure.

Figure 9.3 summarises key economic terms of an LBO.

It is customary in LBO facilities to have a cash sweep mechanism that dictates that all cash generated above a certain threshold (post mandatory debt repayments) is used to reimburse in advance outstanding debt (revolver, Term A, and Term B).

Once the above assumptions have been finalised, it is possible to finalise PL, BS, and CF.

Perform LBO analysis

Assess the Resulting LBO Capital Structure and Critically Review
the Output A base case scenario is now finalised and summary output (in addition to PL and BS) would look like the one depicted in Table 9.6.

Particular attention must be dedicated to interest coverage ratios (see Table 9.7) that illustrate the firm's ability to pay interest on the debt used to finance the acquisition. Common measures of interest coverage (compared to their 'ideal' values) include those in Table 9.7.

Other critical questions to ask when reviewing the LBO output are:

- Is there sufficient cash flow for debt repayment?
- How much cash flow is left?
- How large is the buffer relative to the necessary payments and expenses?
- Does the company have other substantial payment commitments (rents, severance pay outs, and cash payments for post-accounting reserves)?

Sources	% 'Min'	% 'Max'	x EBITDA 'Min'	x EBITDA 'Max'	Fees 'Min'	Fees 'Max'	Cash margin 'Min'	Cash margin 'Max'	PIK margin 'Min'	PIK margin 'Max'	IRR* 'Min'	IRR* 'Max'	Tenor (in years) 'Min'	Tenor (in years) 'Max'	Repayment
Senior A							2.25%	4.75%	n.a	n.a			4	6	Linear / Increasing
Senior B							2.75%	5.25%	n.a	n.a			6	8	Bullet
Senior C							3.25%	5.75%	n.a	n.a			7	9	Bullet
Senior D							3.75%	6.25%	n.a	n.a			7	9	Bullet
Total senior debt	30.00%	55.00%	2.0 x	5.0 x	1.75%	3.50%									
Mezzanine							4.00%	7.50%	4.00%	7.50%	0.00%	5.00%	6	9	Bullet
High-yield							7.50%	12.00%	n.a	n.a			6	9	Bullet
PIK loan							0.00%	2.00%	8.00%	10.00%			6	9	Bullet
Total subordinated debt	0.00%	20.00%	0.0 x	1.8 x	2.00%	4.00%									
TOTAL DEBT	30.00%	75.00%	2.0 x	6.8 x											
Vendor/PIK loan	0.00%						0.00%	2.00%	0.00%	3.00%			3	6	n.a.
Shareholder loan	0.00%						0.00%	1.00%	0.00%	4.00%			3	6	n.a.
Ordinary equity	0.00%												3	6	n.a.
TOTAL EQUITY	70.00%	25.00%	4.7 x	2.3 x	0.00%	1.50%					30.00%	15.00%			
TOTAL SOURCES	100.00%	100.00%	6.7 x	9.1 x											

*For mezzanine, this refers to the percentage of ownership if warrants are fully exercised.

FIGURE 9.3 Summary table of key economic features of an LBO.

TABLE 9.6 Summary output of an LBO model.

Pro forma cash flow statement	2014A	Forecast 2015	2016	2017	2018	2019	2020	2021
Net income		30.0	37.9	49.9	59.2	67.9	77.3	88.0
(+) Initial Depreciation		9.9	10.8	11.8	13.0	0.9	15.0	16.1
(+) Transaction Goodwill Amortisation		10.2	10.2	10.2	10.2	10.2	10.2	10.2
(+) Amortisation of Financing Fees		1.1	1.1	1.1	1.1	1.1	1.1	1.1
(−) Capital Expenditures (No acquisitions)		−10.9	−11.9	−13.0	−14.3	−15.3	−16.5	−17.7
(−) Increase / Decrease in Working Capital		−38.8	−25.7	−29.0	−30.7	−33.0	−35.5	−38.2
(+) Increase / Decrease In Other Assets and Liabilities		11.2	7.3	8.0	8.7	9.4	10.1	10.8
Cash flow available for debt amortisation		**12.7**	**29.7**	**39.0**	**47.2**	**41.2**	**61.7**	**70.3**
Cash Used to Pay Down Bank Debt		−12.7	−29.7	−39.0	−47.2	−41.2	−56.6	−70.3
Check Balance		0	0	0	0	0	17.8	70.3
Cash Used to Pay Down Sub. Debt		0	0	0	0	0	−17.8	−70.3
Change in Cash		0	0	0	0	0	0	0

Pro forma capitalisation (€)	2014A	Forecast 2015	2016	2017	2018	2019	2020	2021
Cash	0.0	0.0	0.0	0.0	0.0	0.0	0.0	0.0
Bank Debt	226.4	213.7	184.0	145.0	97.8	56.6	0.0	0.0
Subordinated	97.1	97.1	97.1	97.1	97.1	97.1	79.3	9.0
Common Equity	248.5	278.5	316.4	366.3	425.5	493.4	570.7	658.7
Total Capitalisation	**572.0**	**589.3**	**597.5**	**608.4**	**620.4**	**647.1**	**650.0**	**667.7**

Pro forma capitalisation (%)	2014A							
Cash (%)	0.0	0.0	0.0	0.0	0.0	0.0	0.0	0.0
Bank Debt ( )	39.6	36.3	30.8	23.8	15.8	8.7	0.0	0.0
Subordinated ( )	17.0	16.5	16.3	16.0	15.7	15.0	12.2	1.3
Common Equity ( )	43.4	47.3	53.0	60.2	68.6	76.2	87.8	98.7
Total Capitalisation ( )	**100.0**	**100.0**	**100.0**	**100.0**	**100.0**	**100.0**	**100.0**	**100.0**

TABLE 9.7 Summary credit statistics of an LBO.

Selected credit statistics	Min.	2014A	Forecast						
			2015	2016	2017	2018	2019	2020	2021
EBITDA/Total Interest (x)	1.80	3.50	3.51	4.07	5.11	6.35	8.15	11.25	18.89
EBITDA/Cash Interest	1.80	3.31	3.63	4.22	5.32	6.65	8.61	12.10	21.13
EBIT/Total Interest		2.57	2.83	3.34	4.27	5.36	6.91	9.58	16.13
EBIT/Cash Interest		2.66	2.94	3.46	4.45	5.61	7.31	10.30	18.11
(EBITDA-Capex)/ Total Interest (x)	1.35	3.33	3.14	3.65	4.62	5.74	7.36	10.15	17.01
(EBITDA-Capex)/ Cash Interest	1.35	3.21	3.26	3.79	4.81	6.01	7.79	10.92	19.10
Bank Debt Repaid		0.00	5.60	18.70	35.90	56.80	80.70	100.00	100.00
Total Debt/Capitalisation		56.60	52.70	47.00	39.80	31.40	22.20	12.20	1.30
Total Debt/ EBITDA (x)	5.75	3.40	3.00	2.40	1.80	1.30	0.90	0.50	0.00
Bank Debt/ EBITDA	4.00	2.40	2.00	1.60	1.10	0.70	0.30	0.00	0.00

In recap, it is important to analyse the effect of the transaction on the projected EPS: EPS in fact will be likely significantly lower than it was before the recap, because of the substantial debt and interest expense post transaction (unless a substantial portion of the cash is used to repurchase stock at attractive valuations). As many public companies trade on earnings, reduced earnings and high leverage will probably reduce the stock price initially, and in so doing lower the P/E multiple slightly. The level of earnings growth over time and comfort that the management team can operate effectively given high levels of debt are critical issues in recap analysis.

Evaluate Equity Returns The analysis of equity returns is the last building block of the LBO analysis. The typical output illustrates cash on cash and IRR for the equity investors (see Table 9.8) as a function of different exit years and different exit multiples (usually multiples of EBITDA). Table 9.8 illustrates a typical summary table.

TABLE 9.8 LBO equity returns.

TOTAL EQUITY RETURNS ANALYSIS				
Cash on Cash		**Year 3**	**Year 4**	**Tear 5**
	7.3x	1.8x	2.1x	2.3x
	8.3x	2.1x	2.4x	2.6x
	9.3x	2.4x	2.7x	2.9x
Equity IRR		**Year 3**	**Year 4**	**Year 5**
	7.3x	13.3%	13.2%	12.6%
	8.3x	16.6%	15.8%	14.6%
	9.3x	19.5%	18.1%	16.4%

There is an important decision with regard to exit valuation multiples: it should usually be assumed that exit multiples will be similar to the entry multiples. Alternatively, one should use multiples consistent to future exit strategy:

- If the exit is an IPO, use P/E multiples.
- If the exit is a trade sale, use EV/EBITDA multiples.

When evaluating exit multiples, consideration should be given to the company's position at the time and to what the market environment will be like at exit.

Determine Valuation In simple terms, an LBO valuation is based on the concept of figuring out how much a financial Sponsor could pay for a company, given the returns which all the capital providers require and the risk constraints they face: total debt is constrained by the value of the assets that can be loaned against and the cash flows required to pay down debt (also measure by coverage ratios), while initial equity put into the deal is constrained by the required equity returns (since, as we saw, less equity put into the deal means higher returns).

LBO valuation methodology neither replaces nor contradicts the discounted cash flow valuation methodology: both methodologies utilise the same forecasts and are based on utilising the required returns for capital providers (in the DCF valuation this is the WACC; in the LBO valuation these are interest rate on debt and the target returns on equity). LBO is preferred by buyout funds because it is based on the actual returns and constraints required by lenders and equity investors whereas, the WACC used in the cash flow valuation is more 'theoretical'.

Traditionally, the valuation implied by LBO analysis is toward the lower end of the valuation techniques (such as comparables transactions and DCF).

LBO structuring: a modeling example

An example of LBO structuring is reproduced in Figure 9.4 (the accompanying Excel file is downloadable from the companion website).

LBO Model

Deal Key Input (€m)

EBITDA 2018	19.7
NFP 2018	0 *assuming purchase of debt/cash free Target*
Entry multiple	8.0x
Envy ratio for management	3.3x
Preferred equity return	10%

Uses	€m	x EBITDA	%
Equity value target	157.6		
Transaction costs	3.5		
Cash overfunding	1.5		
Total Uses	**162.6**		

Sources	€m	x EBITDA	%
Senior debt	65	3.3x	
Term Loan A	25	1.3x	
Term Loan B	40	2.0x	
Fund equity	94.4	4.8x	90%
Ordinary	28.8	1.5x	
Preferred	65.6	3.3x	
Sweet equity	3.2	0.2x	10%
Ordinary (management)	3.2	0.2x	
Total Sources	**162.6**		

P&L Input	2014A	2015A	2016A	2017A	2018A	2019E	2020E	2021E	2022E	2023E	2024E
Sales YoY growth		12.5%	10.4%	11.9%	12.2%	11.0%	11.0%	11.0%	11.0%	11.0%	11.0%
Operating Costs / Sales (%)	(50.0%)	(49.1%)	(49.6%)	(46.9%)	(46.6%)	(47.0%)	(47.0%)	(47.0%)	(47.0%)	(47.0%)	(47.0%)
Personnel Costs / Sales (%)	(19.5%)	(20.3%)	(20.5%)	(21.1%)	(20.8%)	(21.0%)	(21.0%)	(21.0%)	(21.0%)	(21.0%)	(21.0%)
D&A / Sales (%)	(2.5%)	(2.7%)	(2.4%)	(2.3%)	(4.0%)	(4.0%)	(4.0%)	(4.0%)	(4.0%)	(4.0%)	(4.0%)
Tax rate	(26.0%)	(26.0%)	(26.0%)	(24.0%)	(24.0%)	(24.0%)	(24.0%)	(24.0%)	(24.0%)	(24.0%)	(24.0%)

BS Input	2014A	2015A	2016A	2017A	2018A	2019E	2020E	2021E	2022E	2023E	2024E
Days receivables	207.7	194.5	163.2	159.5	150.3	150.0	145.0	130.0	120.0	120.0	120.0
Days payables	91.3	85.9	88.9	93.7	91.6	100.0	110.0	120.0	120.0	120.0	120.0
Days inventories	58.4	52.7	48.5	43.3	46.8	45.0	45.0	45.0	45.0	45.0	45.0

Debt structure	Term (Years)	Amort.	x EBITDA	Amount (€m)	Base rate	Margin	Interest rate
Senior Debt							
Term Loan A	6	Amortising	1.3x	25.00	-0.1%	3.00%	2.90%
Term Loan B	6	Bullet	2.0x	40.00	-0.1%	3.50%	3.40%
Revolving cash facility	7	RCF	0.8x	15.00	-0.1%	2.50%	2.40%

FIGURE 9.4 LBO structuring: a modelling example.

Debt repayment schedule

	2018	2019	2020	2021	2022	2023	2024
Term Loan A							
Interest rate		2.90%	2.90%	2.90%	2.90%	2.90%	2.90%
Amortisation schedule		16.67%	16.67%	16.67%	16.67%	16.67%	16.67%
Opening balance		25.00	20.83	16.67	12.50	8.33	4.17
Principal repayments		-4.17	-4.17	-4.17	-4.17	-4.17	-4.17
Interest expense		-0.66	-0.54	-0.42	-0.30	-0.18	-0.06
Closing balance	25.00	20.83	16.67	12.50	8.33	4.17	0.00
Term Loan B							
Interest rate		3.40%	3.40%	3.40%	3.40%	3.40%	3.40%
Amortisation schedule		0.00%	0.00%	0.00%	0.00%	0.00%	100.00%
Opening balance		40.00	40.00	40.00	40.00	40.00	40.00
Principal repayments		0.00	0.00	0.00	0.00	0.00	-40.00
Interest expense		-1.36	-1.36	-1.36	-1.36	-1.36	-0.68
Closing balance	40.00	40.00	40.00	40.00	40.00	40.00	0.00
RCF							
Interest rate		2.40%	2.40%	2.40%	2.40%	2.40%	2.40%
Commitment fee		1.00%	1.00%	1.00%	1.00%	1.00%	1.00%
Commitment	15.00						

Profit & Loss

(€m)	2014A	2015A	2016A	2017A	2018A	2019E	2020E	2021E	2022E	2023E	2024E
Total Sales	40.0	45.0	49.7	55.6	62.4	69.3	76.9	85.3	94.7	105.1	116.7
Cost of materials	(15.0)	(16.8)	(18.1)	(18.2)	(20.1)						
Cost of service	(3.0)	(3.3)	(4.3)	(5.6)	(6.6)						
Rents and leasing	(2.0)	(2.0)	(2.2)	(2.3)	(2.4)						
Total Operating Cost	(20.0)	(22.1)	(24.6)	(26.1)	(29.1)	(32.6)	(36.1)	(40.1)	(44.5)	(49.4)	(54.9)
Salaries	(5.4)	(6.3)	(7.3)	(8.2)	(9.0)						
Social contributions	(1.6)	(2.0)	(1.9)	(2.4)	(2.6)						
Other personnel costs	(0.8)	(0.9)	(1.0)	(1.1)	(1.4)						
Total Personnel Costs	(7.8)	(9.2)	(10.2)	(11.7)	(13.0)	(14.5)	(16.1)	(17.9)	(19.9)	(22.1)	(24.5)
Other operating costs	(1.8)	(1.2)	(0.7)	(0.8)	(0.6)	(0.7)	(0.7)	(0.7)	(0.7)	(0.7)	(0.7)
EBITDA	10.4	12.6	14.2	17.0	19.7	21.5	23.9	26.6	29.6	32.9	36.6
% Sales	26.0%	27.9%	28.5%	30.6%	31.6%	31.0%	31.1%	31.2%	31.3%	31.3%	31.4%
Depreciation & amortisation	(1.0)	(1.2)	(1.2)	(1.3)	(2.5)	(2.8)	(3.1)	(3.4)	(3.8)	(4.2)	(4.7)

FIGURE 9.4 (*Continued*)

EBIT	9.4	11.4	13.0	15.7	17.2	18.7	20.8	23.2	25.8	28.7	32.0
(Interest expense) / income											
Senior debt	0.2	0.1	0.2	0.2	0.2	(2.2)	(2.1)	(1.9)	(1.8)	(1.7)	(0.9)
Interests on RCF						(0.2)	(0.2)	(0.2)	(0.2)	(0.2)	(0.2)
Mezzanine PIK						(2.0)	(1.9)	(1.8)	(1.7)	(1.5)	(0.7)
Mezzanine cash						-	-	-	-	-	-
Bonds coupon						-	-	-	-	-	-
Bonds under par						-	-	-	-	-	-
Bonds PIK						-	-	-	-	-	-
Non-op income											
Pretax Profit	9.6	11.5	13.2	15.8	17.4	16.5	18.8	21.3	24.0	27.1	31.1
Taxes	(2.5)	(3.0)	(3.4)	(3.8)	(4.2)	(4.0)	(4.5)	(5.1)	(5.8)	(6.5)	(7.5)
Net Income	7.1	8.5	9.7	12.0	13.2	12.6	14.3	16.2	18.2	20.6	23.6
% Sales	17.8%	18.8%	19.6%	21.7%	21.2%	18.1%	18.6%	18.9%	19.3%	19.6%	20.2%

Balance Sheet

(€m)	2014A	2015A	2016A	2017A	2018A	2019E	2020E	2021E	2022E	2023E	2024E
Trade receivables	22.8	24.0	22.2	24.3	25.7	28.5	30.5	30.4	31.1	34.6	38.4
Inventories	6.4	6.5	6.6	6.6	8.0	8.5	9.5	10.5	11.7	13.0	14.4
Trade payables	(5.0)	(5.2)	(6.0)	(6.7)	(7.3)	(8.9)	(10.9)	(13.2)	(14.6)	(16.2)	(18.0)
NWC	24.2	25.3	22.8	24.2	26.4	28.1	29.1	27.7	28.2	31.3	34.7
Tangible fixed assets	17.0	15.5	16.0	16.5	19.0	21.2	23.7	25.8	28.1	28.8	29.2
Intangible fixed assets (goodwill at impairment test)	10.0	12.0	12.5	12.0	118.7	118.7	118.7	118.7	118.7	118.7	118.7
Financial fixed assets	-	-	-	-	-	-	-	-	-	-	-
FIXED ASSETS	27.0	27.5	28.5	28.5	137.7	139.9	142.4	144.5	146.8	147.5	147.9
TOTAL ASSETS	51.2	52.8	51.3	52.7	164.1	168.0	171.5	172.3	174.9	178.8	182.6
(Cash and equivalents)	(5.8)	(9.2)	(13.7)	(14.8)	(1.5)	(6.0)	(12.6)	(23.8)	(35.2)	(47.7)	(23.4)
Short term financing											
Financial debts	-	-	-	-	65.0	60.8	56.7	52.5	48.3	44.2	0.0
Net Debt	(5.8)	(9.2)	(13.7)	(14.8)	63.5	54.9	44.1	28.7	13.1	(3.6)	(23.4)
Provisions	2.0	2.0	2.0	2.5	3.0	3.0	3.0	3.0	3.0	3.0	3.0
Net equity	55.0	60.0	63.0	65.0	97.6	110.2	124.4	140.6	158.8	179.4	203.0
TOTAL LIABILITIES	51.2	52.8	51.3	52.7	164.1	168.0	171.5	172.3	174.9	178.8	182.6

check

FIGURE 9.4 (Continued)

Cash-flow statement

(€m)	2019E	2020E	2021E	2022E	2023E	2024E
EBITDA	21.5	23.9	26.6	29.6	32.9	36.6
Taxes	(4.0)	(4.5)	(5.1)	(5.8)	(6.5)	(7.5)
Change in provisions	-	-	-	-	-	-
Change in NWC	(1.7)	(1.0)	1.4	(0.5)	(3.1)	(3.4)
Cash Flow from operating activities	15.8	18.4	22.9	23.4	23.4	25.7
Capex	(5.0)	(5.5)	(5.6)	(6.0)	(5.0)	(5.0)
FCFF	10.8	12.9	17.3	17.4	18.4	20.7
Cash (Interest expenses) / Income	(2.2)	(2.1)	(1.9)	(1.8)	(1.7)	(0.9)
New debts / (reimbursements)	(4.2)	(4.2)	(4.2)	(4.2)	(4.2)	(44.2)
FCFE	4.5	6.6	11.2	11.4	12.5	(24.3)
Equity injections / (distributions)	-	-	-	-	-	-
Net Cash Flow	4.5	6.6	11.2	11.4	12.5	(24.3)
RCF drawdown/repayment	-	-	-	-	-	-
Cash beginning of period	1.5	6.0	12.6	23.8	35.2	47.7
Cash end of period	6.0	12.6	23.8	35.2	47.7	23.4

Total equity at entry 97.6
Fund equity at entry 94.4

Returns Analysis - Sensitivity exit year vs exit multiple

Year of Exit	2022	2023	2024
EBITDA	29.6	32.9	36.6
Total debt	48.3	44.2	0.0
Closing cash position	35.2	47.7	23.4
Preferred equity value	96.0	105.6	116.2

Proceeds to Ordinary Equity			
EBITDA Exit Multiple	2022	2023	2024
7.0x	98.1	128.5	163.7
8.0x	127.8	161.5	200.4
9.0x	157.4	194.4	237.0

FIGURE 9.4 (*Continued*)

(money multiples – received/paid)

Total proceeds to Fund

EBITDA Exit Multiple	2022	2023	2024
7.0x	184.4	221.3	263.6
8.0x	211.0	251.0	296.6
9.0x	237.7	280.6	329.5

Money multiples for Fund

EBITDA Exit Multiple	2022	2023	2024
7.0x	1.95x	2.34x	2.79x
8.0x	2.24x	2.66x	3.14x
9.0x	2.52x	2.97x	3.49x

IRR for Fund

EBITDA Exit Multiple	2022	2023	2024
7.0x	18.2%	18.6%	18.7%
8.0x	22.3%	21.6%	21.0%
9.0x	26.0%	24.3%	23.2%

Total proceeds to Management

EBITDA Exit Multiple	2022	2023	2024
7.0x	9.8	12.9	16.4
8.0x	12.8	16.1	20.0
9.0x	15.7	19.4	23.7

Money multiples for Management

EBITDA Exit Multiple	2022	2023	2024
7.0x	3.07x	4.02x	5.12x
8.0x	3.99x	5.05x	6.26x
9.0x	4.92x	6.08x	7.41x

IRR for Management

EBITDA Exit Multiple	2022	2023	2024
7.0x	32.3%	32.1%	31.3%
8.0x	41.4%	38.2%	35.8%
9.0x	48.9%	43.5%	39.6%

FIGURE 9.4 (Continued)

REFERENCES AND FURTHER READING

P. Pignataro. 2014. *Leveraged Buyouts: A Practical Guide to Investment Banking and Private Equity*. Wiley.

J. Rosenbaum, J. Pearl, and J. Harris. 2013. *Investment Banking: Valuation, Leveraged Buyouts, and Mergers and Acquisitions*. Wiley Finance.

SUGGESTED CASES

M. Jensen, W. Burkhardt, and B. Barry. 1989. 'Wisconsin Central Ltd. Railroad and Berkshire Partners (A): Leveraged Buyouts and Financial Distress.' Harvard Business School Case 190-062.

A. Perold. 1990. 'RJR Nabisco – 1990.' Harvard Business School Case 290-021.

W.A. Sahlman. 1988. 'Harris Seafoods Leveraged Buyout.' Harvard Business School Case 289-019.

CHAPTER 10

Management of the Portfolio Companies and Exit

INTRODUCTION

The management of an investment by the private equity fund focuses on:

- **reporting:** a periodic report that the investee company prepares for the fund;
- **monitoring:** controls based on reporting and aimed at creating value;
- **creation of value:** the activity implemented by the fund to increase the value of the portfolio company.

Whilst we do not deal in great detail with this topic in this book, it is important to provide a concise outline of the different techniques since value creation is the essence of a private equity transaction.

REPORTING

The goal of reporting is to:

- promptly report the economic and financial performance to the fund;
- monitor key variables for understanding business performance (through the Tableau de Bord);
- verify that the indicators subject to covenants and/or guarantees are in line with contractual expectations and forecasts;
- provide the fund with information that the same in turn will need to provide its investors.

The frequency of the information can vary from monthly (on variables such as turnover and net debt) to quarterly (income statement and Tableau de Bord), to half-yearly (balance sheet).

MONITORING

The monitoring activity is much more intense than that of the public markets or the bank, as the fund does not have a variety of financial instruments (overdrafts, etc.) that allow it to constantly monitor the company's performance.

The monitoring activity of a fund consists, therefore, in frequent and periodic visits to the company and detailed reports.

Monitoring is functional to:

- promptly activate actions to avoid deterioration of performance;
- protect with timely intervention the capital that the fund has made available.

VALUE CREATION

An integral part of the investment of a private equity fund is a plan to create value by addressing the following four areas:

- **Strategic:** this implies
  - identifying non-core assets;
  - implementing growth initiatives (products, geographies, channels, customers);
  - making add-on acquisitions.
- **Operational:** priority is given to
  - sales: take advantage of growth opportunities;
  - assets:
    - optimise capacity utilisation;
    - maximise operations efficiency;
    - outsource non-core activities;
  - managing costs:
    - optimise procurement;
    - increase efficiency of labour costs;
    - optimise plant overhead, sales force efficiency, and G&A;
    - streamline/consolidate R&D;
    - control capex.
- **Organisational:**
  - build management team:
    - select the best management team to maximise value creation;
    - develop high potentials;
  - build processes:
    - identify core processes;
    - define process owner;
    - redesign processes;
  - build structure
    - define corporate centre and services.

- **Financial:**
  - manage balance sheet:
    - sell non-required assets;
    - use off balance-sheet financing;
  - optimise financial structure:
    - find the optimal financing mix;
    - reduce working capital;
    - optimise cash management.

A private equity fund designs initiatives following a structured approach and categorises actions following their impact on the bottom line of the profit and loss and on the balance sheet. A possible action plan is the following:

- **Revenue enhancement:**
  - customers: increase new customers or share of wallet on existing ones;
  - product: prune marginal products, focus on blockbuster, launch new ones;
  - pricing: by far the most used lever for its immediate impact on the bottom line;
  - channel: analyse the effectiveness and performance of the different available channels;
  - branch network: carefully select the ones to keep and those to close.

- **Cost improvement:**
  - selling, general, and administrative (SG&A) expenses: streamline costs in line with needs;
  - purchasing: negotiate with suppliers best terms;
  - supply chain: select the most efficient position in the value chain;
  - manufacturing: look at different plants' performances, optimise processes, close non-performing units;
  - complexity management: reduce relentlessly the complexity that typically can be found in product offering, production, geographical presence, etc.

- **Capital management:**
  - working capital: improve cash generation by optimising the networking capital cycle;
  - asset optimisation: sell under-performing or under-utilised assets;
  - WACC reduction: carefully select the best capital structure and reduce the cost of its components.

- **Add on acquisitions:**
  - M&A: this is usually the most used growth strategy due to its immediate impact on EBITDA increase and due to the fact that there are multiple arbitrages to exploit when buying smaller companies;
  - integration: a crucial area to obtain synergies.

EXIT

IPO and sale to a trade buyer are the two most common forms of exit route.
Trade sales may well be preferable or equal to an IPO, but they will still require
appropriate planning. Financial bidders should be viewed as serious contenders:
although they need more time to learn their sector, they are often prepared to go
through the same bidding and short-listing process as a trade bidder is.

Other exit routes are secondary sale to financial buyers, share buyback,
options, or recap.

Before analysing the different exit alternatives available to a private equity
owner, there are many areas of the exit process that private equity investors can
positively influence:

- plan the exit from the very start of each investment:
- review continuously the portfolio and watch for potential buyers;
- identify opportunities as they come up;
- use marketing effectively;
- be prepared for all possible exit routes.

In order to improve exit performance, private equity should always consider
the following when considering investing in a new opportunity:

- What will the exit route be?
- Who will purchase the firm?
- Is this the right business strategy for the exit desired?
- Is the business structure appropriate for an effective exit?
- Does management want to exit? Can they be given an incentive? How can
  private equity interests be protected?

A summary 'exit checklist' is provided below:

Strategy:
- make sure there is a strategy;
- seek to achieve a strong growth track record;
- reflect exit plans when choosing strategy options;
- make sure new opportunities are being created, to ensure that growth
  continues;
- be aware that potential buyers may be competitors who will pay a premium for a business that can be merged for profit purposes. Even if
  they do not buy, their interest alone will raise the price.

Marketing:
- report accomplishments to the financial press;
- announce new orders and results;
- be aware that advertising and marketing may help to sell the business.

Financial statements:
- present accounts in a professional manner;
- ensure the accounts are informative, and that they reflect the business strategy;
- ensure the financial statements are consistent from year to year.

Reporting systems:
- present dependable, timely, and relevant management information;
- have reporting systems in place from the outset.

Legal structure:
- keep it simple.

Management:
- ensure the team is balanced, experienced, and of good quality;
- do not permit gaps to arise;
- plan for succession;
- ensure each member can demonstrate a good record at exit.

Since exit is a critical phase of any private equity transaction, and because it can be very time consuming, often private equity investors use advisers to support them in this phase. External advisers include investment banks, M&A specialists, or the corporate finance departments of major accounting firms. Advisers may be used in a number of roles ranging from conducting a search for buyers, to preparing an information memorandum and helping with negotiations. It is normal practice to pay the adviser a percentage of the consideration (success fee) by way of incentive. A fixed element (retainer fee) to the fee can help make sure the adviser spends enough time in advance in preparation of the memorandum of information. It is increasingly common to pay a higher percentage success fee on a margin of proceeds over a certain level as a super incentive to go the extra mile. The importance of maintaining confidentiality should be stressed at the outset. A codename can be used in all correspondence, and the adviser can be asked to limit the giving of knowledge to those members of staff who are actually working on the project. Confidentiality letters should be used, although they cannot be enforced. Commercially sensitive information should not be given out if it would damage the business if the deal fails.

When choosing advisers, private equity funds look for the following qualities:

- contacts
- discreet marketing
- knowledge of industry
- independence
- resources
- ability
- enthusiasm and commitment

- nature and size of investment
- experience
- confidentiality.

It may be a good idea to appoint an adviser in the following circumstances:

- the fund does not have the time or resources to do the work in-house;
- management and fund do not know all potential buyers;
- there is a need for discretion and confidentiality;
- an objective view of the value of the business would be beneficial;
- management/partners do not accept the fund's advice as impartial.

A final note is worthwhile regarding the role of management. Management is usually at the centre of any exit decision. Because of this, many proactive investors like to work out detailed exit arrangements with management at the very start of the investment and some investors will only invest if management has the same exit objective as they do.

IPO

Private equity investors (especially those involved in minority investing) generally like IPOs as an exit route because of the returns they may generate, and because management can remain in charge. However, IPOs are not always a viable exit strategy because the lock up agreement requires the private equity investor to retain a material investment so as to provide confidence to institutional investors. Thus, since it will not matter if there is a good IPO price if the price in the market then falls before the private equity can sell off the remainder, some investors opt for the trade sale process instead.

The most compelling argument for IPOs is that necessary preparation may well lead to a pre-emptive bid, thereby allowing the private equity to have the best of both worlds. On the other hand, the correct investigation of the opportunities for a trade sale may have revealed the same buyer, and may have saved some of the professional costs associated with a flotation.

In summary, the following pros and cons of an IPO should be balanced before deciding to start the IPO process.

- **Advantages:**
  - high price if market is in positive sentiment;
  - preferred by managers;
  - primary and secondary issues permit a staged exit;
  - can be a dual-track approach which may encourage a trade bid;
  - possibility of higher price.

■ **Disadvantages:**
  ● more costly than other routes;
  ● the lock up agreement prevents a complete exit;
  ● illiquidity of many European markets;
  ● not available to many small firms.

The main pre-requisites for an IPO are:

■ regulated stock market with good liquidity;
■ size of issue;
■ growth story;
■ profitable trading history.

TRADE SALE

Trade sale is the sale of the investee company to another company. It usually refers to a strategic buyer who intends to grow his business and for this reason is often willing to pay a higher price than the financial buyer due to the presence of synergies.

Amongst the advantages of a trade sale, it is worth citing:

■ purchasers must pay a premium for synergy, market share, or market entry;
■ certainty because it is a 100% cash exit (subject to warranties, escrows, indemnities, and deferred consideration);
■ less costly than IPO;
■ faster and less complex than IPO;
■ available to small companies;
■ buyers bring industry expertise;
■ need only persuade one buyer, rather than a market.

The most common disadvantages of a trade sale are:

■ not favoured by management, who have to give up independence;
■ only a few trade buyers in some countries;
■ most private equity funds are unwilling to give warranties to buyers.

SECONDARY/TERTIARY SALE TO FINANCIAL BUYERS

Increasingly we witness sales to other private equity funds as an exit route. There are several reasons why this exit route has become more common (especially in buyout): amongst them the credit boom and the increase in capital in the leveraged buyout space.

The main reason why private equity firms will pursue a secondary sale to other private equity firms can be summarised as follows:

- sales to strategic buyers and IPOs may not be possible for niche or undersized businesses;
- secondary buyouts may generate liquidity more quickly than other routes (i.e. IPOs);
- target firms might have already achieved some meaningful results in terms of improved reporting, governance, etc.;
- selling to a financial purchaser may enable the firm to re-leverage;
- private equity may assign greater value to a high-cash/low-growth firm than a trade buyer might;
- the seller fund may have achieved the end of its life and is under pressure to divest.

Amongst the advantages of an exit to a financial investor it is worth citing:

- financial investors have usually sufficient financial resources;
- financial investors bring management expertise.

Amongst the disadvantages of an exit to a financial investor it is worth citing:

- financial investors are tough negotiators;
- financial investors have a short-term horizon;
- company financial risk might increase as a result of leverage (usually used for the transaction).

OTHER EXIT ROUTES (SHARE BUYBACK, OPTIONS, RECAP)

Other techniques or exit routes can or should be considered (also when drafting the legal documentation). The most used are:

- **Share buybacks:** Buy back by co-investors or management has been a common form of exit for passive investors, and for funds when alternative routes are unsuccessful. This is often because a weak performance results in a lack of interested buyers, or because management or majority owners of smaller firms have declined to sell to a third party. Aside from insolvency, a buyback is the least popular route because of the lack of competition, and the buyer's strong position results in a low sale price for the current investor.

- **Options:** used to achieve an exit from a transaction where the exit options are limited. In order to be effective, the fund needs to identify the counterparts for a sale and to establish both a time and a price or a formula under which a price is established such as for example:
  - Fixed: per share price or minimum return of Euribor + x%;
  - variable: based on an independent fair valuation of the company's equity;
  - variable: based on trading multiples (e.g. x times EBITDA).

REFERENCES AND FURTHER READING

O. Gadiesh and H. MacArthur. 2008. *Lessons from Private Equity Any Company Can Use (Memo to the CEO)*. Harvard Business Review Press.

C. Zook and J. Allen. 2010. *Profit from the Core*. Harvard Business Review Press.

SUGGESTED CASES

D. Yoffie and A. Mehta. 2015. '$19B 4 txt app WhatsApp...omg!' Harvard Business School Case 812-049.

CHAPTER 11

Private Debt

INTRODUCTION

Quantitative and qualitative details of each transaction; key drivers and adequate allowance for their impact; assessment of management's character and competence; and identification and analysis of risk are the key ingredients illustrated in the previous chapters to properly assess credit risk.

Once all the analysis has been performed, due diligence (site visits; trade checks; interviews with the borrower's competitors, suppliers, customers, and employees; accounting and tax reviews effected by external audit firms, etc.) made, and meetings with the borrower executed, the credit analyst is now in a position to assemble everything as a prelude to developing the structure of the transaction.

Required preliminary financial analysis for this stage includes: analysis of historical financial statements, cash-flow statements, liquidity analysis, capital structure analysis, forecast and sensitivity analysis, and estimation of asset values (both market value and liquidation value).

This chapter deals with long-term debt structuring, which is the dominant product offered by traditional private debt funds.[1]

In this sense, there are several analogies and commonalities with LBO debt structuring (which represents a more sophisticated debt structure).

STRUCTURING A CREDIT FACILITY

The primary objective of structuring a credit facility is to ensure that the structure provides adequate protection for the lender from identified risk and compensates him for the risks taken, whilst allowing the borrower sufficient flexibility to meet his business targets. In this sense, an ideal loan structure combines the specific

---

[1]Thanks to process digitalisation and data analytics, a new breed of private debt funds offering short-term lending (mainly invoice discounting) is making its way onto the market.

need of the borrower with the lender's assessment of the risks; this is then adjusted to take into account the lender's appetite for that specific risk, competitive factors, market conditions, and the existing debt repayment commitments of the borrower.

Structuring a credit facility is both a modelling and 'qualitative' exercise. From a modelling perspective, a forecasting funding profile consists of the following steps.

- **Capital structure:** forecast maximum debt capacity and decide acceptable refinancing risk. Some ratios can be used as 'benchmarks': leverage, gearing, ICR.
- **Debt profile:** use base (also called bank) case to input amount, drawdown, repayment profile, tenor, and interest rate.
- **Cash flow debt service coverage:** check whether cash flow coverage ratios (e.g. debt service coverage ratio (DSCR)) fall within acceptable limits and if not adjust debt profile.
- **Financial covenants (see later):** set covenant levels based on base case and check whether, in a downside case, covenants act as warning indicators and if they are breached.

In parallel to running several iterations of the model, the following elements should be thought through when structuring a credit facility.

- **Amount:** this is the starting point of every credit structuring. The borrower usually quantifies an anticipated future need and the lender has to figure what is his maximum willingness to lend as a function of the borrower debt capacity. Debt capacity is the maximum amount a company can borrow and repay in full at the end of the tenor of the loan. Debt capacity is usually determined using:
  - A cash flow borrowing base: cash flow debt capacity is defined as the amount of debt that can be fully serviced by a business from its cash flows over a period. Full servicing of debt demands that both interest and principal are paid when due and no other conditions of borrowing, such as covenants, are broken. In reality debt may be serviced in a number of ways, from cash flow profits, cash balances surplus to normal business requirements, proceeds from the sale of assets or businesses, and refinancing through debt or equity. If, after calculating the cash flow debt capacity, the loan officer discovers that the borrower cannot support the (existing or proposed level of) debt, then alternative repayment sources should be analysed thoroughly. A 'theoretical' approach is to look at the discounted free cash flows; but the practitioner approach focuses on cash flow coverage ratios (e.g. DSCR) or on comparing, during the assumed tenor horizon, annual cash flow available for debt service with debt service needs. Cash flow methodology is usually used to support credit application where the use of proceeds are: capex, acquisitions, or permanent working capital needs. The primary source of repayment is cash flow (hence the

main risk is insufficient cash flow to service debt) but very often a second line of defence is represented by guarantees on the company's assets. Covenants are usually structured to protect the cash flow stream and both repayment and amortisation are linked to cash flow forecasts. In several instances, asset sale is a secondary source of repayment (with cash flow being the primary source). Examples are: airlines, property investors, hotels, shipping companies, and natural resource companies.

- An asset sale borrowing base: asset sale borrowing base is defined as the maximum amount of debt a bank is willing to lend based on the net realisable value of a pool of assets. It is used to control the drawing amount and preserve asset coverage. The typical loan officer procedure involves:
    - *defining eligible assets:* amongst the most eligible assets (receivables, inventory, fixed assets) it is important to identify the typical non-eligible:
        - *receivables:* inter-company, more than 90 days overdue, assigned to another creditor;
        - *inventory:* perishable goods, obsolete inventory, work in progress, assigned to another creditor;
        - *fixed assets:* old equipment, construction in progress, assigned to another creditor.
- Assign lending margins (see Table 11.1).

    When setting margins, it is important to consider quality and diversity, existence of a secondary market, and cost of collection and liquidation:
    - calculate borrowing base at each drawdown;
    - obtain regular status on assets;
    - monitor borrowing base coverage.

    Asset sale borrowing base methodology is usually used to support credit application where the use of proceeds is a permanent (but revolving) requirement for trading (and tradable) assets. The primary source of repayment is the sale of assets. Since the key risk is the deterioration of quality, value, and liquidity of assets, covenants are usually structured to protect asset quality and value. Repayment is linked to the value of the borrowing base (or individual asset) and thus tenor is usually short or medium term with a clean-up requirement. Key characteristics of the assets are liquidity, wide marketability, ease of valuation, commoditisation, and

TABLE 11.1 Typical lending margins in asset-based lending transactions.

Assets	Margin
Cash	100%
Receivables (applied to eligible ones)	60–80%
Inventory	45–55%
Equipment and real estate	70% for equipment, 80% for real estate
Intangibles	Low/none

standardisation. Typical situations where lending is based on asset value borrowing base are traders, property developers, asset securitisation (not covered in this book).

The main drawback of asset based methods of determining debt levels is that in recessions, asset values in many sectors fall well below even the worst fears: in several instances minimum value clauses have failed to offer protection because asset values fell dramatically and owners were unable either to repay debt or to offer sufficient additional collateral.

- **Currency:** the main factors that determine the currency of the loan are the currency of the need, the currency of the source of repayment, and the currency of the assets that are being financed. In certain instances, borrowers choose to raise funds in certain currencies to expand the range of funding sources available to them or to take advantage of interest rate differentials. Particular attention (and eventual pricing adjustments) should be applied in case of illiquid or shallow currency markets.

- **Tenor:** this is usually determined by the interplay of cash flow profile, lender appetite, borrower request, and existing debt profile. The basic principle of tenor matching implies that long-term or permanent needs should be financed with long-term or permanent funds and, conversely, short-term needs by short-term funds. Short-term funding is not a secure source for the company, and therefore a company which is using short-term funds to finance a permanent need is exposing itself to the risk that it may have to liquidate fixed or permanent assets to repay short-term debt. It should be noted, though, that many companies have a permanent level of working capital which, given its nature and in order to ensure stability in funding, should also be financed with long-term or permanent funds. The cash flow and debt capacity analysis will indicate how much of the long-term funding can be provided by long-term debt as opposed to equity.

- **Repayment profile:** typically either bullet or amortising, the repayment profile is set in order to match the borrower cash flows, reduce the bank exposure in case of default, and take into account the actual repayment obligations under existing debt. The most popular variations to the above are:
  - grace periods: principal repayments do not start until a later specified period;
  - cash sweep mechanism: all cash available for debt service – to be exactly defined – prior to certain payments (e.g., dividend payments, capex, above a pre-agreed amount) are to be used to reduce the principal outstanding;
  - put provision: lender has the right to sell the debt back (i.e., ask for early repayment) to the issuer/borrower at a designated price and on pre-agreed dates;
  - call provision: issuer or borrower has the right to buy the debt back (i.e., repay early) from the investor/lender at a designated price and on pre-agreed dates.

- **Drawdown:** typically driven by client need, level of control desired by the lender, and condition precedent, this will be affected by the borrowing base and eventual performance milestones. It is usually structured as either one lump sum or as drawings over a period. Although subject to eventual conditions preceding drawdown, in the former case the lender has little control, whilst drawdown arrangements can be put in place in the case that more control is required.

■ **Conditions precedent:** these are requirements the borrower must satisfy before the bank has a legal obligation to extend the loan. Conditions may include business transactions (that must be concluded or events that must have occurred), counsel's opinions, satisfaction by the lender of the due diligences, certificate of no default, resolution of the Board of Directors authorising the transaction, and no material adverse changes (MAC) affecting the company prior to the transaction.

■ **Security:** this establishes the lender's control on specific assets and indirectly on the overall cash flow of the company. In this sense, it helps to ensure that the lender is given priority in the distribution of operating cash flow. Determining the correct security to take depends on several factors:
  ● current market value of the assets;
  ● expected future value in liquidation;
  ● reliability of the prediction with which residual values can be predicted over the life of the loan;
  ● liquidity of the collateral;
  ● ability to effectively perfect a lien;
  ● cost of disposing of or maintaining the assets in repossession;
  ● current and prospective participation of other senior secured lenders.

The borrower charges assets typically by means of a mortgage which is registered and enforceable under local laws. Collateral can be seen as an alternative repayment source only if a realistic resale value can be established and collateral can be repossessed and reasonably quickly disposed of. On the one hand, cash in an escrow account pledged to the lender is identifiable and the value is determinable; on the other hand, the realisable value for land and building depends on market demand and may require considerable time to realise, whilst the value of specialised industrial equipment is even more questionable (due to the limited number of buyers for the equipment, the cost of removing and reinstalling the equipment, and the physical condition of the equipment). For all these reasons, the value of collateral as a repayment source is not always a reliable alternative. Looking at the different types of assets, we can summarise as follows:
  ● Physical collateral:
    ○ *inventory/stock:* medium to low (as a function of type) liquidity;
    ○ *transportation/equipment:* low liquidity;
    ○ *real estate:* medium liquidity;
    ○ *equipment:* low liquidity;
    ○ *rights and patents:* low liquidity (unless special cases).
  ● Intangible collateral:
    ○ *contracts and concessions:* medium to low liquidity;

- o *non-traded securities:* low liquidity;
- o *intangible assets (incl. brands):* low liquidity (unless special cases).
- Financial collateral:
- o *cash/bank accounts:* very high liquidity;
- o *traded securities:* very high liquidity (if investments are short-term);
- o *receivables:* medium to high (as a function of type) liquidity;
- o *insurance policies:* medium to high liquidity.

- **Ranking:** determining the ranking of a debt instrument is key to identifying the lender's access to and claim on cash flow in relation to the borrower's other obligations, and to safeguarding a lender's position. In fact, good credit will have a primary and a secondary source of repayment (and, if possible, a third). This is particularly relevant for long-term loans that might encounter changes in operating conditions over the life of the loan. Whereas cash flows generated are the primary source of repayment, reliance on a secondary source may occur if the primary source is impaired: in this case the secondary source of repayment may be from the proceeds of a guarantee, exercise of the share pledge, or sale of assets pledged to the lender. Any lender seeks the highest degree of seniority. Creditors can be divided into five categories (as a function of priority ranking and recovery expectations):
  - Privileged creditors: these must be paid immediately. The claims may include wages and benefits and fees paid to insolvency specialists.
  - Secured creditors: these benefit from collateral security in support of their credit. They include financial creditors and some wages.
  - Unsecured creditors: these are the majority of creditors, and include financial creditors, most suppliers, and wages.
  - Subordinated creditors: these have agreed to be paid after other creditors in return for higher payments, or have been subordinated because of the organisational structure of the group. Ultimate contractual subordination recognises that the holder of more senior debt would recover more in the event of a default. In going-concern subordination, creditors will be paid interest only after the holders of more senior debt have been paid. A number of mechanisms are in place to put off interest payments in the event of non-payment. Certain debt instruments allow interest payment to be capitalised or 'rolled up'; others have a paid-in-kind approach, referring to the practice of having interest payments made with common or preferred stock;
  - shareholders: they get paid last (preferred shares first and then ordinary ones).

Claims can be:

- Senior: a debt financing obligation issued by a bank or similar financial institution to a company or individual that holds legal claim to the borrower's assets above all other debt obligations. The loan is considered senior to all other claims against the borrower, which means that in the event of a bankruptcy the senior bank loan is the first to be repaid, before all other interested parties receive repayment.

- Junior: (also known as subordinated) is debt which ranks after the senior debt if a company falls into liquidation or bankruptcy. Such debt is referred to as subordinate because the debt providers (the lenders) have subordinate status in relationship to the normal debt. Subordinated debt has a lower priority than other bonds of the issuer in case of liquidation during bankruptcy, and ranks below: the liquidator, government tax authorities, and senior debt holders in the hierarchy of creditors. A junior position can be acceptable when the lender is aware of the extra risks and is compensated appropriately;
- *Pari passu* i.e. ranking equally: each creditor is paid pro rata in accordance with the amount of his claim. *Pari passu* status can be achieved via a *pari passu* clause, negative pledge, restriction on sale of assets, restrictions on further borrowing, or inter-creditor agreement (a document spelling out the agreed-upon priority of each party's claims against the company's assets, which may be different to the relative priority that would operate under law).

Seniority or subordination can be achieved:

- Legally: legal seniority or subordination refers to the order of creditors' claims when a borrower's business is liquidated, and can be achieved by contract/agreement (e.g. an inter-creditor agreement that specifies that the debt is senior or subordinated to a particular debt) or by taking security by means of a lien on a company's assets. Senior unsecured creditors will be paid from the liquidator before creditors whose claims are legally junior and, in absence of any junior unsecured claims, all senior unsecured lenders will rank *pari passu* with each other and legally junior to secured creditors. Secured lenders (or creditors) will receive the proceeds of the sale of their collateral in settlement of their claims before unsecured creditors receive payments from the proceeds of liquidation. In case of surplus from the collateral proceeds after secured creditors' claims have been met, it is made available to pay junior claims. In case of deficit of the collateral proceeds to meet the secured creditors' claims, they become unsecured creditors for the shortfall. A 'negative pledge' (prohibiting the borrower from giving security) and/or *pari passu* clause is very often used to maintain existing ranking (i.e. to ensure that no lender can achieve legal seniority over others by taking a security interest in assets of the borrower). When there are various lenders with different security interests, an inter-creditor agreement may be entered into by the different lenders. If some or all of a company's assets have been given as security to lenders, a new obligation may be secured by a secondary security interest in all or some of the same assets, thus placing the new lender ahead of any unsecured creditors and permitting him to achieve a degree of control over what happens to the assets (since his consent will be needed to sell or dispose of those assets).
- Structurally: in contractual subordination (Figure 11.1a), loans are made to the same company but the senior creditor and junior creditor agree

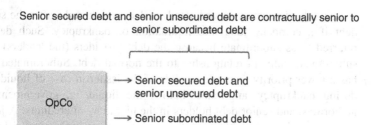

Senior secured debt and senior unsecured debt are contractually senior to senior subordinated debt

OpCo

→ Senior secured debt and senior unsecured debt

→ Senior subordinated debt

FIGURE 11.1a   Contractual subordination example.

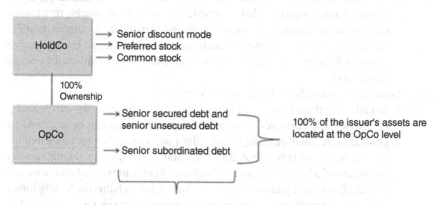

HoldCo

→ Senior discount mode
→ Preferred stock
→ Common stock

100% Ownership

OpCo

→ Senior secured debt and senior unsecured debt

→ Senior subordinated debt

100% of the issuer's assets are located at the OpCo level

Debt obligations at the OpCo level are structurally senior to obligations at the HoldCo level
(as long as the OpCo has not guaranteed any debt at the HoldCo level)

FIGURE 11.1b   Structural subordination.

priority of payment by contract. Structural subordination (Figure 11.1b) arises when there is more than one borrower within a group of companies and one lender is disadvantaged in terms of priority of payment relative to other lenders because of lending to one company in the group rather than another.

- *Contractual subordination:* Although closely tied to legal seniority, structural subordination applies to an ongoing business as well as one in liquidation. A typical example of structural subordination is a loan to the finance holding company ('HoldCo') acting as the 'treasurer' for a group of operating subsidiaries companies ('OpCos'). In such a situation, the lender relies upon the OpCos to repay their inter-company loans, but being 'one degree away' from the assets and cash flows of the OpCos makes lenders to HoldCo structurally subordinated to any lenders to the OpCos. To determine the ranking of a debt relative to other creditors, lenders must analyse the legal structure of the group of companies to which they are lending and understand inter-company transactions (in particular if they are in the form of equity investments or loans). In general terms, the further from the ultimate source of repayment (assets or cash flows), the more deeply subordinated in structural terms the lender will be. In addition to putting limits to the amount of indebtedness of different companies within the group, there are some ways to mitigate subordination such as:

- o *Upstream guarantees:* entities with the most economic substance may irrevocably and unconditionally guarantee the obligations of the parent company or the issuing entity on a senior basis in order to mitigate structural subordination. In the event of a default, the assets of both entities would have to satisfy the obligations of both the guarantor and the beneficiary. At this point, the debt obligations of both entities would then have the same level of seniority and would be *pari passu*. Upstream guarantees may be limited in some jurisdictions because of the potential for fraudulent conveyance.
- o *Inter-company loans:* these involve the use of inter-company loans from the parent to the entities in charge of the operating assets.
- o *Portfolio diversity and concentration of liabilities:* in the former, creditors of the parent company have a better chance of recovery if the operating assets of the subsidiaries are diversified geographically and arranged as separate business entities, whilst in the latter, chances increase if liabilities are not concentrated.
- effectively or economically: by structuring the interest and principal repayment dates of a loan/bond in a way that one group of lenders/investors will be (dis)advantaged relative to other lenders/investors.

- **Covenants:** covenants establish minimum standards of conduct and obligation for the borrower, so as to limit the risk that the loan will not be repaid. The main purpose is to protect the sources of repayment and the lender's access to it, by preserving the nature of the borrower's business, allowing its performance to be monitored, and providing warning and timely signals of unacceptable or deteriorating performance. When the source of repayment is cash flow, then it is essential to maintain adequate cash flows (and a covenant to test the level of cash generated by the company compared to its requirements to pay principal and interest is used), to limit uses of cash flow (thus restrictions on what the company can do with its cash such as dividends, capex, etc. are inserted), and have restrictions on additional indebtedness (so that the cash available to service the existing debt is not diverted by other obligations) and ranking of guarantees (hence there will be safeguards to ensure that the lender's ranking is maintained relative to other lenders). When the source of repayment depends on asset values, safeguards include maintenance of assets (e.g. covenants with restriction on asset sales or negative pledge or adequate insurance or rights to inspection), maintenance of asset coverage (e.g. loan to value mechanisms or minimum net worth clauses or proceeds of sale to be used to reduce loan), and requirements that the company representing it has valid legal title to the assets, that they will be maintained in good condition, that they be insured, that they not be sold without the consent of the lender, and that proceeds of any sale be used to repay debt.

Covenants are usually classified as:

- Affirmative: lay out things the borrower must do (including things it would do even if there were no loan). Examples of affirmative covenants are: application of loan proceeds to the agreed upon purpose; reporting obligations; compliance with laws; right of inspection; preservation of corporate existence; maintenance of insurance, properties, records, and books.

- Negative: established to prevent the borrower from doing things that could harm lenders. Example of negative covenants are restriction of mortgages, pledges, and other encumbrance of assets, limitation of additional or total indebtness, restriction on payments of cash dividends, restriction on mergers, restriction on sale of assets, restriction on sales of subsidiaries, limitation on capex, restriction on engaging in other businesses.

- Financial: establish financial parameters within which the contractual party is required to operate and are designed to discipline or constrain borrowers, guarantors, and other parties. If maintained, they should enhance the protection of the lender's financial interest in its investment – especially its interest in having a loan repaid on a timely basis – and, indirectly, better ensure the institutional objective of the lender in seeing projects completed. On an operational level, they allow for the lender's monitoring of its loan since they allow control over matters that may have an impact on the repayment of the loan (e.g. capital investments, sale of assets, changes in capital structure, etc.). In this sense, financial covenants are only as good as the quality and timeliness of the financial information needed to calculate the ratios. To be understandable, financial statements should be not only prepared on the basis of accounting standards and principles that the lender considers acceptable, but also audited at least annually by auditors acceptable to the lender. Non-compliance with a financial covenant provides the lender with a warning about the deteriorating quality of the borrower and the leverage to force a dialogue with the client and, if necessary, exercise remedies. If no satisfactory solution can be found, the failure to comply with a financial ratio covenant in the case of a loan may require that, to preserve its interests, the lender declare a default and accelerate repayment of the principal amount of the loan and all outstanding interest and other charges. Financial covenants should be set at levels that reflect both a realistic and an acceptable projected financial performance of the borrower. In the case of term loans, such levels should comfortably allow repayment of the underlying debt whilst maintaining the borrower as a healthy going concern. Ratios should be set at levels where failure to meet those levels would trigger a default before the lenders' investment becomes seriously impaired.

The most commonly used financial covenants (and relative indicative values) are:

○ *Liquidity:*
  ▪ Current ratio: a generally acceptable optimal value (with all caveats – especially for different working capital requirements – related to the various industries and firm size) is above 2x (with ratios between 1.5x and 2x still indicating financial stability).
  ▪ Quick ratio (or acid test): a generally acceptable optimal value (with all caveats related to the various industries and firm size) is above 1x–1.5x.

○ *Solvency:*
  ▪ Gearing (or debt to equity) ratio: the purpose of this covenant is to control the capital structure of the borrower and prevent additional borrowing unless there is a proportional increase in capital. A generally acceptable optimal value (with all caveats related to the various industries and firm size) is up to 1x (with ratios between 50% and 80% still indicating an acceptable financial situation).
  ▪ Debt to capital ratio: a generally acceptable optimal value (with all caveats related to the various industries and firm size) is up to 30% (with ratios between 30% and 45% still indicating an acceptable financial situation).
  ▪ Leverage ratio: a generally acceptable value (with all caveats related to the various industries, lifecycle, and firm size) is up to 4x.

○ *Coverage ratios:*
  ▪ Interest cover ratio: although it depends on industry, business risk, and guarantees, a generally acceptable value for senior ICR is above 2x (with 1.5x still acceptable).
  ▪ Debt service cover ratio: the purpose of the DSCR is to provide an indication of the ability to repay debt from internally generated cash on a current basis and of the degree of reduction in cash flow margins that lenders can sustain before not being able to service debt. Although it depends on industry, business risk, and guarantees, a generally acceptable value is above 1.3x. (A lower level is only acceptable for businesses with stable cash flow, whilst for companies with less stable cash flow the DSCR should be a minimum of 1.5x. It should be noted that for turn-around or green-field projects, where performance is expected to improve gradually, the level of the covenant should be stepped up annually.)

▪ **Mandatory prepayment:** this is usually required upon the occurrence of any of the following events:
  ● a listing, issue of securities, public offering, or flotation of the borrower (or its group);
  ● a sale of all or substantially all of the assets or business of the borrower (or its group);

- a change of ownership or control of the borrower;
- illegality;
- disposals, extraordinary receipts, insurance claims.

■ **Financial flexibility:** one of the first areas to consider is the coverage by current assets of current liabilities if the company were to liquidate these assets over the short term; when the sale is not realistic, such analysis is of limited use in judging the liquidity of the firm since it does not measure the company's real access to cash or the cash generating ability of the company. It is therefore important also to consider other sources of cash that may be available to a company: other cash income (such as dividends received) or proceeds from the sale of excess assets, or the ability to raise cash from external sources – particularly committed banking facilities. Whilst commercial paper is a reliable source of short-term liquidity for investment-level companies, for other borrowers committed bank credit facilities are the most reliable source of liquidity; bond and equity capital markets are also other viable sources of liquidity. Finally, realisable proceeds from saleable assets are a regular source of liquidity for many companies. In assessing the short-term needs of a company, credit analysts should evaluate additional funding needs to meet seasonal peaks in conjunction with the availability of cash or near cash resources: a key source of such cash may be a company's own cash reserves as well as its bank facilities. Where possible, the extent to which drawing under committed facilities are conditional upon the company meeting certain criteria (e.g. certain financial or business covenants) and the terms of such conditions should be ascertained. It is important to note that, whilst a facility may be committed, if the company is in breach or close to breaching covenants the funds may not be available for drawing at a critical time. In summary, when evaluating the financial flexibility of a company, the following liquidity checklist may be useful:
- Debt profile:
  - long-term debt maturities;
  - commercial paper outstanding.
- Bank lines:
  - total amount;
  - amount available;
  - maturity of loan;
  - covenants;
  - MAC clause;
  - debt triggers;
  - restrictive covenants (head room).
- Off balance-sheet obligations:
  - subsidiary guarantees;
  - support agreements;
  - joint ventures;

- take-or-pay obligations;
- contingent liabilities.
- Alternative sources of liquidity:
  - free cash flow;
  - cash/liquid assets;
  - asset sales;
  - dividend flexibility;
  - capital spending flexibility;
  - parental support.

Credit analysts should be aware of the following circumstances that could give rise to increases in cash outlays: a crisis in consumer confidence in the product (e.g. mad cow crisis in the beef industry), an important negative litigation judgment (e.g. asbestos), a negative change in commodity prices, and managerial misconduct, real or alleged (e.g. WorldCom). When a company has financial flexibility, it has the means of finding cash and, in so doing, avoiding a default on payment. The best ways for management to avoid liquidity crises include:

- not relying too heavily on short-term, confidence-sensitive debt;
- having well distributed and manageable debt maturities;
- having well-established relationships with the company's banks;
- providing significant headroom in bank loan covenants;
- making sure there is sufficient financial disclosure.

- **Events of default:** this section sets out the circumstances in which the bank has the right to discontinue the loan. These circumstances include:
  - failure to pay interest and principal when due;
  - inaccuracy in representation and warranties;
  - failure to abide by a covenant;
  - bankruptcy, liquidation, appointment of receiver;
  - impairment of collateral, invalidity of a guarantee or security agreement;
  - failure to pay other indebtness when due or perform under related agreements:
    - cross default (right of the bank to declare an event of default when the borrower is in default on another obligation);
    - cross acceleration;
  - change of management or ownership;
  - extraordinary circumstances;
  - expropriation of assets;
  - MAC.

- **Pricing:** pricing is determined by the level of risk, competition, market conditions, internal profitability targets, and alternative sources of financing available to the borrower. Pricing may consist of a number of items, the most important of which are:
  - Fees: these can include a commitment fee (to compensate the bank for committing the capital during the life of the loan), upfront fee (to compensate

the bank for the work done), and an arranging fee (to compensate the bank
for arranging the loan).

- Margin: risk premium is the determinant of sovereign risk, credit risk, and
  specific liquidity risk. When determining the risk premium, the lender
  takes into account general costs, maturity, credit deterioration/migration,
  and unexpected loss.
- Yield protection: this can take the form of a make-whole clause, a
  pre-payment fee, etc;
- Equity kicker: warrant, call option, or other performance related/equity
  value creation instrument.

SANITY CHECKS

Table 11.2 can serve as a high-level guide to credit risk profiles as a consequence
of business risk, financial risk, and liquidity of a company.

TABLE 11.2 Credit risk as a function of business, financial, and liquidity risk.

Credit risk profile	Business risk characteristics	Financial risk characteristics	Liquidity
Very low	■ Undisputed leader in global, established industries with strong demand fundamentals ■ Diverse and stable sources of cash flows ■ Strong record of growth and success organically and through acquisition	■ Growth together with sustained low debt leverage, sometimes even net cash position ■ Stable distribution of dividends	■ Stable and significant free and discretionary cash flow ■ Unhindered access to short- and long-term debt markets and equity markets ■ Undrawn bank and capital market short-term debt facilities
Low	■ Leader in more competitive industry, or in a narrow segment with strong demand ■ May be supported by regulatory protection or incumbent position ■ Diverse sources of cash flows, competitive operations	■ Higher profitability ■ Growth with sustained low debt leverage ■ Debt leverage may be higher because of growth by acquisition if business risk characteristics are favourable	■ Stable cash flow ■ Easy access to debt and equity markets ■ May have committed bank facilities for 3–5 years

(continued)

TABLE 11.2   (*Continued*)

Credit risk profile	Business risk characteristics	Financial risk characteristics	Liquidity
Moderate	▪ Large, established competitors of the industry leaders ▪ Leaders of industries with less attractive characteristics ▪ Successful niche firms with low levels of debt, or benefiting from a competitive factor such as brand	▪ Finances are usually more aggressive, due to capital-intensive business, or to aggressive financial policies ▪ Ability to pay debt over next 3 years ▪ Cash flow may depend on business cycle ▪ Possibility of modest dividend payments	▪ May not have readily available access to debt and equity markets ▪ Consequently, need to have committed bank facilities for 3–5 years
High	▪ Second-tier participants in a global sector, with less attractive characteristics ▪ Companies with a below-average operating profile ▪ Companies with the potential to be industry leaders, with very high levels of debt because of over-investment at the top of the business cycle	▪ Tight debt-repayment ratios ▪ Volatile cash flow ▪ Capital structure is usually leveraged ▪ Acquisitions and dividends are probably not from free cash flow	▪ Generation of cash flow only in strong phase of business cycle ▪ Discretionary cash flow is likely to be marginal, if present at all ▪ Access to debt capital markets could be inconsistent and depends on the credit cycle ▪ Committed credit facilities for 3–5 years are necessary
Very high	▪ Weaker participants in industries with unfavourable characteristics ▪ Companies with operational problems such as outdated equipment, reliance on a high-risk asset or poor business model	▪ Debt repayment ratios are tight ▪ No dividend payments ▪ Capital structure is usually very leveraged	▪ Debt service is unlikely in the short term ▪ Consequently long-dated debt is necessary and short-term debt is both secured and subject to stringent covenants

Source: Based on data from Ganguin and Bilardello (2004).

Step 1 – Define the assumptions of the model

(%)	2017	2018	2019	2020	2021	2022	2023	2024
Sales Growth (%)	17.5%	24.9%	5.0%	5.0%	5.0%	7.5%	7.5%	7.5%
EBITDA Margin (% Sales)	40.8%	38.5%	37.5%	37.5%	37.5%	40.0%	40.0%	40.0%
DA (% Sales)	(3.0%)	(11.0%)	(11.0%)	(11.0%)	(11.0%)	(12.0%)	(12.0%)	(12.0%)
Change in Working Capital (% Sales)	-2.1%	(2.5%)	(3.0%)	(3.0%)	(3.0%)	(5.0%)	(5.0%)	(5.0%)
CapEx (% Sales)	0.0%	(1.8%)	(1.8%)	(1.8%)	(1.8%)	(1.8%)	(1.8%)	(1.8%)
Tax (% EBT)			35.0%	35.0%	35.0%	35.0%	35.0%	35.0%
Cash Sweep (% of Excess Cash)			30.0%	30.0%	30.0%	30.0%	30.0%	30.0%

Step 2 – Define the debt schedule and pricing

Debt Structure	Term (Years)	Amort.	x EBITDA	Amount	Margin	Interest Rate
Senior debt						
Term Loan A	7	Balloon	2.8x	60.0	2.25%	4.25%
Term Loan B	8	Bullet	1.4x	30.0	2.75%	4.75%
Term Loan C	9	Bullet	0.9x	20.0	3.25%	5.25%
Revolver	7		0.9x	20.0	2.25%	4.25%
Mezzanine	10	Bullet	1.4x	30.0		
PIK Interest					5.00%	5.00%
Cash Interest					5.00%	7.00%
EURIBOR						2.00%

Step 3 – Define the senior debt repayment schedule

Senior Debt Repayment Schedule	2017	2018	2019	2020	2021	2022	2023	2024
Term Loan A								
Interest rate			4.25%	4.25%	4.25%	4.25%	4.25%	4.25%
Fixed charges cover			1.4x	1.5x	1.3x	1.4x	1.5x	1.6x
Amortisation schedule (% of total facility)			10%	10%	15%	15%	15%	15%
Opening balance			60.0	52.3	44.2	33.8	22.9	11.5
Principal repayments			(6.0)	(6.0)	(9.0)	(9.0)	(9.0)	(9.0)
Cash sweep			(1.7)	(2.0)	(1.4)	(1.9)	(2.4)	(2.5)
Interest expense			(2.4)	(2.1)	(1.7)	(1.2)	(0.7)	(0.2)
Closing Balance		60.0	52.3	44.2	33.8	22.9	11.5	0.0
Term Loan B								
Interest rate			4.75%	4.75%	4.75%	4.75%	4.75%	4.75%
Amortisation schedule (% of total facility)			0%	0%	0%	0%	0%	0%
Opening balance			30.0	30.0	30.0	30.0	30.0	30.0
Principal repayments			0.0	0.0	0.0	0.0	0.0	0.0
Cash sweep			0.0	0.0	0.0	0.0	0.0	0.0
Interest expense			(1.4)	(1.4)	(1.4)	(1.4)	(1.4)	(1.4)
Closing Balance		30.0	30.0	30.0	30.0	30.0	30.0	30.0

FIGURE 11.2 Modelling example of a private debt transaction.

Term Loan C

	2017	2018	2019	2020	2021	2022	2023	2024
Interest rate			5.25%	5.25%	5.25%	5.25%	5.25%	5.25%
Amortisation schedule (% of total facility)			0%	0%	0%	0%	0%	0%
Opening balance			20.0	20.0	20.0	20.0	20.0	20.0
Principal repayments			0.0	0.0	0.0	0.0	0.0	0.0
Cash sweep			0.0	0.0	0.0	0.0	0.0	0.0
Interest expense			(1.1)	(1.1)	(1.1)	(1.1)	(1.1)	(1.1)
Closing Balance		20.0	20.0	20.0	20.0	20.0	20.0	20.0

Revolver

	2017	2018	2019	2020	2021	2022	2023	2024
Interest rate			4.25%	4.25%	4.25%	4.25%	4.25%	4.25%
Commitment fee			1.70%	1.70%	1.70%	1.70%	1.70%	1.70%
Commitment			20.0					
Undrawn			20.0	20.0	20.0	20.0	20.0	20.0
Opening cash balance			0.0	4.0	8.8	12.1	16.6	22.2
Cash increase/(decrease)			4.0	4.7	3.4	4.4	5.6	7.4
Closing cash balance before Revolver			4.0	8.8	12.1	16.6	22.2	29.6
Drawdown/(repayment)			0.0	0.0	0.0	0.0	0.0	0.0
Minimum closing cash balance		3.0						
Opening balance			0.0	0.0	0.0	0.0	0.0	0.0
Drawdown/(repayment)			0.0	0.0	0.0	0.0	0.0	0.0
Closing Balance		0.0	0.0	0.0	0.0	0.0	0.0	0.0
Interest expense			0.0	0.0	0.0	0.0	0.0	0.0
Commitment fee on Unused Revolver			(0.3)	(0.3)	(0.3)	(0.3)	(0.3)	(0.3)

Step 4 – Define the Mezzanine Loan repayment schedule

Mezzanine Repayment Schedule	2017	2018	2019	2020	2021	2022	2023	2024
Mezzanine								
Interest rate - PIK			5.0%	5.0%	5.0%	5.0%	5.0%	5.0%
Interest rate - cash			7.0%	7.0%	7.0%	7.0%	7.0%	7.0%
Amortisation schedule (% of total facility)			0.0%	0.0%	0.0%	0.0%	0.0%	0.0%
Opening balance			40.0	42.0	44.1	46.3	48.6	51.1
Principal repayments			0.0	0.0	0.0	0.0	0.0	0.0
Interest expense - PIK			(2.0)	(2.1)	(2.2)	(2.3)	(2.4)	(2.6)
Interest expense - cash			(2.9)	(3.0)	(3.2)	(3.3)	(3.5)	(3.7)
Closing Balance		40.0	42.0	44.1	46.3	48.6	51.1	53.6
Total Senior Debt		110.0	102.3	94.2	83.8	72.9	61.5	50.0
Total Debt		150.0	144.3	138.3	130.1	121.5	112.5	103.6

FIGURE 11.2 (*Continued*)

Step 5 – Forecast the income statement

P&L	2002	2017	2018	2019	2020	2021	2022	2023	2024
Revenue	45.1	53.0	66.2	69.5	73.0	76.6	82.4	88.6	95.2
EBITDA	19.8	21.6	25.5	26.1	27.4	28.7	33.0	35.4	38.1
Depreciation & amortisation	(0.9)	(1.6)	(7.3)	(7.6)	(8.0)	(8.4)	(9.9)	(10.6)	(11.4)
EBIT	18.9	20.0	18.2	18.4	19.3	20.3	23.1	24.8	26.7
Interest									
Senior debt (TLa, TLb, TLc, Revolver)				(5.2)	(4.9)	(4.5)	(4.0)	(3.5)	(3.1)
Mezzanine PIK				(2.0)	(2.1)	(2.2)	(2.3)	(2.4)	(2.6)
Mezzanine cash				(2.9)	(3.0)	(3.2)	(3.3)	(3.5)	(3.7)
Total Cash Interest (Senior debt + Mezzanine cash)				(8.1)	(7.9)	(7.6)	(7.3)	(7.0)	(6.7)
Total Interest (Cash interest + Mezzanine PIK)				(10.1)	(10.0)	(9.8)	(9.7)	(9.5)	(9.3)
Interest check				OK	OK	OK	OK	OK	OK

Step 6 – Calculate the cash flow

CF	2017	2018	2019	2020	2021	2022	2023	2024
EBITDA			26.1	27.4	28.7	33.0	35.4	38.1
Adjustments:								
- Change in Working Capital			(2.1)	(2.2)	(2.3)	(4.1)	(4.4)	(4.8)
- Tax			(2.9)	(3.3)	(3.7)	(4.7)	(5.4)	(6.1)
- CapEx			(1.2)	(1.3)	(1.3)	(1.4)	(1.5)	(1.7)
Cash flow before financing			19.8	20.6	21.4	22.7	24.1	25.6
FCF (% EBITDA)			76.1%	75.4%	74.6%	68.9%	68.0%	67.1%
Total cash interest (Senior debt + Mezzanine cash)			(8.1)	(7.9)	(7.6)	(7.3)	(7.0)	(6.7)
Cash flow available for debt repayment			11.8	12.7	13.8	15.4	17.0	18.8
Debt Repayments			(6.0)	(6.0)	(9.0)	(9.0)	(9.0)	(9.0)
Excess cash			5.8	6.7	4.8	6.4	8.0	9.8
Cash sweep			(1.7)	(2.0)	(1.4)	(1.9)	(2.4)	(2.5)
Opening cash balance			0.0	4.0	8.8	12.1	16.6	22.2
Cash increase/(decrease)			4.0	4.7	3.4	4.4	5.6	7.4
RCF drawdown/repayment			0.0	0.0	0.0	0.0	0.0	0.0
Closing cash balance		0.0	4.0	8.8	12.1	16.6	22.2	29.6
Cash balance check			OK	OK	OK	OK	OK	OK

FIGURE 11.2 (*Continued*)

Step 7 – Calculate the credit statistics

Credit Stats	2017	2018	2019	2020	2021	2022	2023	2024
EBITDA			26.1	27.4	28.7	33.0	35.4	38.1
Net Senior debt			98.2	85.5	71.7	56.3	39.3	20.4
Net Total debt			140.2	129.6	118.0	104.9	90.3	74.0
Total Cash interest (Senior debt + Mezzanine cash)			(8.1)	(7.9)	(7.6)	(7.3)	(7.0)	(6.7)
CapEx			(1.2)	(1.3)	(1.3)	(1.4)	(1.5)	(1.7)
Cash flow before financing (CFBF)			19.8	20.6	21.4	22.7	24.1	25.6
Debt repayments			(6.0)	(6.0)	(9.0)	(9.0)	(9.0)	(9.0)
Leverage ratios (maximum)								
1. Net senior debt/EBITDA			3.8x	3.1x	2.5x	1.7x	1.1x	0.5x
Assumed headroom			20.0%	20.0%	20.0%	20.0%	20.0%	20.0%
Adjusted EBITDA			20.9	21.9	23.0	26.4	28.3	30.5
Covenant level			4.71x	3.90x	3.12x	2.14x	1.39x	0.67x
Proposed Covenant			**4.70x**	**3.90x**	**3.10x**	**2.15x**	**1.40x**	**0.65x**
Headroom			19.8%	19.9%	19.5%	20.5%	20.8%	17.5%
2. Net total debt/EBITDA			5.4x	4.7x	4.1x	3.2x	2.6x	1.9x
Assumed headroom			20.0%	20.0%	20.0%	20.0%	20.0%	20.0%
Adjusted EBITDA			20.9	21.9	23.0	26.4	28.3	30.5
Covenant level			6.72x	5.92x	5.13x	3.98x	3.19x	2.43x
Proposed Covenant			**6.70x**	**5.90x**	**5.15x**	**4.00x**	**3.20x**	**2.45x**
Headroom			19.7%	19.8%	20.3%	20.4%	20.3%	20.6%
Interest cover ratios (minimum)								
1. EBITDA/cash interest			3.2x	3.5x	3.8x	4.5x	5.0x	5.7x
Assumed headroom			20.0%	20.0%	20.0%	20.0%	20.0%	20.0%
Adjusted EBITDA			20.9	21.9	23.0	26.4	28.3	30.5
Covenant level			2.58x	2.78x	3.01x	3.59x	4.03x	4.53x
Proposed Covenant			**2.60x**	**2.80x**	**3.00x**	**3.60x**	**4.05x**	**4.55x**
Headroom			19.5%	19.4%	20.3%	19.8%	19.6%	19.7%
2. (EBITDA-CapEx)/cash interest			3.1x	3.3x	3.6x	4.3x	4.8x	5.4x
Assumed headroom			20.0%	20.0%	20.0%	20.0%	20.0%	20.0%
Adjusted EBITDA			20.9	21.9	23.0	26.4	28.3	30.5
Covenant level			2.43x	2.62x	2.83x	3.39x	3.81x	4.28x
Proposed Covenant			**2.45x**	**2.60x**	**2.85x**	**3.40x**	**3.80x**	**4.30x**
Headroom			20.4%	21.5%	20.5%	20.8%	21.1%	20.6%
Cash cover (minimum)								
CFBF/(cash interest + debt repayment)*			1.4x	1.5x	1.3x	1.4x	1.5x	1.6x
Covenant			1.2x	1.2x	1.2x	1.2x	1.2x	1.2x
Headroom			14.9%	19.3%	6.9%	13.6%	20.1%	26.2%

*Also known as fixed charges cover

FIGURE 11.2 (Continued)

STRUCTURING A LOAN FACILITY: A MODELLING EXAMPLE

Compared to the case of a complex loan structure, such as that of an LBO (for which reference should be made to the related chapter), the structuring of a private debt transaction is simpler.

The main phases are:

a) Analysis of sector and company's competitive positioning:
 i. identification of main business drivers and key success factors;
 ii. identification of main risks and related threats.
b) Development of a 'pre-money' business plan of the target company:
 i. forecast of a five to seven year business plan (up to EBIT);
 ii. forecast of a five to seven year balance sheet.
c) Insertion of the loan characteristics and verification of debt sustainability:
 i. insertion of amount, rate, tenor, and amortisation profile;
 ii. check that the benchmark ratios (leverage, gearing, interest cover, debt service cover) are in line with 'ideal' values;
 iii. verify that covenants are complied with during the life of the financing;
 iv. in the event that steps ii and iii of this phase are not complied with, modify some of the hypotheses referred to in step (i) (e.g., amount, duration).
d) Perform a sensitivity test to verify sustainability even in the case of downside.

An example of private debt structuring is reproduced in Figure 11.2 (the accompanying Excel file is downloadable from the companion website).

REFERENCES AND FURTHER READING

B. Ganguin and J. Bilardello. 2004. *Standard & Poor's Fundamentals of Corporate Credit Analysis*. McGraw Hill.

SUGGESTED CASES

M. Baker, A. Sunderam, N. Sato, and A. Kanno. 2013. 'Restructuring JAL.' Harvard Business School Case 214-055.
W.C. Kester and C. Stephenson. 2012. 'Hill Country Snack Foods Co.' Harvard Business School Brief Case 913-517.

CHAPTER 12

Legal Documentation

INTRODUCTION

There are several legal documents that are needed in a private equity or private debt transaction. The typical set of documents is the following:

- confidentiality agreement (non-disclosure agreement or NDA);
- letter of intent or term sheet.

Then, depending on the type of transaction (private equity or private debt), different documents are needed:

- **private equity:** constitutional documents, subscription, share sale and purchase, shareholders' and put and call option agreements;
- **private debt:** facility, intercreditor, security, hedging, and fee agreements.

In this chapter, the main legal documents are briefly illustrated. In Appendix 12.1 and 12.2, examples of a term sheet for a private debt and private equity deal are provided.

Confidentiality agreement (or non-disclosure agreement)

A confidentiality agreement (also called non-disclosure agreement or NDA) is a legal agreement that binds one or more parties to non-disclosure of confidential or proprietary information provided to a private equity or private debt fund. A confidentiality agreement is used in situations where sensitive corporate information is not to be made available to the general public or competitors.

The main terms of a confidentiality agreement are:

- **Identification of the parties:** the party providing confidential information can be referred to as the disclosing party and the recipient of the information can simply be referred to as the recipient. When the recipient provides the confidential information to an affiliated company or to its consultants, then the NDA should also cover those third parties.

- **Definition of what is deemed to be confidential:** this section defines what confidential information means. The disclosing party wants this definition to be as broad as possible to make sure the other side does not use information or secrets.
- **Scope of the confidentiality obligation:** this section deals with the fact that the recipient of the confidential information has to keep it secret and that recipients cannot use the information themselves.
- **Exclusions from confidentiality agreement:** every NDA contains certain exclusions intended to address situations where it would be unfair or too burdensome for the other party to keep the information confidential. The common exclusions include information that is 1) already known by the person or persons who are signing the agreement; 2) already publicly known; and 3) easily learned or could be learned independently outside the company that drafted the agreement. The agreement will also define instances of permissible disclosure (e.g. to law enforcement) and disclosure exceptions.
- **Term of the agreement:** this section indicates how long the NDA will last.

Other provisions contained in a confidentiality agreement include no employee and/or client solicitation and a jurisdiction clause in case of disputes.

Letter of intent

A letter of intent is a pre-contractual written document that defines the parties' preliminary understandings. It is not usually intended to have any binding effect on the completion of the deal.

Whilst the letter of intent is not obligatory, it is useful for the party most anxious to close the deal because it tends to present a moral obligation that people will respect. It also establishes a solid foundation for determining fundamental terms. For the party less anxious to close the deal, the letter provides a chance to obtain concessions that may be harder to obtain later on. The letter also signals that a point has been reached for disclosing an agreement in principle to people outside the immediate negotiations. With a public company, the letter permits a public announcement of the negotiations, so as to avoid insider trading issues.

The letter of intent sets out the contents of verbal negotiations between the parties about the fundamental terms of the deal and the structure of the transaction, the price and financing, the terms of notes or stock to be conveyed as part of the price, and other matters such as tax considerations. A letter of intent is usually recommended, even though it is not binding.

Term Sheet

A term sheet summarises the terms of a deal. It summarises all the important financial and legal terms of the proposed transaction, and it quantifies the value of the transaction or its financing terms.

A term sheet is usually not legally binding. Both parties have an implied duty to negotiate in good faith. After a term sheet has been 'executed', it guides legal counsel in the preparation of a proposed 'final agreement'.

The terms and conditions of a term sheet will vary greatly depending on the type of product (debt or equity) being offered and the situation in which each company finds itself. The usual terms are:

- **Parties:**
  - in a private equity deal: the investor and the investee (or target) company;
  - in a private debt deal: the lender and the borrower.
- **Financial instrument:**
  - in a private equity deal: any of the equity products described in Chapter 3;
  - in a private debt deal: any of the equity products described in Chapter 2.
- **Amount:**
  - a fixed amount; or
  - an amount determined by a formula.
- **Economic terms:**
  - fees;
  - price
    - *in a private equity deal:* valuation of the target company;
    - *in a private debt deal:* margin of coupon.
- **Agreements:** this section indicates the agreement that will comprise the final legal documentation:
  - in a private equity deal: these can include subscription, share sale and purchase, shareholders' and put and call option agreements;
  - in a private debt deal: these can include a facility, inter-creditor, security, hedging, and fee agreements.
- **Governing law:** this indicates the law regulating the agreement.
- **Dispute resolution:** this clause indicates the jurisdiction of the court or arbitration in case of disputes.

PRIVATE DEBT LEGAL DOCUMENTATION

There are a number of legal documents involved in a private debt (and leveraged buyout) transaction. We summarise the key ones in this section.

Mandate (or Commitment) Letter

The borrower usually appoints a lender (the arranger) via a mandate letter to underwrite the debt facility. The provisions commonly covered in a mandate letter include:

- an agreement to underwrite;
- appointment of the arranger, underwriter, facility agent, security agent;

- an indication of commitment amounts and exclusivity provisions;
- conditions to lenders' obligations;
- costs, cover, and indemnity clauses.

Term Sheet

The mandate letter will be signed with a term sheet attached. The term sheet sets out the terms of the proposed financing prior to full documentation. See previous paragraph on term sheet and Appendix 12.2 for details.

Facility agreement

The facility agreement sets out the detailed terms and conditions on which the facilities are made available to the senior borrower. Unlike the letter of intent, the acquisition agreement is a legally binding document. A party that fails to consummate the transaction may be liable for damages. The agreement has four basic objectives:

1. To set out the structure and terms of the transaction.
2. To disclose all the major legal and financial aspects of the target.
3. To oblige both parties to do their best to complete the transaction, and oblige the seller/manager of the Target not to change the Target in any significant way before the deal closes.
4. To determine what happens if the parties discover problems that should have been disclosed either in the agreement or before the closing but were not properly disclosed.

A typical facility agreement contains the following sections:

- **Definitions:** this section defines the main terms that are used throughout the agreement.
- **Borrower:** indicates the beneficiary of the loan.
- **Facility:** this clause describes the type of credit facility (e.g. a term loan or a revolving facility), the amount, the currency, and the cost. It also requires the lender to provide the loan (subject to compliance with the previous conditions). In a syndicated loan, this clause can be very extensive, defining the individual commitment of each bank.
- **Period:** the life of a loan is divided into 'interest periods', determined by the inter-bank rate; the choice is substantially limited to one, three, or six months, i.e. to standard inter-bank periods. The interest periods have two functions: the reference underlying rate (e.g. Euribor, Libor, etc.) is recalculated at the beginning of each period and applies throughout its duration. Therefore, the variable rate is a succession of different fixed rates and the repayments must coincide with the end of a period of interest.

- **Repayment:** indicates the amortisation profile as the loan can be bullet (repayment in a single solution) or be repaid in instalments.
- **Drawdowns:** indicates whether the disbursement of the loan is envisaged in a single solution or in several instalments.
- **Voluntary pre-payment:** indicates the terms (minimum amount and cost) on the basis of which early repayment is allowed on a voluntary basis.
- **Purpose clause:** the creditor will want to exert a certain influence on the use of the funds by the debtor in order to protect his loan. On the other hand, the debtor will try to guarantee flexibility and be sure that his proposals for using the funds do not provoke a violation of the agreement.
- **Conditions:** apply in relation to two situations:
  - those that must be satisfied before the first drawdown. These initial conditions are divided into three categories:
    i. production of various documents (for example legal opinions);
    ii. assurances that the loan is obtained (e.g. board resolution authorising the credit line);
    iii. guarantees that specific events have taken place (for example underwriting of the equity).
  - those that apply in all phases, i.e. commitments that:
    i. all declarations and guarantees remain valid;
    ii. no MAC has occurred;
    iii. there are no default events.
- **Representations and warranties:** in this section, the seller makes detailed statements about the financial and legal state of the company, the property to be conveyed, and the seller's ability to consummate the transaction. The representations and warranties are intended to disclose all the legal and many financial aspects of the business to the buyer. The seller also gives assurances that the transaction will not unfavourably impact the property to be conveyed. The main purpose is to monitor the debtor and cause a default event if they should contravene the declarations made. During the financing, representations and warranties must be kept fulfilled through constant repetition, periodic repetition, and cross-references to covenants and events of default. Representations and warranties are important in loan contracts as they form the contractual basis of the loan; if incorrect, they may constitute an event of default, so that their inaccuracy suspends the drawdown and could trigger 'special circumstances' (e.g. prohibition of payment of dividends). Usually the debtor guarantees:
  - their legal status (for example, that the company is regularly constituted);
  - the powers and authorisations;
  - that the loan contract is not in conflict with by-laws or other financing contracts (debt limits, negative pledges, etc.);
  - the legal validity and applicability of debtor obligations (in acquisition finance, for example, may extend to acquisition agreements);
  - the ranking of *pari passu* for loans with other unsecured debt;

- secured loans, possession of the assets subject to collateral, priority of collateral, etc.;
- the absence of litigation, real or threatened;
- the substantial correctness of the latest financial statements;
- the correctness of the information memorandum, i.e. that the projections are based on reasonable assumptions, that no material omissions occurred (to the best of the knowledge and the good faith of the debtor);
- the legal conduct of the business.

In case of more drawdowns, there are 'evergreen' declarations and guarantees. Legal advisers spend a lot of time qualifying representations and warranties based on their knowledge. The first draft of a loan agreement is usually prepared by the lender's legal counsel, who will try to make the statements as broad as possible. The borrower will tend not to provide statements. If the lender accepts, certain specific exceptions will be included in the declarations or in a side letter (essentially an agreed list of specific elements that would normally prevent a debtor from making a declaration, but to which the lender has agreed to waive) attached to the loan agreement.

- **Covenants:** the commitment to do (or not do) something or to get something to be (or not) done. Covenants should be carefully reviewed by the borrower, since a violation will trigger an event of default. These are a typical topic of negotiations, since on the one hand the lender (who wants to be reimbursed and therefore intends to protect the loan) tries to impose restrictions and obtain information, whilst on the other hand the borrower wants freedom to carry on their business as they see fit and with the least additional burden. The balance to be sought is finalised in covenants that are not too stringent for the borrower – so that they do not have to spend more time requesting waivers than managing the company – but not so large as to prevent the lender from intervening in the business activity. The type of covenant and its invasiveness will therefore depend on the quality of the counterparty, the leverage, the package of guarantees, the nature of the business, and the purpose of the loan. Typical covenants are:
  - Affirmative (indicate what the borrower must do to comply with the loan terms):
    - use of financing for specific purposes;
    - reporting;
    - compliance with the law;
    - conservation of the business purpose;
    - inspection fees;
    - maintenance of insurance on assets, properties, registrations, and accounting books.
  - Negatives (limit the activities of the borrower):
    - restriction of mortgages, liens, and other limitations to assets (negative pledge);
    - limitation of total debt;

- o limitation of the payment of dividends;
- o restrictions on changes in the business;
- o restrictions on the repurchase of shares;
- o merger restrictions;
- o restrictions on the sale of goods;
- o limitations on the sale of subsidiaries;
- o capex limitations;
- o limitations in undertaking other businesses;
- o investment restrictions;
- o limitations to leasing contracts.

■ **Financials:** these represent an obligation to comply with certain financial parameters. To be effective, financial covenants must be based on timely and high-quality financial information. The commitment of the borrower to provide timely and quality information is in itself a standard financial covenant. Financial statements must be prepared on the basis of accounting standards and principles that the creditor considers acceptable (for example, UCI, GAAP, IFRS) and should be reviewed at least once a year by auditors. Financial covenants can remain static or change over the life of the loan. Their violation will trigger an event of default, allowing the lender to request early repayment (so-called acceleration), and can trigger cross-default clauses on other loans. Before being obliged to repay the loan early, the borrower has, in certain cases, the possibility of remedying the breach. In the event of an event of default, the lender may choose to renegotiate the loan documentation or suspend certain violations, imposing strict controls on the debtor.

In LBOs, because of the high degree of leverage involved, lenders usually impose restrictive covenants on the borrower. Any deviation whatsoever is likely to trigger default. Because the buyer cannot always foresee future events, it may not always be possible to adhere to the covenants, and it may have to go back to the lenders to request for covenants to be waived or modified. If the consent of multiple lenders is required, the process can be costly and time consuming. Lenders are most concerned with financial covenants that relate to the company's generation and distribution of cash. They will want to monitor the company's ability to service both current and future debt. They will therefore want to impose limits on cash outflows like dividends and excessive capital expenditures until their claims are satisfied. Lenders will also want advance information about the company's cash inflow. If this ratio begins to decline and approach default levels, the lender will step up monitoring and will inform management of default consequences. The following financial covenants on the borrower are likely to be imposed:

- leverage ratio;
- gearing ratio;
- interest cover ratio;
- debt service cover ratio.

The borrower may also be required to attain specified minimum goals for
- net worth and
- cash flow

and to not exceed specified maximum limits for
- capital expenditures and
- total debt.

- **Events of default:** these are events or circumstances that allow the lender to exercise certain rights. Common default events are:
  - failure to pay on time;
  - the violation of representations and warranties;
  - the emergence of bankruptcy proceedings;
  - a change of control (or the change in the company structure);
  - a material adverse change (MAC: any change, financial or otherwise, that affects the debtor in a manner judged materially negative by the lender);
  - cross-default.

  The consequences of an event of default are:
  - the termination of the loan and the obligation of early repayment;
  - the tightening of guarantees.

  An event of default allows the lender to reduce or freeze its exposure to the borrower and assigns to the lender a greater degree of control over the borrower.

  The latter will try to limit the event of default using:
  - periods of tolerance (cure periods);
  - thresholds of reasonableness and materiality;
  - or tolerance margins (headrooms).

  In the event of an event of default:
  - the borrower may remedy (with the so-called cures); for example, through a capital injection to bring back a covenant to the levels set by the contract;
  - the parties may renegotiate terms;
  - the lender may accelerate the repayment.

- **Transfer:** the transfer of existing financing to another lender is forbidden to the borrower but allowed for the lender. The transfer carried out by the lender can be done by assigning the financing or by sub-participation. With the assignment, the original lender transfers his rights to a new lender. A sub-participation takes place when the lender grants a sub-participant the rights or interests, in a loan, creating new rights and obligations rather than transferring existing rights.

- **Governing law:** the clause set out the law that will regulate the interpretation and application of the contract. The governing law and jurisdiction do not necessarily coincide.

Transaction Security Documents

This is a document entered into by any obligor creating or undertaking to create any security over all or any part of its assets as a guarantee to the obligations of any of the obligors under any of the finance documents (or the mezzanine finance documents). The security is held by a security trustee on behalf of the senior lenders, the second lien lenders, and the mezzanine lenders. The security trustee provisions are typically contained in an inter-creditor agreement between (amongst others) the senior lenders, second lien lenders, and mezzanine lenders.

Inter-creditor Agreement

The inter-creditor agreement (also sometimes known as the subordination or priority deed) is a document which contractually provides that the senior bank debt and the security ranks in priority to the second lien and other subordinated debt as well as to the shareholder debt.

Second Lien and/or Mezzanine Facility Agreement

These agreements set out the terms and conditions on which the subordinated facilities are made available.

Structural Intra-Group Loan Agreement

This agreement contains HoldCo/Topco and its subsidiaries' structural shareholder debt subscription mechanics, rights, obligations, and restrictions.

Hedging Letter

The senior borrower is often required to confirm in a letter to the arranger that interest rate hedging will be obtained (within a certain period of time after completion of the acquisition) for a percentage of the funded debt and for a certain period to create a greater degree of certainty over the funding costs.

Fee Letters

This document contains the fees that the senior borrower must pay to senior lenders, second lien lenders, and mezzanine lenders. Sometimes it also sets out the fees due to those entities which have performed additional work or have taken on greater responsibility in the loan process; primarily the arranger, the facility agent, and the security trustee. Details of these fees are usually included in separate side letters to ensure confidentiality. The senior facility agreement should refer to the fee letters, and when such fees are payable ensure that any non-payment by the senior borrower carries the remedies of default set out in the senior facility agreement.

Highly Confident Letter

In this document, the underwriter declares it is highly confident it can arrange high-yield financing on specified terms (ratings, bank, financing, etc.) subject to market conditions.

PRIVATE EQUITY LEGAL DOCUMENTATION

Constitutional Documents

The constitutional documents for most companies are generally the Memorandum (or Deed) of Incorporation and the By-laws (or Articles of Associations).

The first one, more synthetic, sets out the willingness of the future shareholders to incorporate the company and the relevant details of the organisational structure; whilst the second is more analytic and contains the legal and common provisions for the functioning of the company.

Both documents are generally public and need to be filed with the competent Chamber of Commerce.

Memorandum (or Deed) of Incorporation

The Memorandum (or Deed) of Incorporation is the agreement executed amongst the future shareholders of the company and which is necessary – the name is self-explanatory – to incorporate the company itself.

In some jurisdictions the Memorandum of Incorporation must be signed in front of a public notary, who will then take care to file it with the competent companies' register.

The Memorandum of Incorporation includes, amongst other things, the details of the shareholders incorporating the company (including the indication of the number and nominal value of the shares which will be owned by each of them in the company), the company's registered office location, as well as the specification of the company's corporate purpose (i.e. the activities which the company will carry out during the course of its existence).

Such a document also details the exact composition of the company's share capital. Specifically, the Memorandum of Incorporation sets out the share capital amount, the number of shares it is divided into, the relevant value, as well as the main provisions regulating the profit distribution.

In this regard, it is important to point out that in some jurisdictions it is possible for the company to issue different classes of shares, granting their relevant owners different kind of rights (e.g. each class of shares may grant the shareholders different, either economic or governance, rights which are, indeed, better described in the By-laws).

Finally, since the Memorandum of Incorporation – as previously stated – contains the description of the organisational structure, it also sets out the number of the members of the board of directors, the relevant powers, as well as the rules governing their appointment procedure. The same information is usually provided also with reference to the members of the board of statutory auditors.

Articles of Associations or By-laws

As anticipated, By-laws are the documents setting out in detail the rules governing the relationships between the company and its shareholders as well as the functioning of the company itself.

Although they are formally a different document, separate from the Memorandum of Incorporation, the By-laws are often attached to this such that these two documents eventually form a sole and unique deed setting out the main requirements of the incorporating company and the rules of its functioning.

The provisions contained in the By-laws mainly depend on the number and the quality of the company's shareholders.

Therefore, the By-laws of a company with a sole shareholder will be rather simple and straightforward, and will contain only the provisions regulating the appointment and functioning of the corporate bodies as well as the process for the liquidation of the company.

Conversely, the By-laws of a company with many shareholders – amongst which there are also one or more financial investors – are likely to be more complex and provide more specific provisions regulating rights and obligations of each shareholder toward the others as well as toward the company.

Often, in fact, the private equity investor may require the transposition of some of the shareholders' agreement provision directly into the By-laws.

The reason for any such request is due to the fact that in some jurisdictions the provisions contained in the By-laws are more effective than those – although identical – contained in the shareholders' agreements: whilst a breach of the By-laws is in fact enforceable, a breach of the shareholders' agreement may sometimes only entail a reimbursement of the damaged party.

Accordingly, it usually happens that, besides the fundamental provisions, the shareholders decide to insert in the By-laws some additional provisions aimed at protecting and defending in different ways their investment in the company; such as: lock up, right of first refusal, drag along right, right to appoint a certain number of members of the board of directors or of the statutory auditors, and veto right (for a more detailed description of such clauses, please refer to the section 'Shareholders' agreement' below).

Share Purchase and Investment Agreement

The Share Purchase Agreement The share purchase agreement (SPA), is an agreement executed between two parties whereby one of them, the seller, sells to the other, the purchaser, a stakeholding representing a certain percentage of the – or the entire – corporate capital of a company.

It differs from the asset purchase agreement, whose subject consists of the transfer of the assets – and not the shares – of the company.

The language used in the SPA, regardless of the nationality of its parties – and particularly when they have different nationalities – is usually English; in any case, the parties may decide to use any other different language, at their complete discretion.

The parties may also decide which law governs the SPA and in accordance to which the agreement must be construed and interpreted. Whilst there may not be any such specific obligation upon the parties, the SPAs are usually subject to the law applicable in the country in which the registered office of the target of the transaction is located.

The SPA, in fact, has become increasingly a self-sufficient agreement, which sets out most of the necessary provisions aimed at regulating parties' interests, and therefore there is no need for it to be completed or construed in accordance with any specific law.

A standard share and purchase agreement is usually composed of the following sections.

- **Parties, recitals, definitions, right of designation:** The share purchase agreement opens with the identification of the parties, often followed by some recitals whereby the parties disclose to each other some relevant information and assumptions made for the purposes of the construction and interpretation of the agreement, the agreed definitions of some specific words which are relevant to the agreement, as well as the determination of the exact subject of the agreement.

  In the last section the SPA: (i) regulates the transfer of ownership of the shares from the seller to the purchaser; (ii) sets out the purchase price and the exact timing when the transfer of the ownership of the shares will take place (so called 'closing date'); and (iii) usually, provides for the right for the purchaser to designate another entity (or person), in its place, which (or who) shall assume all its relevant rights and duties provided therein. The right of designation is usually provided when the buyer, executing the SPA, is a private equity investment fund, which intends to execute the purchase through a subsidiary newly incorporated for the purposes of the carrying out of the investment.

- **Interim management:** the timeframe, if any, between the signing of the SPA and the closing date, upon which the transfer of the ownership over the shares will be effective, is called 'interim period' and is often regulated in the share purchase agreement by an ad hoc clause – 'interim management' – providing the rules aimed at regulating the management of the Target in this specific timeframe. During such period, in fact, the purchaser is not yet the owner of the shares and its interest is to ensure that the seller does not deteriorate, with its actions, the position of the Target. For such reasons the SPA provides for some undertakings with respect to the buyer, aimed at preserving the liquidity of the target and its ordinary course of business. By way of exemplification, the buyer often undertakes, amongst other things, to not: (i) purchase or otherwise acquire real estate properties; (ii) purchase, sell, transfer, encumber, lease (as lessor or lessee), license (as licensor or licensee), or otherwise acquire or dispose of tangible or intangible assets; (iii) hire or dismiss any executive; (iv) increase the rate of compensation payable or to become payable to any employees, other than those made in accordance with normal past practice and in the ordinary course of business or mandatory under applicable law; (v) waive any substantial right or entitlement; (vi) change the accounting methods, principles, practices, or policies, other than as provided for by applicable law; (vii) delay the payment of any amount due; and (viii) make any distribution of profits.

- **Conditions precedent:** When the closing date is not contextual with the signing of the SPA, the transfer of the ownership of the shares is sometimes subject to some conditions, named 'conditions precedent', which, if not duly fulfilled, may prevent the obligation of the purchaser and seller to affect the closing. Sometimes, for example, it may happen that the transfer of the shares of the Target must be authorised by a competent authority. In such events, the parties, since they cannot envisage whether the transaction will or will not receive the required approval from the authority (technically called 'clearance') have an interest in subjecting the execution of the closing to the obtainment of the relevant authorisation.

- **Purchase price:** The ownership of the shares of the Target is transferred against the payment of the price. The determination of the purchase price and the regulation of the relevant payment mechanism in the sale and purchase agreement is, subsequently, of paramount importance in private equity transactions.

The sale and purchase agreement usually provides for one of the following typical categories of clauses, aimed at determining the purchase price:

- clauses whereby the purchase price is determined and agreed from the beginning and it consists of a fixed and unchangeable amount (so called 'lock box');
- clauses pursuant to which the purchase price is not yet determined, but determinable by means of a formula previously agreed upon by the parties, and subject to a further adjustment after closing (so called 'closing accounts');
- clauses pursuant to which only a part of the purchase price is determined in advance by the parties, being the payment of the other part possible or, in any case, subject to subsequent quantification (e.g. earn out clauses, whereby a part of the purchase price is calculated upon, and subject to, the results of the Target within an agreed timeframe).

The formulas used by the parties to determine the purchase price may be very different since they are conceived in such a way as to take into account all the various factors contributing to the determination of the price.

In some cases, the purchase price is calculated on the basis of the net asset value of the company, whose items are not always easy to be evaluated (e.g. inventory, receivables, and intellectual property rights) and, therefore, are subject to a very attentive regulation by the parties. Very often the parties use some formulas which determine the purchase prices, such as the EBITDA multiplied by a fixed factor that depends on the specific market sector in which the target operates.

In the event that the purchase price is not yet determined at the date of the signing of the SPA, or only part of the same has been determined by the parties, the sale and purchase agreement often provides for a price adjustment mechanism. In such cases, the purchase price is calculated on the basis of the net financial position of the target as at a specific deadline, usually coinciding with the closing date, which, subsequently, can only be verified after the closing date. Therefore, the purchaser pays, at closing, a 'temporary' amount to the seller, which will be then finally determined based on the results of a price adjustment mechanism.

Such adjustment procedure is typically divided in the following phases: (i) preparation by the buyer of the financial position of the Target as at the closing date; (ii) verification of such financial position by the seller; (iii) in case of disagreement among the parties, submission of the verification of the financial position to a third and independent party; and finally (iv) payment of the balance of the purchase price (or reimbursement of the relevant part of the purchase price already paid in excess by the buyer).

- **Representation and warranties:** Representation and warranties are a series of statements of fact usually given by the seller with respect to the Target (and, eventually to its group companies).

    Representation and warranties are sought for three reasons: deciding whether to proceed with the transaction, negotiating price adjustments, and inserting specific clauses.

    The extent and the scope of the representation and warranties depends on negotiation between the parties and of the type of the company which is going to be acquired. Usually, representation and warranties are given as at the signing date and, if signing and completion of the transaction are split, repeated at the closing date.

    The SPA, when addressing the representation and warranties, usually covers the following:

    - Fundamental representation and warranties, such as the existence and good standing of the Target (and, eventually, its group companies), power and capacity of the seller and its full title.
    - Commercial representation and warranties with respect to the business, contracts, liabilities, and assets of the Target company (and, eventually of its group companies), covering, inter alia:
        - Employment and social security matters; for example, with respect to key terms of the employment contracts with senior employees and directors. The investor may also require a list of all employees with details of

applicable collective bargaining agreements, and key financial terms of employment, including bonuses and other economic benefits.

○ Existence of assets and absence of liabilities.

○ Validity of commercial contracts, including as to the applicability of any change of control provision possibly acknowledged during the performance of the legal due diligence activity carried out on the Target.

○ Absence of related parties' transactions.

○ Validity of intellectual property rights and confirmation that they are not infringed by any third party.

○ Accounting and tax aspects, whereby sometimes the purchaser may require the seller to provide the last financial statement approved by the Target and, eventually, any of its group companies (as well as the last consolidated financial statements, where applicable).

○ In general, compliance with law (including under environmental, health and safety, data protection, anti-bribery regulations, etc.).

○ Absence of litigation.

All the exceptions to the representation and warranties are set out in specific schedules. In case of breach of the representation and warranties, the purchaser can claim from the seller the relevant suffered damages, which are aimed at restoring the buyer from losses suffered by the buyer that he would have not suffered if the seller's representation and warranties had been true and accurate.

The indemnification obligations for the breach of the representation and warranties are often limited by a liability cap (the maximum amount in relation to which the seller will be liable), a *de minimis* (the amounts in relation to which the seller will never be liable and which will never be taken into account for the calculation of damages), and a threshold (the amount under which the seller will never be liable).

▪ **Jurisdiction or arbitration clause:** parties may choose to submit disputes either to arbitration or to national courts. Arbitration tends to be the preferred choice due to both the speed of the proceedings and the ability to appoint arbitrators who are recognised experts in the relevant practice area. However, there are still some downsides, such as the fact that arbitration procedure is most often more expensive than ordinary proceedings before national courts.

▪ **Replacement of directors and/or auditors:** in most transactions – usually when the purchaser acquires the majority or the entire capital of the Target – the investor may have an urgent interest in assuming control of the managing and controlling structure of the Target. Thus, the SPA commonly provides for some undertaking of the purchaser, which, before or upon the closing date must promptly cause the resignation of some or all the directors and/or statutory auditors of the company and, eventually, call the shareholders' meeting to resolve upon the appointment of the new members of the administrative and/or controlling bodies, designated by the investor prior to the closing.

Investment Agreement Sometimes the investment can be carried out by the investor, not through the acquisition of a stakeholding of the Target from the seller, but through the subscription of a capital increase of the Target specifically reserved to the investor itself. In such an event, the agreement between the current shareholder of the Target and the investor is called 'investment agreement'. Such an agreement also provides for, besides the other provisions contained in an SPA (interim period, representation and warranties, indemnification provision, directors' change obligations, etc.), the undertakings of the existing shareholders of the Target and of the investor to, respectively, resolve upon a capital increase of the company and to subscribe it and fully pay it up.

The Shareholders' Agreement

Shareholders' agreements (SHA) are agreements whereby the parties regulate their relationships as shareholders of a company.

These agreements can be entered into at any time during the company's lifetime amongst all or some of its shareholders, which are the only persons bound by their content.

Such agreements are typical in private equity investments and are aimed at minimising the risk that a disagreement amongst the shareholders might force the investor to accept a fundamental change to the business plan or to the capital structure (including its dilution) and to sell its participation at an inopportune time, or at unsatisfactory conditions, or make it impossible to exit at all.

The main provisions included in the shareholders' agreements are typically the following:

- **Lock up:** by means of the lock up provision, the parties agree not to sell their shares before a pre-established period has expired. Such a clause allows, accordingly, the crystallisation of the structure of the company.
- **Right of first refusal:** the right of first refusal clause applies when a shareholder receives an offer from a third party aimed at purchasing his/her shares. Pursuant to such a clause, before the relevant acceptance, the offeree must first propose to sell his/her own shares to the other shareholders on the exact same terms agreed with the potential buyer. If the remaining shareholders do not opt to buy the offeree's shares, then the sale to the third party could be concluded, in any case, on the same terms.
- **Tag-along right:** the 'tag-along' clause is often used in conjunction with the right of first refusal. If the shareholders decide not to buy the offeree's shares, they can choose to exercise their right to require the third party to buy their shares as well. This clause is often used in scenarios where the remaining shareholders wish to join business with the third party and/or they represent a minority stake in the company. The minority shareholder has the right to join the sale of majority shares and sell the minority stake, preferably at the same terms. It is a contractual obligation used to protect a minority shareholder.

- **Drag-along clause:** the 'drag-along' clause is used in the event the majority shareholder intends to sell their share package, to compel the other shareholders to sell their portion of the corporate capital to the same third party. The other shareholders are therefore forced to join the transaction at the same price and conditions. This clause is clearly in favour of the majority shareholders who, in such a way, are able to increase their bargaining power towards the buyer.

- **Put and call options:** the put option and the call option are agreements – or clauses of the SHA – that set a limit on the free circulation of shares. In particular, they have the function of assigning to one of the parties, respectively, the right to sell or buy a certain amount of shares, at a pre-established price or otherwise determinable, at a fixed time, upon payment of a premium that constitutes the price of the option.

- **Veto rights:** the inclusion of veto rights provisions protects shareholders who hold less than 50% of the shares in the company; this could be made possible by giving them more input into fundamental resolutions. However, this right may also be recognised to only one shareholder (or the investor). Obviously, it regards matters of key importance for the parties. In such a way, since certain resolutions are crucial (e.g. issuing of new company's shares, sale of the going concern, etc.) for the functioning of the business, the same cannot be adopted by the other shareholders, in case of shareholders' resolution, or by the board of directors, in case of board of directors' resolution, without the prior consent of the relevant holder of the veto right.

- **Appointment rights:** generally, this clause refers to the appointment of the board of directors and/or of the board of the statutory auditors and it may specify both the number of directors and/or auditors as well as the right of certain shareholders to designate some or all of the relevant members. This is the tool that investors commonly use as: (i) they do not want to be involved in the day-to-day management of the company; and (ii) they may need to appoint a trusted member to these corporate bodies in order to have an indirect, full view over the business.

- **Information rights:** through this clause, information requirements are imposed on the management towards certain shareholders (or the investor). Typically, this information concerns the financial aspects and the performance of the company. Monthly management accounts and related reports, quarterly financial statements, and, on an annual basis, financial statements certified by an auditor chosen by the investor may be required.

These are just some of the clauses that can be included in these legally binding and enforceable private documents. Generally, they may also include non-competition and dispute resolution clauses.

As previously anticipated, in light of the major effectiveness which the By-laws have in some jurisdictions, often the investor – and specifically the private equity investor – are required to reflect the main provisions of the SHA into the By-laws. In such an event, the shareholders' agreement should also provide for how to handle a conflict between its content and the contents of the company's By-laws (which can be solved in favour of the first or of the latter, depending on the willingness of the parties).

REFERENCES AND FURTHER READING

J. Coallier. 2018. *Loan and Security Agreement*. Business - Secured Transactions, Legal Forms Book.

S. Mock, K. Csach, and B. Havel. 2018. *International Handbook on Shareholders' Agreements*. De Gruyter.

A. Wilmerding. 2006. *Term Sheets & Valuations – A Line by Line Look at the Intricacies of Term Sheets & Valuations*. Aspatore.

APPENDIX 12.1: EXAMPLE OF AN EQUITY TERM SHEET

NOTE: Please note that this term sheet is just a sample document which has been prepared for learning reasons only and therefore the terms set out herein are indicative only and this document cannot be intended in any way to replace the assistance of a lawyer or a legal adviser in the negotiation activities.

DRAFT TERM SHEET
[COUNTRY]
[Target Company]
Draft Date: [•]

Target Company	*[insert the name of the Target Company]*
Shares	Common shares of the Target Company issued and outstanding at any time and from time to time.
Seller	*[insert the name of the seller]*
Shareholders	*[list of all shareholders of the Target Company which are to be parties to the Shareholders' Agreement, other than the investor]*
Investor	*[insert the name of the Investor (usually a private equity fund)]*
Investment	*[insert a brief description of the specific investment (e.g. the acquisition by the Investor of an interest in the Target Company through the purchase of such interest from the Seller and/or the subscription of a capital increase)]*
Legal Agreements	To include:

1. [Subscription Agreement between the Shareholders and the Investor] (*if the Investment is carried out as a subscription by the Investor of a capital increase of the Target Company*).
2. [Share Sale and Purchase Agreement between the Seller and the Investor] (*if the Investment is carried out as a purchase of shares/quotas*).
3. Shareholders' Agreement between the Shareholders and the Investor.
4. Put and Call Option Agreement between the Investor and the Shareholders.

(*continued*)

Language	All Legal Agreements will be in the [English] language. All other documents submitted to the Investor and all correspondence between the Investor and the Seller and between the Investor and the Target Company and between the Investor and the Shareholders will be in the [English] language or will be accompanied by a certified [English] translation and the [English] version will govern.
Financial Information	All financial information shall be prepared in accordance with [Generally Accepted Accounting Principles in [●]] or [International Financial Reporting Standards (IFRS) consistently applied], as amended from time to time.
Fees and Expenses	[●] will pay the fees and expenses of the Investor associated with the negotiation and execution of the Legal Agreements, any protection/enforcement of rights and any amendments/waivers.
Governing Law	[●] Law.
Dispute Resolution	[Exclusive jurisdiction of the courts of [●]] or [Arbitration clause]
Material Adverse Change	Means any change or event which materially and adversely affects the carrying out of the Investment or the Target Company's business prospects, assets, or financial condition, or which makes it improbable that the Seller or the Target Company or the Shareholders will be able to fulfil any of their obligations under any of the Legal Agreements.

Principal Terms of the Subscription Agreement (in summary)

Share Subscription	The Investor will subscribe in a single transaction the [Subscription] Shares.
[Subscription] Shares	[ordinary voting] [shares] or [participation interests] of the Target Company with a par value of [●], representing the [●]% of the capital of the Target Company post subscription.
Subscription Price	[●] per share for a total consideration of $ [●].

Representations and Warranties of the Target Company

1. **Representations regarding the Target Company and its Subsidiaries:** the Target Company is duly incorporated and has the power to own its properties and carry out its business; the Target Company has no subsidiaries different from [•] ('**Subsidiaries**'); details of share capital of the Target Company; directors and officers of the Target Company; financial statements of the Target Company are true; the Target Company has title to its assets; there are no material contracts; there is compliance with law; there are no bribes, undue influence, fraud, or corruption; there are no defaults; there is compliance with environmental and social laws; and there is no litigation (including any other Representation and Warranties as may be required and deemed appropriate in connection with the specific transaction).

2. **Representations regarding the Agreements:** the Target Company has corporate power to perform the Legal Agreements; there has been due authorisation; Legal Agreements are enforceable and don't conflict; there are necessary governmental approvals; Legal Agreements are in full force and effect and not in breach; the By-laws given to the Investor are correct; there is no insolvency; no taxes are payable; the Target Company owns its Subsidiaries; and there has been waiver of any pre-emption rights.

3. **Representations regarding the Shares (made by the Seller):** the Shares represent all the [issued voting share capital][participation interests] and there are no other [shares][participation interests]; the Seller is the owner of the [Purchase] Shares free of liens and able to sell; on the Closing Date the Seller will own the [Purchase] Shares free of liens and restrictions; the shareholders' registry of the Target Company is in good order; and the [Purchase] Shares will rank *pari passu* with other Shares.

(*continued*)

Subscription	**Subscription Date:**
	1. the Seller shall cause the Target Company to provide evidence of By-laws amendments etc. for the capital increase;
	2. the Investor shall subscribe and transfer the Subscription Price to the Target Company; and
	3. the Seller shall cause the Target Company to take all necessary action to register the [Subscription] Shares.
	If the Target Company fails or is unable to register the [Subscription] Shares, the Investor may require return of the Subscription Price with appropriate interest.
	Anti-dilution: Prior to subscription, the Target Company shall not issue shares, increase capital, change rights attached to shares, or otherwise dilute the interest represented by the [Subscription] Shares.
Suspension and Cancellation	The Investor will have the right to suspend or cancel its obligation to purchase and/or pay for the [Subscription] Shares if:
	1. Subscription has not taken place by [●];
	2. any Legal Agreement is breached;
	3. a Material Adverse Change occurs; or
	4. a breach of any of the Representation and Warranties occurs.
Conditions Precedent	The Investor shall have received the following, in form and substance satisfactory to the Investor:
	1. original Legal Agreements;
	2. certified copies of all corporate authorisations;
	3. copies of any necessary resolution of shareholders' meetings and/or board meetings, including any required for the Investor's right to appoint a member of the Target Company's Board of Directors;
	4. certified copies of all relevant governmental and other licences/approvals etc.; and
	5. legal opinions,
	and all of the foregoing agreements are in full force and effect; all Representations and Warranties are true; neither the Target Company nor any Shareholder is in default; there is no event which might have a Material Adverse Effect; use of proceeds; [Subscription] Shares will represent [●]% of the Shares free of liens after transfer; and the Investor has received other documents it reasonably requests.

Company Undertakings	The Seller shall cause the Target Company to conduct its business with due diligence and efficiency, in accordance with sound engineering, financial, and business practices, and in compliance with all applicable laws; and not engage in fraud or corruption.
Investor Nominee to the Target Company's Board of Directors	The Investor shall have the right to appoint a member/a certain number of members of the Target Company's Board of Directors at all times whilst the Investor is a shareholder.

Principal Terms of the Share Sale and Purchase Agreement (in summary)

Share Purchase	The Investor will purchase from the Seller [in a single transaction] the [Purchase] Shares.
[Purchase] Shares	[[ordinary voting] shares of the Target Company][participation interests] with a par value of [•], representing the [•]% of the capital at Signing and Closing.
Purchase Price	[•] per share for a total consideration of $ [•].
Representations and Warranties	1. **Representations regarding the Target Company and its Subsidiaries (made by the Seller):** the Target Company is duly incorporated and has the power to own its properties and carry out its business; the Seller is duly incorporated and has full power to sell the [Purchase] Shares; the Target Company has no subsidiaries other than [•] ('**Subsidiaries**'); details of share capital of the Target Company; directors and officers of the Target Company; financial statements of the Target Company are true; Target Company has title to its assets; there are no material contracts; there is compliance with law; there are no bribes, undue influence, fraud, or corruption; there are no defaults; and there is compliance with environmental laws; there is no litigation (including any other Representation and Warranties as may be required and deemed appropriate in connection with the specific transaction).

(continued)

2. Representations regarding the Agreements (made by the Seller): each party has corporate power to perform the Legal Agreements; there has been due authorisation; Legal Agreements are enforceable and don't conflict; there are necessary governmental approvals; Legal Agreements are in full force and effect and not in breach; the By-laws given to the Investor are correct; there is no insolvency; no taxes are payable; the Target Company owns its Subsidiaries; and there has been waiver of any pre-emption rights.

Sale and Purchase

Closing:
1. The Seller will deliver a notice of closing specifying a closing date ('**Closing Date**').
2. If conditions precedent are fulfilled, the Investor will transfer the Purchase Price to the Seller on the Closing Date.
3. Simultaneously to the receipt of the Purchase Price, the Seller shall deliver to the Investor documents – and shall carry out all fulfilments required for transfer of title, including the delivery of any necessary powers of attorney of the Seller.
4. The Seller shall cause the Target Company to record the transfer of the [Purchase] Shares to the Investor and satisfy all other legal requirements in connection with the transfer of the [Purchase] Shares to the Investor.
5. The Seller provides the Investor with documents of title.

Anti-dilution: Prior to transfer, the Seller shall cause the Target Company to not issue shares, increase capital, change rights attached to shares. or otherwise dilute the interest represented by the [Purchase] Shares.

Suspension and Cancellation

The Investor will have the right to suspend or cancel its obligation to purchase and/or pay for the [Purchase] Shares if:
1. Closing will not take place by [●];
2. a breach of any Legal Agreement occurs;
3. a Material Adverse Change occurs; or
4. a breach of any Representation and Warranties occurs.

Conditions Precedent	The Investor shall have received the following, in form and substance satisfactory to the Investor: 1. original Legal Agreements; 2. certified copies of all corporate authorisations; 3. evidence of its right to appoint a member of the Board of Directors; 4. certified copies of all relevant governmental and other licences/approvals etc.; 5. certified copies of shareholders' registry extract showing Seller's title; evidence that the Target Company's By-laws are duly registered; Seller's share certificates; other evidence relating to the Investor Purchase Shares; 6. legal opinions; and all of the foregoing agreements are in full force and effect; all Representations and Warranties are true; the Seller is not in default; there is no Material Adverse Change; the [Purchase] Shares will represent [•]% of the Shares free of liens after transfer; there has been no dilution of the interest of the [Purchase] Shares; the Investor has received notice of closing; waiver of any pre-emption rights in favour of third parties; all sums due to the Investor are paid; and the Investor has received other documents it reasonably requests.
Seller undertakings	The Seller shall provide the Investor with information relating to Representations and Warranties; allow the Investor access to books and premises; notify the Investor of breach of Representation and Warranty; execute any other documents which the Investor deems necessary or desirable; procure that the Target Company's business is carried on as usual prior to the Closing Date; pay any taxes; and [comply with the Shareholders' Agreement].

Principal Terms of the Shareholders' Agreement (in summary)

Undertakings of the Shareholders	The Shareholders shall procure that the Target Company's business is conducted on a commercial, independent basis in accordance with good practice, and shall exercise their respective rights as a shareholder to protect and promote the long-term interests of the Target Company.

(continued)

General Meeting of Shareholders	**A** [A quorum of at least [●] members holding not less than [●]% of the voting Shares and an affirmative vote of not less than [●] of all members present will be required for decisions on the following resolutions:]
	OR
	B [Whilst the Investor is a shareholder, no shareholder resolution in respect of the following shall become effective without the affirmative vote of the Investor:] 1. amendment of By-laws or other constitutional documents; 2. change in Shares or voting rights attached to Shares; 3. transform, merge, liquidate, etc. the Target Company; 4. approval of dividends, share redemption, share split, or share dividend; 5. change directors and auditors; or 6. approval of capital increases and sale of going concern.

Board of Directors	1. there shall be [●] members;
	2. the Investor shall be able to nominate [●] members;
	3. the Shareholders shall be able to nominate [●] members;
	4. a quorum of [●] for meetings and [●]votes are needed for the following resolutions:
	   a. approval of business plan;
	   b. appointment of key officers;
	   c. approval of financial expenditure over [●];
	   d. approval of transactions with related parties;
	   e. approval of agreements on intellectual property;
	   f. approval of debt over [●];
	   g. approval of proposals of merger; and
	   h. approval of loans or guarantees over [real estate properties, going concerns, and stakes].

Other Operational Matters	Appointment/confirmation of Board of Directors' members; auditors; annual business plan; adequate record-keeping.
Furnishing of Information	The Shareholders shall procure that the Target Company will furnish to the Investor: **a)** For each quarter, within [60] days after its end, unaudited financial statements, a management discussion and analysis, a statement of transactions with its affiliates and shareholders in excess of [●].

b) For each financial year, within [120] days after its end, audited financial statements and a management letter from the Target Company's auditors.

c) Current insurance certificates.

Prompt notice of any incident or accident which has or is likely to have a significant adverse effect on the environment or on public or occupational health or safety.

Information on fraud and corruption.

All notices, reports, and other communications to the Target Company's shareholders [and access to the Target Company's shareholders' meetings as an observer].

Upon the Investor's request, extracts of the Target Company's share register showing the Investor's stake in the Target Company and such other information as may be reasonably requested by the Investor from time to time.

A Transfer of Shares

[•] shall retain legal and beneficial interest in [all] the issued and outstanding shares in the Target Company and shall:

1. cause the Target Company not to increase its capital or issue Shares;
2. not transfer any equity interest to anyone other than the Investor or a party approved by the Investor;
3. not otherwise dispose/encumber any Shares;
4. not permit the Target Company to change par value/rights of Shares; and
5. not otherwise dilute any shareholder's interest in the Target Company.

OR

B Restrictions on Transfer

No Shareholder shall transfer Shares except as agreed below.

B Transfers to Affiliates

Transfers to affiliates are permitted provided the affiliate adheres to the Shareholders' Agreement.

B X Right of First Offer

A Shareholder (the '**Offeror**') may transfer Shares if it gives the other Shareholders (the '**Offerees**') a right of first offer as follows:

1. the Offeror gives the Offerees an offer notice (the '**Offer Notice**') relating to all the Shares to be transferred, containing proposed terms and conditions including pricing;

(*continued*)

2. the Offerees may accept or decline all (but not some of) the offered Shares [pro-rata to their existing shareholdings (unless they agree otherwise)] *[to be possibly inserted if more than one offeree]*;

3. if only some Offerees accept, the remaining Shares shall be offered to the accepting Offerees in the same manner, save that they may accept any number of Shares, and if too many are accepted they shall be distributed [pro-rata] *[to be possibly inserted if more than one offeree]*; and

4. if there is a failure in the above (not due to the Offeror) then the Offeror may sell the Shares to a third party on terms and conditions no more favourable to the purchaser, provided that the third party adheres to the Shareholders' Agreement.

AND/OR

B Y Right of First Refusal

A Shareholder other than the Investor (the '**Offeror**' may transfer Shares if it gives the other Shareholders (the '**Offerees**') a right of first refusal as follows:

1. the Offeror obtains a written offer from a proposed third party transferee, containing proposed terms and conditions including pricing;

2. the Offeror offers the shares to the Offerees on the same terms and conditions and giving notice of the proposed transferee;

3. the Offerees may accept or decline all (but not some) of the Shares [(pro-rata to existing shareholdings)] *[to be possibly inserted if more than one offeree]*;

4. if only some Offerees accept, the remaining Shares shall be offered to the accepting Offerees in the same manner, save that they may accept any number of Shares, and if too many are accepted they shall be distributed [pro-rata] *[to be possibly inserted if more than one offeree]*; and

5. if there is a failure in the above (not due to the Offeror) then the Offeror may sell the Shares to a third party on terms and conditions no more favourable to the purchaser, provided that the third party adheres to the Shareholders' Agreement.

Pre-emptive Rights

The Investor [and the Shareholders] shall have the right to subscribe for its pro-rata share of any new Shares issued by the Target Company.

Tag-along Rights	If [•] (or [•] and [•] together) propose to transfer [any][a controlling interest of] Shares to a potential transferee, the Investor shall be given prior notice (with all relevant details) and shall have the right to sell to the potential transferee on the same terms and conditions [a percentage of the Investor's Shares equal to the percentage of [•]'s shares which are to be transferred]. The only Representations and Warranties that the Investor may be required to give in relation to its Share sale are those relating to title, the absence of security interests, and authority.
Drag-along Rights	If [•] (or [•] and [•] together) propose to transfer [a controlling interest of] Shares to a potential transferee, the transferor(s) can compel the Investor [and the other Shareholders] to sell [all of] their Shares to the potential transferee on the same terms and conditions. The only Representations and Warranties that the Investor may be required to give in relation to its Share sale are those relating to title, the absence of security interests, and authority.

Principal Terms of the Put And Call Option Agreement (Straight Equity)

Call Option	The Investor shall have the right at any time and from time to time during the Call Period to purchase the Shareholder Shares.
Call Period	The period commencing on [•] and terminating on [•].
Call Price	To be determined based on the following: [discounted cash flow][multiples of EBITDA/sales][book value][average price traded on [•] Stock Exchange][prices of comparable companies acquired within [•] months from the notice of call (the 'Call Notice')][other][and taking into consideration [•]].
Exit Put Option	The Investor shall have the right at any time and from time to time during the exit put period to sell the Investor Shares to the Shareholder.
Exit Put Period	The period commencing on [•] and terminating on [•].

(*continued*)

Exit Put Price	To be determined based on the following: [discounted cash flow][multiples of EBITDA/sales][book value][average price traded on [●] Stock Exchange][prices of comparable companies acquired within [●] months from the notice of put (the '**Put Notice**')][other][and taking into consideration [●]].
Accelerated Put Option	The Investor shall have the right at any time and from time to time during the Accelerated Put Period to sell the Investor Shares to the Shareholder.
Accelerated Put Period	The period commencing on the date of occurrence of an Accelerated Put Event and terminating on the date when the Investor no longer holds any Investor Shares.
Accelerated Put Price	To be determined based on the following: [discounted cash flow][multiples of EBITDA/sales][book value][average price traded on [●] Stock Exchange][prices of comparable companies acquired within [●] months from the notice of put ('**Accelerated Put Notice**')][other][and taking into consideration [●]].
Accelerated Put Events	1. The Target Company defaults on any Financial Debt in excess of [●]. 2. Breach of any covenant by the Target. 3. The Shareholder ceases to own directly [or indirectly] at least [●]% of the Shares of the Target Company. 4. Any representation made by the Target Company or the Shareholder was false or misleading when made or confirmed.
Representations and Warranties	No Representation and Warranties other than title.
Currency Indemnity	The Shareholder to indemnify the Investor against any losses due to payment of the Call Price, Exit Put Option, or the Accelerated Put Price on any currency other than [●].
Impossibility or Frustration	The Shareholder to pay the Call Price, Exit Put Price, or Accelerated Put Price despite the inability of the Investor to transfer the Investor Shares due to any reason not the fault of the Investor.
Default	The Shareholder to pay interest on any Call Price, Exit Put Price, and Accelerated Put Price not paid when due.

APPENDIX 12.2: EXAMPLE OF A DEBT TERM SHEET

NOTE: Please note that this term sheet is just a sample document which has been prepared for learning reasons only and therefore the terms set out herein are indicative only and this document cannot be intended in any way to replace the assistance of a lawyer or a legal adviser in the negotiation activities.

DRAFT TERM SHEET
[COUNTRY]
[Target Company]
Draft Date: [•]

Summary Of Indicative Terms And Conditions [*Currency*] [*Amount*] Million [Mezzanine] Term Loan Facility

Company	[*name of principal company*] (the 'Company')
Borrower(s)	The Company
	[*list subsidiaries that are to be original borrowers if known*]
	[*if unknown, list criteria such as material subsidiaries/jurisdiction*]
Lender(s)	[•] ('[•]') [*Insert details of any co-Lender*].
Mandated Lead Arranger	[•] [and [*Insert details of any other arranger*].

[NOTE: sometimes the role of Lender and the Mandate Lead Arrangers can be assumed by the same person.]

Security [Agent/ Trustee]	[TBD]
Facility Agent	[TBD]
Expiration Date	The terms outlined in this summary of indicative terms and conditions are valid until [•] after which they will expire.

FACILITY

Facility	[Mezzanine] term loan facility [, of which [●] is drawn immediately following the Signing Date].
Purpose	[●] for the first drawdown. [●] for any subsequent drawdowns.
Amount **[Ranking]**	[*Insert amount*] to be drawn in [*Insert currency*]. [Second-]ranking [to existing/proposed [Senior Facilities], otherwise first-ranking security.]
Signing Date **Termination Date**	The date the Finance Documents are signed. [●] years after the Signing Date.
Availability	Subject to satisfaction of the conditions precedent, may be drawn down [in full or in part on/or within [3] days] of [Signing Date/date on which conditions precedent to funding are satisfied]. Any Commitments undrawn following such date shall [be cancelled/remain as standby for a period of [12] months] [excluding any committed but undrawn [mezzanine] facility].
Repayment	All outstandings under the Facility shall be repaid in full on the Termination Date.
Guarantors	Unconditional and irrevocable guarantees to be provided by: (i) The Company and Borrower(s); (ii) To the extent legally possible, any [wholly-owned] [non-dormant] member of the Group from time to time. *[NOTE: Other guarantors could be added depending on the specific transaction. In any case, all guarantees are subject to limitations due to corporate benefit and financial assistance.]*
Obligor	The Borrower(s) and the Guarantor(s).
Group	The Company and its material subsidiaries from time to time, which together represent at least [95%] Group EBITDA and [95%] of Group total assets.
[Observer Rights]	The Lender(s) shall receive reasonable notice of, and have the right, at its (their) option, to send an observer to any board meeting of the Company.

[Equity [Warrants/ Options]]	[Free and detachable [warrants/options] in respect of the shares of the Company which on exercise give the holders thereof [●] % of the fully-diluted share capital/[●] %, which, when aggregated with the Margin, results in the Lender(s) achieving an IRR of [●]% per annum] (i.e. after the exercise of any management ratchets and employee and management options). For the avoidance of doubt, the IRR calculation shall be performed excluding any fees or prepayment premia. The exercise price of the [warrants/options] will be [nominal] and the [warrants/options] will have the benefit of anti-dilution protections, and liquidity rights including tag-along and drag-along rights.

Pricing

Interest	The aggregate of the applicable:
	(i) interest rate benchmark (i.e.: Euribor, Libor, other), set by reference to Telerate or, if not available, on the basis of rates provided by Reference Banks;
	(ii) [Cash Margin]/[PIK Margin];
	(iii) Mandatory Costs, if any.
	Drawdown subject to [7] business days' notice for drawdown amounts of up to € [●] or [15] business days' notice for drawdown amounts in excess of € [●].
	[Note: very often the interest rate benchmark is subject to a zero-floor provision.]
Cash Margin	[Subject to the Margin Ratchet] [●] % per annum payable in cash.
	[Note: sometimes the Margin is subject to a margin ratchet with reduction/increase of the margin on the basis of the leverage ratio.]
PIK Margin	[●] % per annum.

(*continued*)

Interest Period	*[One], [three], or [six]* months or *[any other period agreed between the relevant Borrower and all the Lender(s) under the relevant Facility, but no greater than six months]* ending on or before the relevant Termination Date.
Payment of Interest	Interest is payable on the last day of each Interest Period. [For that part of the Interest forming the PIK Margin, this is capitalised at the end of each Interest Period and added to the principal amount of the Facility.] Default interest will be charged on overdue sums at the [1]% above the aggregate interest rate payable in cash.
[Call Protection:]	[Within 12 months from Signing Date: [•] %; Within 24 months from Signing Date: [•] %; Within 36 months from Signing Date: [•] %.] *[NOTE: Other call protections could be added depending on the specific transaction.]*
Upfront Fee	[•] % of the aggregate amount of the Facility payable out of the proceeds of the first drawdown.
Arrangement Fee	[As provided for in Mandate Letter] *or* [[•]% of the aggregate amount of the Facility payable on the Signing Date to the Mandated Lead Arranger.]
Commitment Fee	[Commitment Fee of [•] % per annum on the undrawn and uncancelled amount of the Facility for the period from the Signing Date.]
Agency Fees	[Agency Fees [as set out in the Fee Letter]/[in amounts and on terms to be agreed with the Facility Agent and the Security Agent]].
Expenses	[As provided for in Mandate Letter, which will include all] [All] costs and out of pocket expenses including, without limitation, legal fees, due diligence costs, travel, accommodation and subsistence and fees payable to third parties (in addition to any irrecoverable VAT) incurred by the Lender(s) and/or Mandated Lead Arranger shall be reimbursed by the Company.

Terms

Documentation	Documentation shall be based on this Term Sheet and otherwise based on terms and conditions customary for facilities of this nature and in form and substance acceptable to the Lender(s) ('**Finance Documents**').
Mandatory Pre-payment	(i) Mandatory pre-payment of all amounts outstanding under the Facilities and cancellation of all commitments shall be required upon the occurrence of any of the following events: **a.** a listing, issue of securities, public offering, or flotation of or by any member of the Group; or **b.** a sale of all or substantially all of the assets or business of the Group; or **c.** a change of ownership or control of the Company; or **d.** illegality. (ii) Mandatory pre-payment from the net proceeds of: **a.** disposals; **b.** receipts under acquisition agreements or other extraordinary receipts; or **c.** insurance claims; or **d.** excess cash flow. [as applicable subject to a minimum threshold amount to be agreed and] [subject to agreed exceptions in respect of (a) disposals of trading assets in the ordinary course of business; (b) net proceeds of insurance claims where the net proceeds of such claims are used to remedy the cause of the claim within an agreed period.]
Application of Mandatory Pre-payment Proceeds:	Mandatory pre-payment proceeds will be applied in the following order: [first [pro rata] against outstandings under Facility [●] [and Facility [●]]; [then against outstandings under Facility [●]] [against repayment instalments [in chronological order]/[*pro rata*]/[in inverse chronological order]].

(*continued*)

Voluntary Pre-payment	Loans outstanding may be pre-paid on the last day of the Interest Period relating thereto in whole or in part [subject to a minimum of € [•] or 100% of the outstandings if less than € [•])] subject to the terms of the Call Protection clause. Any such pre-payments may not be redrawn. Any mandatory or voluntary pre-payment shall be made with accrued interest on the amount pre-paid and shall be subject to breakage costs.
Security	[First priority] security over the issued share capital of each Obligor and [First priority] asset security (including pledges over bank accounts, fixed assets, mortgages, trademarks, intellectual property, inventory, receivables and/or guarantees) from all Obligors [where permitted/practical having regard to the potential benefits to the Lender(s) and the cost to the Group].

[NOTE: Transaction security could be reduced or increased depending on the specific transaction.]

Hedging	An interest rate hedging policy is to be agreed between the Lender(s) and [the Company] and, if required, the Company shall have entered into the relevant hedging documents prior to the [Signing Date/first drawdown].
Representations, Undertakings and Events of Default	Each Obligor shall give representations and undertakings (in respect of itself and, as the case may be, in respect of each member of the Group), and each Facility shall be subject to Events of Default, in each case, as is customary for facilities of this nature and in form and substance satisfactory to the Lender(s).
Financial Covenants	All covenants to be calculated and certified by management. [Interest Cover Ratio: Consolidated EBIT[DA]] to Total [Net] Interest Costs; Cash flow Coverage: Consolidated Cash flow to Total Funding Costs; Leverage Ratio: Total [Net] Debt to consolidated EBITDA; Measured [quarterly] on a rolling 12-month basis; [Capital Expenditure not to exceed, during stipulated periods, the relevant specified amounts].

[NOTE: Other financial covenants could be added depending on the specific transaction.]

Information Covenants	To include, with reference to each Obligor and Group member:
	Monthly financial statements 30 days after month end [including management commentary]; Quarterly [consolidated] financial statements 30 days after quarter end [including management commentary]; Annual audited [consolidated] financial statements [120] days after year end; Annual budget provided [7 days] prior to the forecast year for which it refers.
	[NOTE: Other information covenants could be added depending on the specific transaction.]
General Undertakings	To include, with reference to each Obligor and Group member: Dividend [Prohibition] *or* [Limitation]; Restriction on share redemption; Additional Indebtedness [Prohibition] *or* [Limitation]; Restrictions on loans and credit in favour of other parties, as well as to guarantees and indemnities; Negative Pledge that no security to be given other than our facilities and agreed senior debt security; Restrictions on acquisitions and disposals; At least *pari passu* ranking with all other debt; Compliance with laws (including not putting Lender(s) and/or its (their) Affiliates in breach of any law); No deduction of tax on payments to Lender(s) and/or Mandated Lead Arranger; Group having and maintaining relevant authorisations; Sanctions, anti-money laundering, anti-corruption; No change of business.
	[NOTE: Other undertakings could be added depending on the specific transaction.]
Events of Default	To include, with reference to each Obligor and Group member: Non-payment; Full cross-default into all other senior and subordinate debt facilities; Creditors' process;

(continued)

Change of Control of Company or by Company of other
Obligors;
Material Adverse Change;
Breach of any Representation and Warranty;
Material litigation;
Insolvency and insolvency proceedings;
Breach of any undertaking;
Breach of Financial Covenants.

*[NOTE: Other events of default could be added
depending on the specific transaction.]*

**Conditions
Precedent to
Signing**

To include conditions precedent usual and customary for
transactions of this kind including:
Copy of the constitutional documents of each Obligor
and other providers of security;
Evidence of the corporate powers of each Obligor and
other providers of security to entry into the finance
documents;
Good standing certificates of each Obligor and other
providers of security, as well as of any target company,
if any;
Financial, legal, and commercial due diligence to the
satisfaction of the Lender(s);
Structure memorandum of the transaction;
Historical financial statements for the past [five] years,
including audited annual income statements, balance
sheets, and cash flow statements;
[Business plan/Base case]/[Five-]year financial forecast;
Latest available monthly and year to date management
accounts;
Confirmation of balance sheet and cash position at
Signing Date;
Director's certificate with certification of copy
documents;
Execution of the finance documents, fee letters, hedging
letter, and the transaction security documents;
Legal opinions on power and capacity of the Obligors
and the other providers of security;
Legal opinion on validity and enforceability of the
finance documents;
Completion by the Lenders of all the applicable KYC
procedure requirements.

*[NOTE: Other conditions precedent to Signing could
be added depending on the specific transaction.]*

Conditions Precedent to First Drawdown	Representation by the Obligor(s) that: immediately prior to and immediately following the first drawdown and for a period of [four] quarters following the first drawdown no Default (including an Event of Default) is continuing or would result from the proposed Loan; It is (they are) not in breach of its (their) Financial or General Covenants and other Undertakings; The repeated representations to be made by each Obligor are true in all material respects and no change of control has occurred.

[NOTE: Other conditions precedents to the First Drawdown could be added depending on the specific transaction.]

Conditions Precedent to Subsequent Drawdowns	Representation by the Obligor(s) that: immediately prior to and immediately following the first drawdown and for a period of [four] quarters following the first drawdown no Default (including an Event of Default) is continuing or would result from the proposed Loan; It is (they are) not in breach of its (their) Financial or General Covenants and other Undertakings; The repeated representations to be made by each Obligor are true in all material respects and no change of control has occurred.

[NOTE: Other conditions precedents to the Subsequent Drawdown could be added depending on the specific transaction.]

[Standstill Periods for Mezzanine]	[Target to use LMA Standard Terms: *If payment default 90 days standstill, financial covenant breach 120 days, any other event of default 150 days.*]
Lender Decision Making	[*For syndicated facilities.*] consent of all Lenders: changes to price, security, tenor, amount, etc. Majority Lenders: 2/3 of Total Commitments or if Loans outstanding, 2/3 of Loans under each Facility.

(*continued*)

Assignments and Transfers	A Lender may assign any of its rights or transfer [by novation] any of its rights and obligations to any [person]/[to another bank or financial institution or to a trust, fund, or other entity which is regularly engaged in or established for the purpose of making, purchasing, or investing in loans, securities, or other financial assets], subject to a minimum amount of [●] (and if a Lender's participation is less than [Insert minimum amount], such Lender may only assign all of its rights or transfer all of its rights and obligations).
	[Note: depending on the deal, the assignment/transfer can be subject to prior consent of the Borrower, which will not be required in case of assignment/transfer made to a potential lender included in a pre-approved white list or if an event of default (or a major event of default) is continuing. Sometimes it is also provided the absolute prohibition to assignments/transfers in favour of industry competitors of the Borrower's group.]
Miscellaneous Provisions	The facility agreement will contain provisions relating to, amongst other things, market disruption, breakage costs, tax gross-up and indemnities, material adverse events, increased costs, set-off, and administration.
Anti-Money Laundering	The Group shall comply with all anti-money laundering requirements and these need to be satisfied prior to execution of any facility agreement.
Governing Law	[●] law in respect of the principal Finance Documents. The security documents will be governed by [●] law or, if appropriate, the local law governing the jurisdictions on which the assets charged are located.
Jurisdiction	The parties hereby agree to submit to the exclusive jurisdiction of the courts of [●] [save where inappropriate for guarantees and security documents].

CHAPTER 13

Distress Symptoms and Remedies

EARLY WARNING SIGNALS

Detecting early indicators of distress is critical in order to implement promptly corrective actions. It is often very difficult, though, to distinguish between symptoms and problems, between temporary and seasonal swings, and between permanent and cyclical difficulties.

A preliminary deep dive should always start the analysis of the financial statements: key questions to investigate are whether:

- earnings are being generated from core business;
- accounting policies increased profitability and/or reserve accounts;
- there are continuous changes for restructuring/reorganisation;
- creditors are showing signs of concern;
- bad debts are being written off;
- tax charge is low relative to reported earnings.

The main distinction in symptoms of credit deterioration is between financial and non-financial indicators. The key ones are:

- **Financial danger signals:**
  - covenant breaches;
  - late submission of financial statements;
  - creative accounting (frequent acquisitions and disposals, deferred consideration, off balance-sheet financings, contingent liabilities);
  - earning enhancements (sale and lease back, asset write down and subsequent profit on disposal, capitalised expenses, accelerating revenue, suppliers' discounts, deferral of costs, sale of subsidiary with recourse).
- **Non-financial danger signals:**
  - unnecessarily complex corporate structure;
  - board and/or senior management resignations;
  - change in financial year end;

- change in auditors;
- failure to meet commitments on time;
- change in attitude towards banks;
- change in risk aversion (either becoming too aggressive or too conservative).

CAUSES

Companies default for different reasons. Some companies have the wrong business model; others take on too much debt; others still have very complicated businesses. Sometimes the problem is a combination of too much debt and the wrong business model; sometimes there are internal or external unexpected crises. It is vital to understand the reason for the distress and how it influences the investment strategy. The analyst should err on the side of great caution for this section of the analysis.

Typical causes of distress are as follows.

- **Leverage and business performance:** the interplay between debt and operating performance. At risk of over-simplification, in practice we observe the following three situations:
  - Excessive leverage but sound business model: in this case, all debt facilities are fully drawn, there are overdrafts and the cost of debt repayment increases. The point of default is during a cyclical downturn (EBITDA – cash taxes – capex < interest expense + scheduled service of debt). In this case, cash flows usually stabilise at no more than 10% below the point of default and we usually witness an increase in revenues and margins within three years after downturn.
  - Average leverage, poor operating performance: revenues and margins reduce drastically and there is a small increase in debt repayment. Default may (but not necessarily) occur in a cyclical downturn, otherwise it remains the same. In this case it is difficult to assess stabilisation of cash flows; they may go down to 30–50% below point of default, or more. Any increase in revenues may occur 5–10 years after downturn.
  - Excessive leverage and poor operating performance: reduced revenues and margins, debt facilities fully drawn, overdrafts, and cost of debt repayment increases. Default likely to occur in a cyclical downturn. Hard to assess stabilisation of cash flows; they may go down to 50–70% below point of default, or more.
- **Unexpected liabilities:** there may be situations in which a firm is performing well, but unexpectedly significant non-debt claims are made against it. The most common sources of such liabilities are tort claims and contract liabilities:
  - Tort liabilities: associated with liability linked, for example, to asbestos, breast implants, and tobacco. Management usually underestimates the number of potential claims and their financial liability because the probability of the event is very low and claims usually exceed all reasonable

expectations. The available insurance may not be enough to cover the liability, or the insurer contests coverage. When a firm becomes associated with potential personal injury or tort exposure, the market tends to assume the worst and discounts its securities.

- Contract liabilities: associated with bad or uneconomic contracts. These may have been entered into deliberately in the normal course of business, but went bad following a change in circumstances. On the other hand, such contracts may have come with a newly purchased firm and were not entered into consciously. It is difficult for investors to protect themselves against such liabilities.

■ **Performance materially below expectation:** the most common reason for financial distress is that the company performs less well than expected. There are various reasons why performance can fall below expectations:

- Economic downturn: economic cycles, including recessions, are unavoidable. Few businesses are entirely protected against economic downturns. However, the challenge for the distressed investor is to determine whether this is the true cause of the distress – it is easy to blame the economy when things get tough. But is the problem the economy, or is it the management?
- Uncompetitive product or service: because no business is static and due to rapid technological progress, it is possible that businesses that once satisfied consumer needs may be rendered obsolete by advances in technology. Therefore. when a business starts to deteriorate, it will be necessary to examine whether the product or service being offered is still viable.

■ **Crisis of confidence:** these are usually linked to fraud and other events that create financial uncertainty (e.g. WorldCom, Enron). There are two main issues to focus on when the crisis of confidence event occurs:

- Reliability of historical financial information: discoveries of fraud or the need for accounting restatements obviously render historical financial data questionable. Once any particular data has been called into question, all the remaining data should be viewed with scepticism. Nevertheless, it is important to carefully analyse the nature of the alleged issue to see if it is still possible to make a valuation, however tenuous that valuation might be.
- Liquidity and likelihood of bankruptcy: it is important to consider whether the information event in question will lead to a major liquidity crisis or to a bankruptcy. To assess this, the following factors should be considered: cash available, availability of credit lines, risk of loan acceleration.

■ **Unrealistic business plans:** there are three main types of business plan that often prove unrealistic:

- Leveraged buyouts: the financing structure used to make the acquisition is structured on the assumption that either proceeds from asset sales or funds generated internally could be used to deleverage. When these monies do not materialise, the company becomes financially distressed.
- Roll ups: the rationale behind the attempt to consolidate small businesses into a larger entity through acquisition and merger is that the consolidated

entity will have improved economics, mainly due to economies of scale. If savings do not materialise, the consolidated entity might be inefficient to the point of becoming distressed.

- Place in growing sector: this refers to the scenario whereby the success of a new entrant is based on a market environment that is so fast that it is believed there will be space for almost any new entrant. Problems arise when dozens of businesses enter a market, but the demand for the service or product in that sector is not sufficient to support them all.

RESTRUCTURING OPTIONS

In a restructuring case, different options, tools, and funding sources (see Table 13.1) exist as a function of whether the performance deterioration is temporary, a first, and whether a turnaround has already failed or not. Table 13.1 categorises the different situations.

In case debt is traded, price levels of traded debt (Table 13.2) often provide useful indications of the underlying problems and possible solutions.

TABLE 13.1 Restructuring options as a function of its causes.

	Temporary decline	First turnaround failed/delayed	EBITDA slips again
Restructuring options	▪ Buy covenant headroom ▪ Debt reduction ▪ Equity cure/injection	▪ Amend covenants and extend maturities ▪ Discounted debt buyback ▪ Credit bid the entire debt structure	▪ Super senior funding ▪ Debt to equity exchange
Restructuring tools	▪ Amendment ▪ Debt buyback by auction ▪ M&A to explore value and/or disposals	▪ Distressed credit bid or debt exchange ▪ Distressed M&A ▪ Consensual cram down or debt to equity exchange	▪ Bankruptcy driven cram down or flushing out of junior/old equity ▪ Bankruptcy driven debt to equity exchange ▪ New super senior funding
Funding sources	▪ Mostly: sponsor or shareholder ▪ Rarely: new external sources	▪ Mostly: new external sources ▪ Rarely: sponsor or shareholder	▪ Almost exclusively: lenders (old, new, distressed) – lender led process

Source: Based on data from Whitman and Diz (2009).

TABLE 13.2 Debt trading levels and potential solutions.

Problems	Debt trading level	Solutions
Inability to meet capex or operating costs, but sound growth story	80–100	▪ Rights issue ▪ Financial investor
Debt burden too high, no solvency problem	80–100	▪ Rights issue ▪ Financial investor
Equity price decline, ratings downgrade, no solvency problem	70–90	▪ Restructure convertibles
Debt burden too high, but sound business with current cash pile	50–80	▪ Bond exchange ▪ Tender offer
Debt burden too high, solvency problem	20–50	▪ Debt for equity swap ▪ Possible ICR
Debt burden too high, week business	0–20	▪ Insolvency proceeding

Source: Based on data from Moyer (2005).

FINANCING SOLUTIONS

Different restructuring tools can be used depending on whether the gaps are in short-term liquidity or long-term capital requirements.

If there is a shortfall of liquidity that can be considered of a short-term nature, the most commonly used restructuring tools are a temporary extension of existing overdraft or credit line facilities, a redefinition of covenant ratios and implied debt conditions, and a rescheduling of debt repayment.

If there are gaps in long-term capital requirements, there are two main strategic options to resolve financial distress outside bankruptcy.

a) **Raise additional finance:** this is the most obvious strategy for the distressed firm. More cash will not resolve the crisis, but it will buy time. Managers tend to believe more time is good, perhaps because they hope the business will improve, or maybe because they will continue to receive paychecks. For investors, raising more cash can be good if it will boost credit support for the particular debt under consideration. However, it will not be good if it reduces credit support or if it gives bad management more time to erode the business. The following are the most common ways to raise extra cash:
  - Asset sale: price is a critical factor when considering whether asset sales will benefit the distressed investor. If the firm gets a good price, the sale is potentially a value-enhancing event. If, for example, bank lenders are demanding an asset sale, and the cash is used to pay off bank debt, then most creditors will be better off. Holders of the secured debt will benefit because they will receive partial repayment. Holders of unsecured debt will generally benefit because the amount of the secured debt above them is

being reduced and there is a greater chance of getting a good price on the asset sale before, rather than after, filing for bankruptcy.

- Secured financing: if a firm has unencumbered assets, the firm could raise cash by borrowing against those assets. This is not usually a practical option, however. In situations where credit has always been lower than investment grade, the bank lender will probably already have insisted on collateral in the form of almost all the assets. Even if this were not so to begin with, a collateral pledge would probably be demanded by the bank as part of an early restructuring as soon as the business started performing below forecast and technical covenant defaults began to occur. Therefore, by the time the company is in serious distress, the bank will probably have done all it can to protect itself, to the detriment of unsecured creditors.
- Sale and leaseback: in sale and leaseback financing, the firm will sell an asset on the understanding that the new owner will immediately lease it back to the vendor firm. This is more beneficial than a straight sale, because the firm may still need the asset to carry on business. Moreover, the lease can be structured as an off balance-sheet liability so that from a GAAP perspective, leverage will appear lower. The proceeds received may also be higher, depending on the terms of the lease.
- Equity sponsor: the presence of a controlling 50%+ institutional equity holder is generally good news for debt holders. An equity holder can usually only realise value on its equity investment after satisfying the debt claim, so there is a strong common interest. Whilst this is true with regard to equity, when the equity is widely held by public shareholders, usually no single shareholder is willing or motivated enough to work out how to resolve the financial distress alone, if at all.

b) **Reducing leverage:** companies can try to resolve financial distress by reducing leverage through an equity increase or a purchase of debt (at a discount).

- Equity increase: an equity injection is the most common way to reduce debt and is often required by lenders as part of a debt restructuring process. Usually provided by incumbent equity holders, it can be provided by new equity investors (although the timing is longer due to the due diligence process required).
- Debt purchase: there are several ways to execute this. If the purchases are going to be relatively small (around the lesser of 20% of the bonds outstanding) open market purchases are preferred because they are simpler, faster, less costly, more discreet, and they can be achieved without unnecessarily moving market prices. A tender offer is the common-sense route if the repurchase is for a large quantity, or if consideration other than cash will be used for some or all of the purchase price.
  - *Open market repurchases*: this is the easiest way to purchase debt at a discount. Discount debt repurchases can only usually be effected with regard to bonds. If the firm has bank debt that is so distressed that it is sold at a significant discount, lenders will probably have enough power to insist that any available cash be used to repay the debt up front.

  o *Direct purchases from holders*: a firm can make individually negotiated
   purchases directly from holders. In such cases the holder, anticipating
   the firm may be interested in buying, normally calls and offers to sell
   the securities. Holders, which may include distressed investors, do this
   in the hope they can get a higher net price, given that there would be no
   fee payable to an intermediary broker.
  o *Cash tender offers*: a tender offer is the most public way to repurchase
   bonds in the market. Here, the firm will propose to purchase bonds under
   a strict set of conditions. Such conditions normally include a deadline
   by which tenders must be received, the maximum amount that will be
   purchased, and the price.
  o *Exchange offers*: a firm is usually in distress because it does not have
   much cash. Therefore repurchasing debt, even at great discount, may
   not be practical. In this case, de-leveraging can be achieved through an
   exchange offer using new securities of the distressed firm as consideration. Exchange offers can be structured in many ways, but they can be
   distinguished by looking at whether they are coercive or non-coercive.
   Exchange offers are coercive when they force cooperation by 'threat-
   ening' to place participants at the risk of losing out. A non-coercive
   exchange offer does not threaten the participants, but rather it will try to
   present a relatively attractive opportunity so as to encourage cooperation
   by the participants.

Whilst the options above are available to any firm in theory, in practice there
may be limits on their actual implementation. The most important are:

- **Liquidity:** if a firm has limited excess liquidity, it will probably be unable to
  make discounted note purchases. This eliminates the easiest way of reducing
  leverage, and a source of price support or appreciation for debt.
- **Time-to-liquidity event:** it is important to determine how much time is available until the firm's next liquidity event. This is critical because many of the
  options available take time to take effect. For example, it would be difficult to
  sell a business unit in just two months, but it would be viable if one had six
  or more months to spare.
- **Magnitude of problem:** the size of the problem can be relative to time and
  resources. For example, if liquidity is limited and time is short, a small problem such as a coupon repayment can become a big problem.
- **Complexity of capital structure:** it is generally more difficult for firms to
  restructure the more layers they have in their capital structure. If there is a
  considerable amount of secured bank debt, the available options will be limited because of the burdensome covenants that are usually present in these
  facilities. If assets are sold, the proceeds will be needed to pay off bank debt
  rather than to repurchase junior debt at a discount. Coercive exchange offers
  will probably not offer first liens, and there may be limits on the maturity
  structure that could be employed. Moreover, the free use of cash may be limited by constraining payment tests. It is critical that analysts carefully consider

the provisions of all significant capital instruments when assessing the firm's options.

- **Severability of business units:** in a diversified business with core and non-core operations, there could be many opportunities for sales. However, if the firm consists of just one business, there may not be any non-vital units that could be sold off.

LEGAL ALTERNATIVES

Correct analysis of the firm's options is vital in predicting the course of restructuring. When a company is in financial distress and cannot pay its creditors, it can either restructure its debt under the supervision of a bankruptcy court (in-court restructuring, or ICR), or it can try to restructure its debt out of court (out-of-court restructuring, or OCR). Either way, the firm will face complex legal, tax, and accounting issues as it considers its options.

Court supervised debt restructuring is time consuming and costly, and it carries the risk of damage to the company's reputation with all that that entails. Therefore, an OCR is generally a better solution for a distressed company. In an OCR, the company and its main creditors work out a modification in the terms of current obligations, or they complete a voluntary exchange of financial interests. A debt-free solution is often best for companies that are not making enough cash or that will probably need an extra cash infusion at a later date. It will be easier for them to borrow the additional cash if they have no other debt. One of the main limitations to the OCR is that the interests of a claimant who is not taking part in the restructuring cannot be changed. For example, there may a situation where a participating bondholder is free to do anything he wants with his own bonds, but he will not be able to do anything to another creditor or shareholder. The bondholder would not be able to alter the fact that a current shareholder owns a certain number of shares. Nor could he alter the fact that a non-participant bondholder will continue to own a bond. The bondholder could, with the company's consent, change the economic value of the old interest, but he could not expunge the interest unilaterally.

Below is a synthetic comparison of the two alternatives:

1. **Out-of-court (OCR) restructuring:** OCR normally begins with a negotiation that finally leads to an agreement by the parties on the terms of a deal that will then be put into practice, or there will be an effort made to put it into practice. Key elements of an OCR are:
   a. *The parties involved:* where much of the debt capital structure is made up of bank debt, it will be quite easy to decide who will negotiate on behalf of the creditors. In the case of a loan made by one lender or a small group of lenders, it will be obvious who the participants are. Where there is a large syndicated loan, the loan agreement will specify an 'agent' to carry

out these duties in exchange for compensation, though other bond holders may also participate. In the case of bonds, the representative will usually be a small group of key bondholders who form a committee. Technically, the legal representative of the bonds is the indenture trustee, but as a legal matter the indenture trustee will only get involved when it believes it is acting on behalf of all or a certain number of the bonds. Therefore, bondholders must usually reach a consensus before the trustee can act. Trustees typically do not like risk and will usually only do what they are obligated to do under the indenture.

b. *Implementing the restructuring:* if the debt is in the form of a bank loan, implementation is fairly simple; it normally involves an amendment of the loan agreement signed by all or some of the bank debt holders. Bank loans generally permit holders of the majority of the debt to make amendments to most of the provisions that are binding on lenders. However, loan agreements require 100% consent to make certain amendments, such as a extending the maturity date, reducing the amortisation rate, reducing the interest rate, and changing collateral security. If the debt is in the form of bonds and the restructuring can be achieved by involving only the bondholder committee, then implementation may be quite simple. However, because the participants usually have to give up something (by changing the form or reducing the amount of the claim), the participants will usually want all the bondholders to be involved and therefore to also give something up. To engage the participation of non-committee investors, there will normally be a formal exchange or tender offer.

c. *Feasibility and the holdout problem:* OCR is often based on voluntary participation and therefore may not be feasible due to a lack of cooperation. The 'holdout problem' is that the non-participants may be better off than the participants. However, if too many hold out, everyone will be worse off. If there are too many holdouts, the restructuring may not succeed and the company may be forced to file for bankruptcy. In that case, if there are few other benefits from ICR other than the ability to bind the holdouts through either approval by the class or the operation of the Bankruptcy Code's cram-down provisions, the recoveries will be unavoidably lower. Bankruptcy will only add costs that ideally should have been avoided. There are two ways of dealing with holdout: the first essentially involves the threat of applying economic leverage in the future. The major distressed participants usually know each other. They are involved with each other in transactions over time, and will therefore consider the future implications of what they do in any particular deal. Therefore, although each restructuring is independent, the overall market involves a process where the regular participants will work with or against each other in a series of deals. Because of the probability of future contact and the risk that the financial leverage positions might be different at some later date, groups may be able to 'force' cooperation. The second way of dealing with holdouts is via coercive structural devices. These are more appropriate when seeking an exchange offer for bonds than in bank debt cases. The most commonly used form of coercion is to remove the covenant protections of non-tendering bonds. The exchange offer will include a provision that tendering bonds will be considered to have voted to authorise an amendment to the indenture of the original bonds that essentially cancels all protective covenants. Therefore, in a majority tender, holdouts will have a significantly less attractive bond. Another tactic, used when bankruptcy reorganisation is the only obvious choice, is to combine an exchange offer with a request for support for a prepackaged ICR. This legitimises the threat of bankruptcy to holdouts and, in the event of an ICR filing, it minimises costs and reduces the amount of time the firm is in bankruptcy. Pre-packaged bankruptcies can be concluded in less than a month and half.

2. **In-court restructurings (ICR):** it is important to understand two essential points about bankruptcy: first, it is now common for companies to signal to the market ahead of time that they will be filing for bankruptcy. Second, original creditors will typically incur some financial loss in the process. Therefore, experienced distressed debt investors must be able to discern which companies will probably end up in bankruptcy or distress, and the implications of that for a particular claim. A bankruptcy case starts when a petition is filed with the bankruptcy court. There should be well thought out strategic decisions concerning both the jurisdiction of the bankruptcy filing, and the timing of it. Key elements of an ICR are:

a. The plan of reorganisation: the plan is a legal document that sets out what will happen to the debtor, its assets, and the constituent liabilities, including equity interests, when the debtor is released from bankruptcy. There are two basic parts to the plan. The first identifies the claimants and puts them in classes. Classification is related to commonality of interests; claims within a class must be of a similar nature. The second part of the plan sets out what, if anything, each class will receive. All claims within a class must be dealt with similarly. A hypothetical plan of reorganisation may include the following:

   ○ *Class 1 – Administrative claims*: includes post-petition fees, costs of lawyers, accountants, and other professional advisers;
   ○ *Class 2 – Super secured claims*: all amounts extended under the Debtor in Possession facility;
   ○ *Class 3 – Priority claims*: allowed amounts payable to employees relating to pre-petition costs;
   ○ *Class 4 – Super secured claims*: pre-petition claims of senior secured lenders and note holders;
   ○ *Class 5 – Senior unsecured claims*: pre-petition claims of trade creditors and senior unsecured lenders and note holders;
   ○ *Class 6 – Equity*: equity interests of pre-petition shareholders.

b. Operating under Chapter 11: there are four main objectives in bankruptcy proceedings:
  - ○ to stabilise the company's operations and provide liquidity such that the company can work effectively on a post-petition basis;
  - ○ to develop a forward-looking business plan to maximise the value of the firm or its assets;
  - ○ to identify the liabilities of the firm and their relative priority;
  - ○ in the case of a reorganisation, to create and allocate a new capital structure.

If it is not possible to arrange an agreed restructuring, or such a reorganisation will not deal with the main cause of distress, ICR restructuring may be the only realistic option. Bankruptcy proceedings are complex matters that will often involve a good deal of negotiation and gamesmanship. The distressed investor therefore needs to have an understanding of both the other participants and all the parties' sources of negotiating power. There may be considerable risk that if unsecured claims are able, through working together with the debtor's management, to proceed with a conservative valuation, it will be difficult to get a fair recovery. This risk is especially pertinent when considering investments in unsecured claims. Secured claims are likely to have a better chance of recovery, but the commensurate return potential will be lower. Plus, they may be required to share what they recovered with junior classes in order to conclude the reorganisation in a timely manner.

A final note of caution regarding the key legal risks for creditors in insolvency:

- **Stay on claims:** this is an order from the bankruptcy court preventing creditors from collecting their claims or enforcing collateral against an insolvent company. These stays can last from a few months to a few years.
- **Preference or twilight period:** the period before the crisis is recorded will be closely examined by the courts to make sure that no stakeholders try to benefit at the expense of others.
- **Limitations on upstream guarantees:** in some jurisdictions, the law imposes restrictions on, or is not clear about, upstream guarantees.

REFERENCES AND FURTHER READING

S. Moyer. 2005. *Distressed Debt Analysis. Strategies for Speculative Investors*. J. Ross Publishing.

M.J. Whitman and F. Diz. 2009. *Distress Investing: Principles and Technique*. Wiley Finance.

SUGGESTED CASES

C.Y. Baldwin and W. Wang. 2014. 'Paramount Equipment, Inc.' Harvard Business School Case 914-557.

M. Jensen, W. Burkhardt, and B. Barry. 1989. 'Wisconsin Central Ltd. Railroad and Berkshire Partners (A): Leveraged Buyouts and Financial Distress.' Harvard Business School Case 190-062.

R.S. Ruback. 1991. 'Southland Corp. (B).' Harvard Business School Case 291-039.

Index